SHIP TO SHORE, INC.

SLIM TO SHORE

CARIBBEAN CHARTER YACHT RECIPES

All the Low's and No's

Author ....Capt. Jan Robinson
Editor ....Jan Martin, RN, BS, MA
Associate Editor ....Barbara Lawrence, Dietitian, BS, MS
Nutrition Consultant ....Carol Bareuther, RD
Artist ....Raid Ahmad

If you are unable to obtain *SLIM* **TO SHORE**
through your local bookstore, please write to:

SHIP TO SHORE, INC.
10500 Mount Holly Road
Charlotte, North Carolina 28214-9219

or call

1-800-338-6072

First Printing: October, 1993
Second Printing: December, 1993

SLIM **TO SHORE** Copyright 1993

Library of Congress catalog card number: 93-92636

Printed in the United States of America

ISBN 0-9612686-5-4

ACKNOWLEDGMENTS

My sincerest thanks and warmest appreciation to all you wonderful Caribbean Charter Yacht Chefs and Captains who were, once again, willing to share your treasured recipes. The *Ship to Shore* cookbook collection has only been possible because of your continued support.

Also, many thanks to my many friends for testing and tasting the recipes and to Alicia Stack and Mary Goodwin for proof reading. Special thanks to Jan Martin and Vicky Northmore for their knowledge, enthusiasm and support in the test kitchen.

Notice: *This book is intended as a guide to healthy eating and a guide to cooking without fat and salt. If you suspect that you have a medical problem, we urge you to seek competent medical help. Persons who wish to change their diet and are on medication should do so only under the direction of a physician or dietitian. Diabetics should also check with their physician or dietitian before incorporating new foods into their plan. Keep in mind that nutritional needs vary from person to person, depending on age, sex, health status, and total diet. The information in* **Slim to Shore** *is intended to help you prepare healthy delicious dishes.*

TABLE OF CONTENTS

ADD A LITTLE SPICE TO YOUR LIFE !

Removing the fat and salt from a recipe and keeping it tasty is *not* easy. As you are reading this book you are probably thinking "how is it possible to prepare delicious dishes without the use of *fats and salt?*" You may have noticed that most of the other "healthy," "light," and "low-fat" cookbooks have used *some fats and salt* to enhance the flavor. We have eliminated those additions completely and kept all the color, texture, *and* flavor!

I was inspired to write **Slim to Shore** as I reached my 50th birthday. Having decided it was time to pursue a more healthy lifestyle, my quest began by spending two informative, invigorating weeks at the National Institute of Fitness (NIF) in Utah. There I learned the basics of eating more and healthier foods. With these basics under my belt, I have been able to shed twenty-five pounds in the past year while consuming more and feeling better, more energetic, and happier.

As I began research for my sixth cookbook, I discovered, in light of my personal health commitment, there were almost no truly low fat cookbooks on the market. Readers, beware of the words "low" and "light" in a cookbook's title. If you see whole eggs, margarine, or oil, stop right there and put that book back on the shelf -- it's not going to do you *any* favors.

Armed with a mission, I began **Slim to Shore**; a collection of Caribbean charter yacht recipes that were adapted for a healthier life style. After doing considerable research, I chose only recipes low in fat, sugar, cholesterol, and sodium. Every recipe provides under 20% calories from fat, to keep your daily intake low. This percentage is an average based upon my personal experience with NIF's 10% recommendation and the USDA recommendation of 30%.

Slim to Shore takes you from breakfasts to desserts, from grocery store to final presentation. Along the way, *you* will be creating dishes that are delicious as well as ultra-low in fat, sodium, cholesterol, and sugar. You'll find complete nutritional information as well as workable substitutes, week-long menus, even shopping lists! Unlike *any* other cookbook on the market today, **Slim to Shore** actually shows you the tools to rework your life style.

Bon voyage on your healthy and happy cooking journey!

Capt. Jan Robinson

PREFACE

By now you probably know that eating fat makes you fat. Eating food *without* fat is a big adjustment. Most people find the transition is best accomplished by going cold turkey, which is easy for some and difficult for others. Once you have started, you'll discover how easy it is. Motivation is often the key to success, and the good taste of these recipes is motivation to try more and keep at it. In the spirit of this cookbook, indulge yourself in planning a vacation on a charter yacht in the Caribbean! See the chapter "Participating Yachts," for more information and to fuel your motivation!

Eating without salt is another obstacle. Added salt has been omitted from all recipes in *Slim to Shore,* and you will probably miss it for awhile; try the many salt-free herbs and spices that are available.

The **Nutrient content per serving** is based on the list of ingredients shown in the recipe. Nutrient values are rounded to the nearest whole number, except for *fat, fiber, and iron*, which are rounded to the nearest tenth. Zero value is reported for true zero value; if there is any nutrient in the recipe, it is reported.

Almost all of the recipes throughout the book use easy-to-find ingredients. Check "Stocking A Healthy Kitchen" in the back of the book for the products we used while testing (and re-testing) the recipes. Keep in mind that new products come on the market daily; don't be afraid to try them, but be sure to read the labels carefully.

Suggested recipes (shown in *Bold Italics)* may be found in another part of the book, page numbers are listed.

In *Slim to Shore* you will find easy-to-understand answers to some common questions about calories, fat, cholesterol, sodium, weight control, time-saving preparation techniques, and more. Each chapter has delicious recipe and menu ideas. Discover easy-to-prepare and make-ahead recipes, as well as a selection of microwave recipes. For every recipe, you will find preparation time, garnish, and nutrient content per serving.

Note: If you've gained 10, 20, 30 lbs. over the last 5 or 10 years don't try to lose it all at once. Changing your eating habits and losing 1 or 2 pounds per week is more than enough. So, we've created this exciting cookbook for you, the person who is serious about eating better. It's easy, too.*Enjoy!*

Living Healthy

HEALTHY COOKING

Eat better, feel better. Below is an introduction to preparing healthful meals and ingredient substitutions to reduce sodium, fat, cholesterol, sugar, and calories plus adding fiber to one's diet.

To Reduce Sodium:
- Use *fresh* or frozen ingredients in recipes. If you must use canned, drain and rinse in fresh water before using.
- Use low-sodium cheese.
- Use the following flavor enhancers:
  Fresh herbs and spices
  Dried herbs and spices (See pages 256 - 260)
  No-salt or low-sodium vegetable or tomato juice to flavor soups and stews.
  Grated lemon, lime, or orange peel to flavor chicken, fish, salads and vegetables, or one to two tablespoons of apple or orange juice concentrate.
- Make homemade stocks with leftover vegetables rather than broth bases or bouillon.
- Spray popcorn *lightly* with a nonstick cooking spray to make seasoning adhere. Flavor with chili, garlic or onion powder.

To Reduce Fat and Cholesterol:
- Use nonfat, and no or low cholesterol dairy products.
- Remove skin from chicken and fish.
- Substitute two egg whites, or 1/4 cup egg substitute for each whole egg.
- Replace one cup whole milk with one cup nonfat milk.
- Use nonfat mayonnaise or nonfat yogurt in place of mayonnaise.
- Broil, bake, roast, boil, or steam in order not to add any fat. Sauté in a small amount of water or broth instead of butter or oil.
- Use nonfat yogurt with fresh chives in place of sour cream on baked potatoes.
- Use fat-free cream cheese.
- Season foods with salsas rather than butter-based sauces.
- Use skimmed evaporated milk instead of cream.
- Use crushed high-fiber cereal flakes in place of buttered bread crumbs.
- Make gravy from bouillon, stock, or wine and herbs.
- Thicken gravy, stock, or stew with arrowroot powder or agar agar, or try thickening by reduction (cooking to remove water).

- Use fat-free cottage cheese in place of mayonnaise or sour cream in dips.
- Refrigerate stocks, soups, or stews so the fat can float and condense on the top; skim off before reheating and serving.

To Reduce Sugar:
- Choose canned fruits in their own juice or water-packed.
- Scan product labels for words on ingredient labels such as dextrose, sucrose, corn syrup solids, fructose or high fructose corn sweetener. These are all words for sugar.
- Use 100% fruit juice.

To Add Fiber:
- Substitute whole-wheat flour (half the quantity) for all-purpose flour when baking;
- Add 2 tablespoons wheat germ or unprocessed bran for each cup of flour;
- Use brown rice, whole wheat, or vegetable-base noodles and pastas.
- Serve fresh fruits and vegetables with their skin on.
- Add sunflower, sesame, poppy seeds for crunch and taste.
- Use wheat germ, unprocessed bran, or uncooked oats in salads, casseroles, and muffins or as a light coating for baked chicken or fish.
- Add dried fruits to recipes.
- Make your own high-fiber granola with oats, seeds, nuts, and dried fruits. (Nuts are rich in fat, so do not go overboard.)

Saving The Vitamins In Cooked Vegetables:
- Leave peels on.
- Cut, slice, dice, etc. after cooking.
- Steam, stir-fry, microwave, or boil in a little water; cover while cooking.
- Cook until tender but crunchy.

Healthy eating!

WALKING

Walking can lower blood cholesterol, burn calories, strengthen bones, reduce blood pressure, and perhaps lessen risks for certain types of cancer. It can help one feel more relaxed and sleep better. All these benefits come from walking. Other forms of exercise can offer these advantages too, but none are as universally accepted, can be so easily accomplished, and incur a minimum of injuries as walking.

Brisk or fitness walking is best accomplished at a speed of three to fives miles per hour. Less than this speed will not help increase heart capacity or help weight loss. Greater than this speed increases the risk of injury with little added benefit. It is better to walk briskly for 40 to 60 minutes than extremely fast for only 20. Likewise, it is better to take a fitness walk from three to five times per week. Less than this number leads to little gain, and more adds the risk of injury.

If a person is overweight, past age 40, or has a health disorder, he/she should check with a doctor before starting any kind of exercise program. The benefits of walking are presented in a theoretical model developed by the Rand Corporation; each mile of fitness walking performed by someone who does not usually do so adds 21 minutes to his/her life span.

Calories Expended Per Hour For Various Activities

Calories Expended	Activities
80 - 100 per hour	Reading, writing, eating, watching TV, listening to music, sewing, playing cards and typing.
110 - 160 per hour	Preparing and cooking food, doing dishes, dusting, ironing, walking moderately fast.
170 - 240 per hour	Making beds, mopping and scrubbing, sweeping, light gardening, walking fast.
250 - 350 per hour	Heavy scrubbing and waxing, walking fast, bowling, golfing, and strenuous gardening.
350 per hour and over	Swimming, playing tennis, running, bicycling, dancing, and skiing.

DINING OUT

General Tips

- Plan a restaurant meal when you are not overly hungry.
- Do not hesitate to ask wait staff questions about how a menu item is prepared. Many times you can request a dish be prepared without added salt, butter, sauces, or gravies.
- Look for and seek out restaurants that offer lighter dishes, fresh foods, moderate portions, and good value for the dollar.
- If you enjoy an alcoholic beverage, partake in moderation and consider something like a sparkling white or blush wine.
- If there is something you would like to eat and you do not see it on the menu, ask for it. Many restaurants will have fresh fruit on hand which can be eaten as a lunch or dinner, appetizer or dessert.
- If you do not see items that you would like, ask for them.
- If portions are too large, request a take-home container.

Best Bets

- Appetizers: Fresh fruits, vegetables, and clear juices.
- Poultry and Fish Entrees: Roasted, baked, and broiled poultry, fish and shellfish. Omit gravy, butter, sauces, and batter-dipped fried items. Remove skin from chicken (if not done in the kitchen).
- Potatoes, Starches: baked, boiled, or steamed potatoes, plain rice, pasta with vegetable based sauces, boiled or baked sweet potatoes, and yams.
- Vegetables: Steamed, boiled, or grilled; request no butter added.
- Salads: Fresh fruit or vegetable based, dressed with fresh lemon, vinegar, or reduced calorie salad dressing. Beware of added bacon, cheese, seasoned croutons, and other high-fat, high-salt items.
- Fats: Omit or ask for side servings of regular salad dressing, butter, sauces, and gravies.
- Breads: Rolls, sliced whole grain breads, French bread, Italian bread, plain and whole-grain crackers, bread sticks, and plain muffins.
- Desserts: Fresh fruit, fresh fruit ices, and sorbets.
- Beverages: Sparkling water, herbal teas, decaffeinated coffee, fresh fruit juice, and nonfat milk, or soy milk.

READING FOOD LABELS

Food labels provide a wealth of information. Over the last three years, nutritionists and consumers nationwide, in cooperation with the Food and Drug Administration (FDA) and Food Safety and Inspection Service of the U. S. Department of Agriculture, have developed a system to make food labels more user-friendly. Their new labeling will go into effect on July 6, 1994.

The new food labeling regulations will ensure the following:
* Nutrition information will appear on almost all foods.
* Labels will guide consumers on how the food fits into their daily diet.
* Labels will now provide nutrition information for saturated fat, cholesterol, dietary fiber, and other nutrients that are of particular concern today.
* Confusing terms like light and fat-free will meet specific definitions.
* Health claims about a food's nutrient content and particular diseases will be backed up by scientific evidence
* Serving sizes will be expressed in common household measures that consumers are likely to eat

The Food and Drug Administration's new labeling will be mandatory on about 90% of all the processed foods. Where labeling is exempt, like on small packages, the manufacturer must include a telephone number or an address for consumers who want to get information.

Nutrition information on the new labels will be given not only in amount per serving but also as a percent of a new reference called Daily Value. Basically, the Daily Value tells consumers what percent of a nutrient the food provides.

Mandatory nutrients which must be listed on the new labels by manufacturers are total calories from fat, total fat, saturated fat, cholesterol, sodium, total carbohydrate, dietary fiber, sugars, protein, vitamin A, vitamin C, calcium, and iron. Terms like "free," "low," "light" or "lite," "reduced," "less," and "high" are now acceptable terms for package labeling but must fit certain criteria and must be consistent from food to food. "Lean" and "extra lean" have been defined also and specifically apply to the fat content of meat, poultry, and fish.

Though the new food labels may look confusing at first, they will be beneficial to those who want to choose healthy foods. One should take the time to read the label.

CHOOSING SUPPLEMENTS

Nutritionists say that all the body's vitamin and mineral needs can be met each day by eating a healthy diet. While this may be true for a person who can and does always eat right, many people find today's hectic lifestyle causes them not to eat the way they should. For this reason, a vitamin and mineral supplement can be beneficial. However, a supplement should never be used in place of choosing healthy foods or as a remedy for a junk-food diet.

Tips for choosing supplements:

- Look for a multi-vitamin and multi-mineral supplement that offers quantities of nutrients at or near 100% of the Recommended Daily Allowance. In addition, it may be helpful to choose extra supplements of vitamins A, E, C, B-carotene, selenium, chromium, calcium, and magnesium. The first six of these nutrients can often be found in one tablet called an antioxidant formulation. Woman especially need to pay attention to their calcium and magnesium intake. Usually one supplement will provide both of these nutrients. Try to get as many of these nutrients in one bottle as possible as this will prevent potential problems with overdosing and keep cost down.
- When taking more than one supplement, make sure that the total of the individual nutrients does not exceed ten times the Recommended Daily Allowance. This is the level where most toxicity can set in.
- Read package labeling carefully.
- Check the expiration date on a bottle of supplements.
- Supplements of amino acids, proteins, and enzymes are generally not necessary because the average American diet supplies these nutrients in abundance.

LIVING WITH DIABETES

Diabetes is a collection of diseases that involve a hormone from the pancreas called insulin. Generally speaking, it is a condition caused by a lack of insulin.

Diet is one of the important areas used to treat diabetes. As more is learned about nutrition, one finds that eating well-balanced and nutritious meals meets the requirements of the diabetic diet.

The recipes in *Slim to Shore* are based on low fat, low cholesterol, high fiber nutrition that can be used in a diabetic meal plan.

Diabetics should check with their physician or dietitian before incorporating new foods into their plan.

Listed with each recipe in *Slim to Shore* are the food exchanges.

Food Exchanges

Food Group	Carbohydrate (grams)	Protein (grams)	Fat (grams)	Calories (grams)
1. Starch/Bread	15	3	trace	80
2. Meat:				
Lean	—	7	3	55
Medium-Fat	—	7	5	75
High-Fat	—	7	8	100
3. Vegetable	5	2	—	25
4. Fruit	15	—	—	60
5. Milk				
Skim	12	8	trace	90
Low-Fat	12	8	5	120
Whole	12	8	8	120
6. Fat	—	—	5	45

Understanding Nutrition

CALORIES

The calorie is a technical calibration of heat transfer. In nutrition it is used to measure the transfer of energy in and out of the body. It is a measurement used in weight control that provides a simple method of controlling the amounts of food consumed.

Knowing which foods have more calories than others is helpful, but only counting calories neglects other aspects of foods, namely, fat, cholesterol, fiber, vitamins, and minerals. For example, a 3-ounce bag of peanuts and 7 fresh apples contain 500 calories each. It is much more likely that someone would munch his/her way through this amount of peanuts than eat this quantity of apples. The key to weight control and an overall healthy diet is learning to eat a variety of foods in moderation.

To determine the amount of calories your body needs to sustain it for a day, you must first establish your ideal body weight. (Use the chart on the next page.) Take this weight and multiply by 10. This figure is the approximate calories needed to sustain the body each day. To adjust for physical activity multiply this number by one of the following:

   1.3 - if not exercising regularly
   1.5 - if exercising for an hour 3 or 4 times per week
   1.8 - if engaging in heavy physical activity every day

The resulting number of calories is the approximate number needed to maintain the body at the ideal weight. Use this figure as a guide, watch the scales, eat nutritious meals, and exercise daily.

Eat more calories than your activity and gain weight. Eat a calorie level that matches your activity and maintain your weight. Eat fewer calories than you expend and lose weight. Eat only *20% calories from fat* per day and live a healthier lifestyle.

Slim to Shore provides the total calories and percentage of calories from fat with each recipe.

Metropolitan Height and Weight Tables

WOMEN:

Height Feet Inches	Small Frame	Medium Frame	Large Frame
4 ..10	102 - 111	109 - 121	118 - 131
4 ..11	103 - 113	111 - 123	120 - 134
5 ..0	104 - 115	113 - 126	122 - 137
5 ..1	106 - 118	115 - 129	125 - 140
5 ..2	108 - 121	118 - 132	128 - 143
5 ..3	111 - 124	121 - 135	131 - 147
5 ..4	114 - 127	124 - 138	134 - 151
5 ..5	117 - 130	127 - 141	137 - 155
5 ..6	120 - 133	130 - 144	140 - 159
5 ..7	123 - 136	133 - 147	143 - 163
5 ..8	126 - 139	136 - 150	146 - 167
5 ..9	129 - 142	139 - 153	149 - 170
5 ..10	132 - 145	142 - 156	152 - 173
5 ..11	135 - 148	145 - 159	155 - 176
6 ..0	138 - 151	148 - 162	158 - 179

MEN:

Height Feet Inches	Small Frame	Medium Frame	Large Frame
5 -- 2	128 - 134	131 - 141	138 - 150
5 -- 3	130 - 136	133 - 143	140 - 153
5 -- 4	132 - 138	135 - 145	142 - 156
5 -- 5	134 - 140	137 - 148	144 - 160
5 -- 6	136 - 142	139 - 151	146 - 164
5 -- 7	138 - 145	142 - 154	149 - 168
5 -- 8	140 - 148	145 - 157	152 - 172
5 -- 9	142 - 151	148 - 160	155 - 176
5 -- 10	144 - 154	151 - 163	158 - 180
5 -- 11	146 - 157	154 - 166	161 - 184
6 -- 0	149 - 160	157 - 170	164 - 188
6 -- 1	152 - 164	160 - 174	168 - 192
6 -- 2	155 - 168	164 - 178	172 - 197
6 -- 3	158 - 172	167 - 182	176 - 202
6 -- 4	162 - 176	171 - 187	181 - 207

Source of data: *Build study*, Society of Actuaries and Association of Life Insurance Medical Directors of America.

PROTEIN

Most Americans eat twice the amount of protein they need each day. The effects of excess protein include potential kidney damage, loss of calcium in the urine, and an excessive fat and cholesterol intake. On the other hand, insufficient protein may lead to loss of muscle, slow healing, and increased risk of infections.

The Recommended Dietary Allowance for protein is 0.8 grams of protein per kilogram of ideal body weight per day. This is, for example, 45 grams of protein daily for a 120-pound woman and 65 grams of protein daily for an 180-pound man. The average American diet supplies 80 to well over 100 grams of protein daily.

Both animal and plant foods contain protein. Animal protein is called "complete" since it provides all the essential building blocks to maintain the body's protein in one food. Combining two or more plant foods can also make a "complete" protein.

A perfectly adequate protein intake can be achieved with plant foods alone. For the non-vegetarian, nutritionists are urging a reduction in lean red meat, poultry, and fish to a 3-ounce serving or less at a meal. Vegetarians, especially those following a diet which excludes all animal protein, should remember to combine dried beans, peas, nuts, lentils, and sprouts with rice, wheat, corn, rye, barley, oats, millet, bulgur, or buckwheat to provide a "complete" protein.

Slim to Shore includes daily menus that provide a balanced "complete" protein diet for non-vegetarians and vegetarians.

Protein-Rich Foods
Examples of foods and portions providing
approximately 7 grams of protein each

Plant Foods: 1 cup cooked millet, whole-wheat macaroni, 100% cereal, oatmeal, spaghetti, wild rice, green peas, or cooked spinach; 1-1/4 cups brown rice, broccoli, brussel sprouts, or wheaten; 1/2 cup cooked lentils, pigeon peas, black beans, Grape Nuts, or All-Bran cereals; 1/3 cup almonds, sesame seeds, or cooked soybeans; 3 tablespoons wheat germ, pumpkin seeds, or tofu.

Animal Foods: 1 ounce poultry, fish, or cheese; 1 skim cup milk.

CARBOHYDRATES

Carbohydrates are the body's main source of energy. Like protein, carbohydrates supply only *four* calories per gram. This is unlike fat which provides *nine* calories per gram. It is the high-fat ingredients added to carbohydrates that have hidden the true caloric value of carbohydrates. For example, a medium baked potato (220 calories) plus one tablespoon of butter (132 calories) and one tablespoon of sour cream (30) is a total of 382 calories.

Carbohydrates are divided into two categories, simple and complex. The simple carbohydrates are sugars such as sucrose, fructose, and lactose. These sugars are found in table sugar, foods made with table sugar, honey, fruit, and milk. The complex carbohydrates are starches and are found in whole-grain breads, cereals, pastas, rice, and vegetables including corn, peas, beans, squash, potatoes, and yams.

A healthy diet contains both simple and complex carbohydrates with the emphasis on the complex. The complex carbohydrates are excellent sources for fiber, B-vitamins, vitamin E, iron, zinc and many other trace nutrients.

Slim to Shore features a host of recipes containing the simple and complex carbohydrates.

DIETARY FAT

Dietary fat is an essential nutrient that provides twice the calories as proteins and carbohydrates. The type and amount of fat consumed plays a big role in the difference between health and disease.

Dietary fats come from either a plant or animal origin. Plant fats contain no cholesterol and, in general, are composed mainly of poly-unsaturated fatty acids. Animal fats do contain cholesterol and are chiefly composed of saturated fatty acids. Both plant and animal fats contain monounsaturated fatty acids. Polyunsaturated fats are found in plant oils like corn, safflower, peanut, olive, and canola. Olive oil is also rich in monounsaturated fats. Saturated fats come from egg yolk, whole milk, whole milk cheeses, dairy products, red meat, poultry, and fish.

In general, most Americans eat a disproportionate quantity of saturated fat. Not only can saturated fat increase the health risk for heart disease, stroke, and cancer; but saturated fats also contain cholesterol. An elevated cholesterol level in the blood contributes to a health risk in itself.

To achieve a healthy fat intake, calories from fat should not exceed 30 percent. 10 percent of this quantity should come from polyunsaturated fatty acids, 10 percent from monounsaturated fatty acids, and 10 percent from saturated fatty acids.

Today medical research in the area of heart disease suggests that the intake of calories from fat be limited to between 10 to 20 percent. In order to decrease the amount of saturated fat and cholesterol in the diet, one should at least reduce intake of red meat and trim fat before cooking. Skin should be removed from poultry and only white meat should be eaten. Only egg whites or egg substitute should be used. (See discussion on Cholesterol for additional information.)

Note: To find out what percentage of the calories come from fat, multiply the fat grams by 9 then divide by the total calories of the product, then multiply by 100 percent. e.g. 4 gm fat x 9 = 36 calories ÷ 150 (total calories of product) = 0.24 x 100 = 24 percent calories from fat.

Each recipe in **Slim to Shore** contains less than 20 percent of calories from fat.

Fat Goals

For limiting dietary fat to 20 percent of total calories daily.

Your Weight (Pounds)	Calorie Intake	Fat Limit (Grams)
Women		
110	1.300	29
120	1,400	31
130	1,600	36
140	1,700	38
150	1,800	40
160	1,900	42
170	2,000	44
180	2,200	49
Men		
130	1,800	40
140	2,000	44
150	2,100	47
160	2,200	49
170	2,400	53
180	2,500	56
190	2,700	60
200	2,800	62

FIBER

Fiber is a type of carbohydrate found in plant foods. The term crude fiber applies to the indigestible portion of plant foods. Dietary fiber, on the other hand, is made up of both the indigestible portion of plants foods and other substances in plants, which are semi-digestible. The importance of fiber is that since it is mostly indigestible, but as it moves through the entire gastrointestinal tract providing beneficial functions along the way. A good diet should contain both soluble and insoluble sources of fiber on a daily basis.

Soluble fiber is found in oats, oat bran, barley, rice bran, dried beans and peas, and fruits like apples and oranges. Soluble fiber has the ability to trap excess fats and cholesterol in the intestine and make them less easily absorbed.

Insoluble fiber is found in wheat and bran. This type of fiber works best at preventing simple sugars from being absorbed. For persons with diabetes, adding insoluble fiber to the diet is helpful. Increasing insoluble fiber in combination with an adequate fluid intake of 6 to 8 glasses of water (or other healthful beverages) a day is the perfect natural cure for constipation.

Fresh fruits and vegetables, whole grain breads, cereals, rice, beans, and pastas contain the greatest amounts of fiber and should be used to increase the intake of fiber. If fiber intake has been low, increase slowly.

All the recipes in *Slim To Shore* contain dietary fiber.

Dietary Fiber–Rich Foods
Foods and portions that providie a
approximately 10 grams of dietary fiber

Cereal and Grains: 1/3 cup All-Bran; 1/2 cup Bran Buds; 1 cup each wheat germ, oat bran cereal, or corn meal; 3 cups cooked brown rice or cooked whole-wheat macaroni

Vegetables: 1 cup cooked lima beans, kidney beans, boiled, mashed sweet potato, lentils, or corn; 1-1/4 cups avocado, cooked broccoli, or peas and carrots; 1-1/2 cups cooked green peas or cooked spinach; 2 cups cooked carrots

Fruits: 1/2 cup dried apricots, dried figs, or chopped dates; 1 sugar apple (cherimoya); 1 cup raspberries or dried prunes; 2 guavas or small mangos

CHOLESTEROL

Cholesterol is a yellowish wax-like substance that is essential for life. It is one of the building blocks of tissues and membranes, so essential that the liver manufacturers enough for the body's needs. The American diet adds an additional 400 to 700 milligrams daily, considerably more than the Recommended Dietary Allowance (RDA) of 300 milligrams per day.

The normal cholesterol level in the U.S. is considered desirable if it is slightly under 200 milligrams. However, in heart studies, there are no reported cases of heart attacks in people with cholesterol levels of under 150 milligrams or lower. For every one percent that cholesterol rose above 150 milligrams, the chance of coronary heart disease increased about two percent. There is much discussion today about high-density lipoprotein (HDL) the *good* cholesterol and low density lipoprotein (LDL) the *bad* cholesterol, which will hopefully lead to better insights into the effects of cholesterol.

Cholesterol is found in fat from animal foods: red meats, poultry, fish, shellfish, eggs, cheese, milk, dairy products, and butter. Cholesterol is *not* found in any plant foods. The closer one's diet gets to less animal products and more (carbohydrate) plant products, the nearer it is to better nutrition.

Slim to Shore provides recipes and menus to help lower your cholesterol level while enjoying the foods you eat.

Cholesterol Content Of Common Foods
Foods and portions which contain approximately
100 milligrams cholesterol each

2 tablespoons cooked chopped chicken livers
3/4 ounce cooked beef liver
1/2 boiled egg
1-1/2 ounces cooked squid
1/2 cup cooked shrimp
1 pound lobster, cooked
3/4 cup cooked crab meat or vanilla soft-serve ice cream
1 cups oysters or shredded cheddar cheese
3 ounces pot roast of beef
4 ounces cooked pork shoulder
5 ounces light meat chicken, no skin or light meat turkey, no skin
6 ounces baked fish, no butter

SODIUM

Sodium, along with its counterpart potassium, regulate the amount of water in the body and in the nerve and muscle function. The body's basic requirement is only 500 milligrams per day, but it is reported that the average sodium intake is a whopping 6,000 to 10,000 milligrams daily.

Surprisingly, the salt shaker is not the true culprit in this high-sodium scenario. A survey indicated that in the average diet 13% of sodium is found naturally occurring in foods, 8% comes from salt added in cooking or at the table via shaker, and 79% is contributed by processed foods containing salt and/or sodium-containing additives. For example, a fresh tomato contains 10 milligrams of sodium. If 1/8 teaspoon of salt is added to that tomato, the sodium content rises to 266 milligrams. A commercial manufacturer makes tomato juice, and the sodium content soars to 882 milligrams per cup.

Nutrition professionals recommend that a prudent intake of sodium is between 2,000 to 3,000 milligrams daily. This recommendation is designed to help prevent health disorders such as heart disease, high blood pressure, stroke, and kidney disease.

The simplest way to avoid excess sodium is to avoid processed foods as much as possible. At the grocery store, one should read labels to determine if salt or sodium-based additives like sodium sulfite or sodium nitrate are in the top five ingredients listed. To further define if a food has an excess sodium content, one needs to look at the nutrition information on the food label. For example, a one-half cup serving of canned yellow corn contains 286 milligrams of sodium, but the same size serving of frozen corn provides only 14 milligrams of sodium. One must beware of foods labeled "low-sodium," "low-salt," and "reduced-sodium"; for they may not be as good as they appear.

Prepare food at home with fresh unprocessed ingredients. Dishes made with fresh foods need not be bland. In fact, the absence of excess salt gives other natural flavors a chance to shine through. Experiment with fresh herbs and spices, onion, garlic, lemon, lime, and even hot peppers. See pages 256 - 260 for *Herb and Their Uses.*

Slim to Shore lists the sodium content of all recipes.

POTASSIUM

Potassium is vital for muscle contraction, nerve impulses, and the proper functioning of the heart and kidneys. Together with sodium, calcium and magnesium, it helps regulate blood pressure and water balance in cells. There is increasing evidence that a high-potassium diet may reduce the risk of hypertension and stroke.

It is known that most people eat far more salt than they should and far too little potassium. In a national nutrition survey conducted in 1991, 30% of people who responded said that they had eaten no fruits or vegetables on the survey day. As well as missing vitamin A, vitamin C, many trace minerals and dietary fiber, these survey participants also missed out on their potassium.

Research indicates that if a person were to eat just one additional serving of fresh vegetables or fruit a day, it would drastically reduce the risk of stroke and hypertension. Although fresh fruits and vegetables provide a good source of potassium, this mineral is found in nearly every food. Whole-grain, beans, nuts and protein foods like poultry and fish also can provide rich sources of potassium.

Even though there is no Recommended Daily Allowance (RDA) for potassium, nutritionists recommend about 3000 milligrams per day.

Slim to Shore lists the potassium content of all recipes.

Potassium-Rich Foods
foods and servings which provide
approximately 500 milligrams of potassium.

Vegetables: 1-1/2 raw tomatoes; 1/3 cup cooked beet greens, cooked mashed yams, or no-salt added tomato sauce; 1/2 cup cooked lima beans cooked Swiss chard; 2/3 cup cooked pumpkin; 3/4 cup cooked spinach, succotash, chicory, or carrot juice; 1 medium plantain or baked potato

Fruits: 1/4 cup dried apricots; 1/3 cup dried figs; 1/2 cup dried prunes, dates, or raisins; 1 cup passion fruit juice, soursop pulp, orange juice, cantaloupe, or honeydew melon; 1 banana; 1-1/4 cups papaya

Grains, Beans, and Nuts: 1/3 cup Bran Buds; 1/2 cup All-Bran or wheat germ; 3/4 cup cooked white beans, navy beans, or pigeon peas; 1/3 cup pistachios; 1/2 cup peanuts or pumpkin seeds

Fish and Shellfish: 3 ounces cooked rainbow trout or coho salmon, 20 small steamed clams, 3 ounces whelks

IRON

Iron is essential to the formation of hemoglobin and myoglobin (the body's blood supply). Hemoglobin carries oxygen from the lungs to the tissues throughout the body. Myoglobin is involved in producing energy from carbohydrates and fats.

Iron, like calcium, is an essential mineral which women find difficult to consume in great enough quantity. The most recent version of the Recommended Dietary Allowance (RDA) suggests a daily intake of 15 milligrams for women in their childbearing years. For adult men and women, the requirement is 10 milligrams daily.

Coffee and tea can reduce iron absorption. In fact, studies have shown that drinking black tea with a meal can lesson iron absorption by fifty percent. Regular coffee has the same effect, with a thirty-nine percent reduction in iron absorption. Better beverages are decaffeinated coffee or herbal teas.

When taking an iron supplement, always take it with foods. This will prevent any possible side effect from nausea and also help the amount of iron which is absorbed from the supplement.

Slim to Shore lists the iron content of all recipes

Iron-Rich Foods
*Foods and portion sizes which provide
approximately 5 milligrams of iron*

Grains and Beans: 1/4 cup Total or Product 19; 1/3 cup All-Bran, Bran Flakes, or cooked Cream Of Wheat; 1/2 cup wheat germ; 3/4 cup rye flour or cornmeal; 1/3 cup quinoa; 3 tablespoon tofu; 1 cup white beans, Great Northern beans, or pigeon peas; 1-1/2 cups lima beans

Fruits and Vegetables: 1 cup cooked spinach, dried peaches, or dried apricots; 1-1/2 cups cooked Swiss chard; 1-1/4 cups dried figs, dried prunes, or raisins

Fish: 1 ounce cooked oysters

Note: Eating vitamin C rich foods such as citrus fruits, strawberries, melons, tomatoes, potatoes, green peppers, and broccoli along with the foods containing iron helps to increase the absorption of iron. Using cast-iron cookware also aids in the absorption of iron.

CALCIUM

Calcium is the most abundant mineral in the human body with approximately 95% in the bones. Calcium is important for building bones and provides a role in nerve signal transmission, muscle contraction, and hormone secretion.

The Recommended Daily Allowance (RDA) for calcium is 800 milligrams per day. Some health professionals suggest 1200 to 1500 milligrams per day. Due to the high sodium, high protein American diet there is a problem in absorption that causes a rapid rate of urinary excretion of calcium leading to a deficiency. Vitamin D helps to counteract this deficiency by increasing the absorption of calcium. Use nonfat milk, nonfat yogurt, and low-fat cheese when choosing dairy foods; these actually contain more calcium than their higher fat counterparts.

Loss of calcium can lead to osteoporosis, the number one cause of debilitating bone breaks and fractures in women over age 60. Prevention of osteoporosis centers on an adequate calcium intake all throughout life and regular exercise.

Calcium carbonate products have a much greater rate of absorption than calcium gluconate. Tums, for example, a calcium-carbonate antacid, makes a great supplement. There is no difference in calcium whether it comes from a natural source like oyster shells or is synthetic, and chelated minerals are not absorbed any better than the nonchelated variety.

Slim to Shore lists the calcium content of all recipes.

Calcium-Rich Foods

Foods and portions which provide approximately
300 milligrams calcium each

Milk and Dairy Products: 1 cup nonfat milk, 1/4 cup dry nonfat milk powder or Parmesan cheese, 1/2 cup skimmed evaporated milk or skim ricotta cheese, 3/4 cup nonfat yogurt, plain or flavored

Beans, Grains, and Seeds: 1/2 cup tofu, 3 tablespoons sesame seeds, 3/4 cup stone-ground cornmeal or whole-wheat flour, 1 cup amaranth

Fruits and Vegetables: 1 cup cooked collard greens, rhubarb, spinach, or dried figs; 1-1/4 cups cooked turnip greens; 2 cups cooked kale, broccoli, or raw chicory

Fish: 4 ounces salmon with bones or sardines with bones

Breakfast and Breads

TROPICAL FRUIT COMPOTE
WITH RASPBERRY SAUCE

Preparation time: 15 minutes　　　　　　　*Chef: Fiona Dugdale*
Chilling time: 30 minutes　　　　　　　　*Yacht: Promenade*
Serves: 8

1 small pineapple, peeled and cored (approx. 2-1/2 cups)
1 papaya, peeled, seeded, and cubed (approx. 1-1/2 cups)
3 kiwi fruit, peeled and sliced (approx. 1-1/2 cups)
2 bananas, peeled and sliced (approx. 1 cup)
1/4 cup Kirsch, or apricot brandy

Raspberry Sauce:
1 (10 oz.) pkg. unsweetened frozen raspberries, thawed
1 tsp. fructose
Garnish: **Fresh mint leaves**

Prepare all fruit and mix in a large bowl with half of the Kirsch. Chill for 30 minutes, or longer. Purée the raspberries in a food processor or blender, add fructose while blending. Strain through a nylon sieve or cheesecloth to remove seeds. Stir in the remaining Kirsch. Spoon the fruit into individual serving bowls and top with Raspberry Sauce.

Fresh mint leaves make an attractive garnish.

Nutrient content per serving:

Calories	130	Cholesterol	0 mg
Protein	1 g	Sodium	3 mg
Carbohydrates	29 g	Potassium	370 mg
Fat	0.6 g	Iron	0.7 mg
Fiber - Dietary	3.8 g	Calcium	24.16 mg

4% calories from fat

Food Exchanges: 1.8 Fruit

POWER BREAKFAST # 1

Preparation time: 2 minutes   *Chef: Jan Robinson*
Serves: 1   *Yacht: Vanity*

1/3 cup rolled oats, uncooked
1 Tblsp. seedless raisins
1/3 cup unsweetened applesauce
1/4 cup orange juice
1/3 cup GrapeNuts

Place ingredients in a breakfast bowl in order given. Then eat! Good Morning!

POWER BREAKFAST #2

1/3 cup rolled oats, uncooked
1/3 cup sliced strawberries
1/3 cup nonfat strawberry yogurt, or applesauce
1/4 cup orange juice
1/4 cup GrapeNuts

Place ingredients in a breakfast bowl in order given.

Note: Nutrient contents in parenthesis.

Nutrient content per serving:

Calories	(309) 330	Cholesterol	(2) 0 mg
Protein	(9) 10 g	Sodium	(84) 268 mg
Carbohydrates	(67) 72 g	Potassium	(507) 469 mg
Fat	(1.8) 2.0 g	Iron	(2.1) 3.1 mg
Fiber - Dietary	(8.4) 5.2 g	Calcium	(149) 30 mg

(5%) 5% calories from fat

Food Exchanges: (1.2 Milk), (1.8) 1.5 Fruit, (1.5) 3.1 Bread, (0.3) 0.3 Fat

THREE MELON BREAKFAST SALAD

Preparation time: 20 minutes   *Chef: Dara Drew*
Serves: 12   *Yacht: Eclipse*

1 cantaloupe (2 cups)
1/4 watermelon (4 cups)
1 honeydew melon (3 cups)
2 cups seedless, green grapes
1-1/2 cups strawberries, cleaned and sliced

Cut melon balls out of all the melons. Mix together with remaining fruits. Chill or serve immediately. *Garnish with sprig of mint.*

Nutrient content per serving:

Calories	57	Cholesterol	0.0 mg
Protein	1 g	Sodium	8 mg
Carbohydrates	14 g	Potassium	320 mg
Fat	0.5 g	Iron	0.3 mg
Fiber - Dietary	1.5 g	Calcium	15 mg

7% calories from fat

Food Exchanges: 0.8 Fruit

MANGO FRENCH TOAST

Preparation time: 10 minutes
Cooking time: 6-8 minutes
Serves: 4

Chef: Judith Pear
Yacht: Valkyrie

1 cup fat-free egg substitute
1/4 cup orange juice
1/4 tsp. cardamom
1 large ripe mango
4 Tblsp. fat-free cream cheese
8 slices fat-free sourdough bread
Vegetable cooking spray
Garnish: Mango slices and sprigs of mint

Heat nonstick griddle or skillet. Mix together egg substitute, orange juice and cardamom. Slice mango into thin slices. Spread 1/2 Tblsp. cream cheese on each bread slice and place mango slices between 2 slices to make a sandwich. Pour egg mixture on a flat plate, then lay each sandwich in egg mixture, turning to moisten both sides. Spray nonstick skillet with vegetable cooking spray. Over medium heat cook long enough to brown evenly on both sides.

Cut the Mango French Toast and garnish with reserved mango slices in decorative flower pattern and a sprig of mint or other greenery.

Hint: *Any fruit can be used if Mangos are not available.*

Nutrient content per serving:

Calories	165	Cholesterol	2.5 mg
Protein	12 g	Sodium	461 mg
Carbohydrates	31 g	Potassium	127 mg
Fat	0.5 g	Iron	0.1 mg
Fiber - Dietary	1.2 g	Calcium	7 mg

3% calories from fat

Food Exchanges: 0.6 Fruit, 0.8 Meat

LAYERED HEALTHY FRUIT SALAD

Preparation time: 30 minutes   *Chef: Dara Drew*
Serves: 8   *Yacht: Eclipse*

1 red apple
1 green apple
2 bananas
1 pear
1 peach
1 cup seedless grapes
1 cup sliced strawberries
8 whole strawberries
2 (8 oz.) cartons plain nonfat yogurt
1/2 cup raisins
1/2 cup GrapeNuts

Wash and remove pits or cores of all fruits. Cut into cubes. Mix together and set aside. Combine raisins and GrapeNuts. Using a parfait glass, place a layer of fruit then yogurt, sprinkle raisin and GrapeNuts mixture over that. Then start again with the fruit. End with a topping of yogurt and add a whole strawberry.

Instead of making in parfait glasses, mix together all ingredients and make a big fruit salad.

Nutrient content per serving:

Calories	242	Cholesterol	1.3 mg
Protein	7 g	Sodium	128 mg
Carbohydrates	55 g	Potassium	737 mg
Fat	1.4 g	Iron	1.3 mg
Fiber - Dietary	5.3 g	Calcium	178 mg

5% calories from fat

Food Exchanges: 0.4 Milk, 2.7 Fruit, 0.5 Bread

OATMEAL AND RAISIN PANCAKES

Preparation time: 10 minutes   *Chef: Doug Pfaff*
Cooking time: 15 minutes   *Yacht: Flash Vert*
Serves: 8

1/2 cup old fashioned rolled oats
1/2 cup seedless raisins
1 tsp. cinnamon
1/4 tsp. vanilla
2 tsp. honey
2-1/2 cups pastry flour
2 Tblsp. no sodium baking powder
1/2 tsp. baking soda
3/4 cup fat-free egg substitute
2-1/2 cups nonfat skim milk
1/2 cup *lite* pancake syrup
Garnish: Twisted orange slice and sprig of mint

In small bowl, mix together oats, raisins, cinnamon, vanilla, honey and enough water to cover oats, let soak 5-10 minutes. Mix flour, baking powder, baking soda, egg substitute and milk in a large bowl, batter should not be too thin. Drain liquid off oat mixture and stir into batter. Use a 1/3 cup measure to ladle out batter. Cook in nonstick skillet or griddle, coat lightly with vegetable cooking spray if necessary. Makes about 16 six inch pancakes. *Serve with lite syrup.*

Nutrient content per serving:

Calories	243	Cholesterol	1 mg
Protein	9 g	Sodium	123 mg
Carbohydrates	49 g	Potassium	358 mg
Fat	1.3 g	Iron	3.3 mg
Fiber - Dietary	2.6 g	Calcium	115 mg

5% calories from fat

Food Exchanges: 0.2 Milk, 0.4 Fruit, 2.1 Bread, 0.2 Meat

CORNMEAL PANCAKES

Preparation time: 12 minutes   *Chef: Candice Carson*
Cooking time: 10 minutes   *Yacht: Freight Train II*
Serves: 8

1-1/2 cups cornmeal
1 cup pastry flour
2 tsp. fructose
1/2 tsp. baking soda
2 Tblsp. no sodium baking powder
2 cups plain nonfat yogurt
1/2 cup nonfat skim milk
1/2 cup fat-free egg substitute
Vegetable cooking spray

Topping:
1/2 cup plain nonfat yogurt
1 cup pure fruit jelly spread

Mix together the first five ingredients. Combine and add next three ingredients, stirring with a wooden spoon until just mixed. Batter will be thick. Pour 1/3 cup of batter on hot nonstick griddle or frying pan, coat with vegetable spray if necessary. *Serve with plain yogurt and pure fruit jelly spread.*

Nutrient content per serving:

Calories	272	Cholesterol	1.5 mg
Protein	9 g	Sodium	135 mg
Carbohydrates	56 g	Potassium	345 mg
Fat	0.8 g	Iron	2.1 mg
Fiber - Dietary	1.7 g	Calcium	166 mg

3% calories from fat

Food Exchanges: 0.4 Milk, 2.0 Bread, 0.1 Meat

UPSIDE-DOWN APPLE PANCAKE

Preparation time: 10 minutes　　　　　　*Chef: Marion Vanderwood*
Cooking time: 35-45 minutes　　　　　　　　*Yacht: Ocean Voyager*
Serves: 6

3 Tblsp. honey
2 Tblsp. brown rice syrup
2 tsp. allspice
3 cups sliced apples
1 cup peaches, sliced, or nectarines

Topping:
1/3 cup pastry flour
2 tsp. no sodium baking powder
1/2 cup fat-free egg substitute
1/3 cup nonfat skim milk
2 Tblsp. fructose
4 egg whites
Garnish: Orange twist and sprig of mint

Preheat oven to 350°F. Spread honey in a 9 inch pie pan, stir in allspice and sugar. Carefully arrange fruit on top. Bake 15 minutes or until apples are soft.

While fruit is baking, combine flour and baking powder, blend in egg substitute, milk and fructose. In separate bowl, beat egg whites into peaks. Fold carefully into egg mixture. Remove pan from oven and pour mixture over fruit. Bake 25-30 minutes, until lightly browned. Remove from oven, let stand 5 minutes. Invert on platter, cut into six pieces. *Garnish and serve immediately.*

Nutrient content per serving:

Calories	144	Cholesterol	0.2 mg
Protein	5 g	Sodium	59 mg
Carbohydrates	19 g	Potassium	242 mg
Fat	0.4 g	Iron	0.8 mg
Fiber - Dietary	1.8 g	Calcium	34 mg

2% calories from fat

Food Exchanges: 0.7 Fruit, 0.3 Bread, 0.5 Meat

RAISIN BRAN MUFFINS

Preparation time: 20 minutes　　　　*Chef: Sheila Kruse Boyce*
Cooking time: 20 minutes　　　　　　*Yacht: Victorious*
Yield: 16 muffins

Vegetable cooking spray
2 cups pastry flour
1-1/2 cups whole wheat flour
4 Tblsp. baking powder
1 tsp. baking soda
1/2 tsp. mace
3-1/3 cups Raisin Bran flakes
2 cups nonfat plain yogurt, or nonfat skim milk
1-1/2 cups unsweetened applesauce
1/2 cup fat-free egg substitute
2/3 cup honey

Preheat oven to 400°F. Spray muffin tins or use paper liners. Blend dry ingredients, stir in flakes. Mix liquid ingredients, add to dry ingredients. Stir until dry ingredients are *just* moistened. *Do not stir again.* Fill prepared muffin tins 3/4 full. Bake 15-20 minutes. Cool 5 minutes. Remove from pan.

Nutrient content per muffin:

Calories	211	Cholesterol	0.6 mg
Protein	6 g	Sodium	158 mg
Carbohydrates	47 g	Potassium	599 mg
Fat	0.6 g	Iron	6.4 mg
Fiber - Dietary	3.5 g	Calcium	227 mg

2% calories from fat

Food Exchanges: 0.1 Milk, 0.4 Fruit, 1.7 Bread

Be aware of 'hidden fats' in breads, even though flour contains no fat.

FRUIT AND OATMEAL MUFFINS

Preparation time: 20 minutes   *Chef: Fiona Dugdale*
Cooking time: 25 minutes   *Yacht: Promenade*
Yield: 24 muffins

Vegetable cooking spray
1 cup puréed fruit, applesauce, bananas *
1 Tblsp. fresh lemon juice
2 cups canned in own juice fruit, or unsweetened frozen
    fruit, thawed and in small pieces: berries, pineapple*
1 cup nonfat skim milk
3 egg whites
3 cups old fashioned rolled oats
3 cups pastry flour
1/3 cup fructose
3 Tblsp. baking powder
1 tsp. baking soda
1 tsp. nutmeg
2 Tblsp. grated orange rind

Preheat oven to 375° F. Spray muffin cups or use paper liners. Blend puréed fruit with lemon juice, milk, egg whites and cut fruit. Mix together all dry ingredients and orange zest; combine with fruit mixture. *Do not over mix.* Fill muffin cups. Bake for 20-25 minutes, cool in pan 5 minutes then turn out.

* *A note about puréed fruit. This is a chance to be inventive: try different varieties of cooked fruit; canned fruit works well, too. Try pears, peaches, apricots or applesauce. One chef uses bananas in the purée and pineapples for the cut fruit for tropical muffins.*

Nutrient content per muffin:

Calories	162	Cholesterol	0.2 mg
Protein	5 g	Sodium	156 mg
Carbohydrates	32 g	Potassium	177 mg
Fat	1.6 g	Iron	2.0 mg
Fiber - Dietary	3.4 g	Calcium	97 mg

9% fat from calories

Food Exchanges: 0. 2 Fruit, 1.5 Bread

OAT BRAN BLUEBERRY MUFFINS

Preparation time: 15 minutes   *Chef: Julie Simpson*
Cooking time: 15-20 minutes   *Yacht: Adela*
Yield: 12 muffins

Vegetable cooking spray
1-3/4 cups oat bran
1-1/2 cup pastry flour
1/2 tsp. baking soda
2 Tblsp. baking powder
1/4 cup fat-free egg substitute
1/2 cup nonfat skim milk
1/3 cup honey
1/2 cup unsweetened applesauce
1 cup unsweetened frozen blueberries, thawed

Preheat oven to 425° F. Spray muffin cups or insert paper liners. Mix dry ingredients, add egg substitute, milk, honey and applesauce. Mix until just moistened. Gently fold in blueberries, *do not over mix.* Fill muffin cups 2/3 full. Bake 15-20 minutes. Let cool in pan 5 minutes. *Serve warm.*

Nutrient content per muffin:

Calories	131	Cholesterol	0.2 mg
Protein	4 g	Sodium	193 mg
Carbohydrates	31 g	Potassium	131 mg
Fat	1.3 g	Iron	1.8 mg
Fiber - Dietary	3.2 g	Calcium	116 mg

7% calories from fat

Food Exchanges: 0.1 Fruit, 1.3 Bread

HEARTY BREAKFAST MUFFINS

Preparation time: 15 minutes
Cooking time: 18-20 minutes
Yield: 12 muffins

Chef: Donna Clark
Yacht: Domus

Vegetable cooking spray
1/4 cup nonfat skim milk
1/4 cup fat-free egg substitute
1/2 cup unsweetened applesauce
1/4 cup shredded raw carrot
1/2 cup raw apple, peeled and shredded
1/4 cup seedless raisins
2 cups pastry flour
1/4 cup rolled oats
2 tsp. ground cinnamon
2 Tblsp. no sodium baking powder

Preheat oven to 375° F. Spray 12 muffin cups or use paper liners. In a medium bowl, mix milk, egg substitute, applesauce, apples, carrots, honey and raisins. Add remaining ingredients and stir until *just* moistened. Fill muffin cups 1/2 full. Bake 18-20 minutes. Cool 5 minutes. Remove from pan.

Nutrient content per muffin:

Calories	126	Cholesterol	0.1 mg
Protein	3 g	Sodium	11 mg
Carbohydrates	28 g	Potassium	150 mg
Fat	0.5 g	Iron	1.8 mg
Fiber - Dietary	1.5 g	Calcium	20 mg

4% calories from fat

Food Exchanges: 0.3 Fruit, 1 Bread

AUTUMN MUFFINS

Preparation time: 15 minutes
Cooking time: 15-20 minutes
Yield: 12 muffins

Chef: Beth Avore
Yacht: Perfection

Vegetable cooking spray
1/4 cup fat-free egg substitute
1/2 cup nonfat skim milk
1/4 cup light brown sugar
1 cup canned pumpkin
1 cup pastry flour
3/4 cup whole wheat flour
2 Tblsp. baking powder
1/2 tsp. baking soda
1 tsp. cinnamon
1/2 tsp. nutmeg
1/4 tsp. allspice

Preheat oven to 400°F. Spray 12 muffin cups or use paper liners. Beat together egg substitute, milk, sugar and pumpkin. Mix together the flours, baking powder, soda and spices. Fold wet and dry ingredients together *until just moistened.* Fill prepared muffin cups 1/2 full. Bake 15-20 minutes. Cool 5 minutes. Remove from pan.

Serve with a fresh fruit platter.

Nutrient content per muffin:

Calories	96	Cholesterol	0.2 mg
Protein	3 g	Sodium	52 mg
Carbohydrates	20 g	Potassium	369 mg
Fat	0.6 g	Iron	1.6 mg
Fiber - Dietary	1.6 g	Calcium	135 mg

5% calories from fat

Food Exchanges: 0.9 Bread

EGG - A - MUFFIN

Preparation time: 10 minutes   *Chef: Ann Glenn*
Cooking time: 5-10 minutes   *Yacht: Encore*
Yield: 16 open-faced sandwiches

2 Tblsp. nonfat mayonnaise
1-1/4 cups fat-free egg substitute
1 Tblsp. lemon juice
1 tsp. dry mustard
1/2 cup low fat grated cheese
1/2 tsp. black pepper
2 Tblsp. chopped parsley
8 English muffins, split and toasted
16 (1/2 oz. each) slices turkey ham
5 egg whites
Garnish: Sprigs of parsley

In a small bowl blend mayonnaise, egg substitute, lemon juice, mustard, cheese, pepper and parsley. Arrange English muffins on a warm serving dish. Warm slices of turkey ham in a nonstick skillet then place one on top of each muffin. Beat egg whites until stiff and fold mayonnaise mixture into egg whites. Scramble egg mixture in a nonstick skillet over medium-low heat for 5-10 minutes or until cooked. Gently spoon mixture on top of muffins. Garnish.

Fresh fruit such as pineapple completes the morning menu.

Nutrient content per serving:

Calories	85	Cholesterol	1 mg
Protein	5 g	Sodium	256 mg
Carbohydrates	14 g	Potassium	183 mg
Fat	0.7 g	Iron	0.9 mg
Fiber - Dietary	0.7 g	Calcium	48 mg

8% fat from calories

Food Exchanges: 0.8 Bread, 0.3 Meat, 0.1 Fat

OFF- THE- HIPS OMELET

Preparation time: 5 minutes   *Chef: Regina Jordan*
Cooking time: 5-10 minutes   *Yacht: Prelude*
Serves: 1

Butter-flavored vegetable spray
1/4 cup sliced fresh mushrooms
1/4 cup diced onions
2 fresh basil leaves, chopped, or 1/4 tsp. dried basil
1/2 cup fat-free egg substitute, or 3 egg whites
1/2 tsp. butter-flavored seasoning
2 tomato slices, or 2 cantaloupe slices

Spray omelet pan and sauté mushrooms, onions and basil until soft,
remove from pan. Spray again and add egg substitute, when it begins
to set, lift edges to let uncooked portion run under. Cook until it is a
soft consistency overall. Add mushroom, onions and basil combination
down the center of the eggs. Sprinkle with butter seasoning. Fold two
sides of omelet into center and slide onto plate. Serve with sliced
tomatoes, cantaloupe slices or both.

Note: *For a spicy omelet, sprinkle the omelet with dried red pepper or
serve with fresh salsa over top of omelet.*

Nutrient content per serving:

Calories	91	Cholesterol	0 mg
Protein	11 g	Sodium	168 mg
Carbohydrates	9 g	Potassium	276 mg
Fat	1.1 g	Iron	0.7 mg
Fiber - Dietary	1.7 g	Calcium	19 mg

11% calories from fat

Food Exchanges: 1.1 Veg., 1.2 Meat

Now try that
again! —

CARIBBEAN LOW FAT FRITTATA

Preparation time: 10 minutes   *Chef: Jan Robinson*
Cooking time: 25 minutes   *Yacht: Vanity*
Serves: 6

1 red bell pepper, julienne
1 yellow bell pepper, julienne
1 green bell pepper, julienne
1-1/2 cups thinly sliced red onion
1-1/2 tsp. dried rosemary, or 4 sprigs of fresh, crushed
1/4 cup fat-free chicken broth (page 80) or water
1 cup sliced fresh mushrooms
3 cups fat-free egg substitute
1/2 cup nonfat skim milk
1/4 tsp. Tabasco
1 tsp. black pepper
Vegetable cooking spray

Preheat oven to 400°F. Simmer peppers, onion and rosemary in chicken broth or water until vegetables are soft, about 10 minutes. Add mushrooms and cook 3 minutes more, turning mixture gently. Remove from skillet and set aside.

Beat egg substitute and milk together. Add Tabasco and pepper. With heat on low, coat large skillet heavily with vegetable cooking spray. Pour in egg mixture, increase heat to medium-high. Lift skillet above burner, rotate in a circular motion to move the eggs to the sides.

When egg mixture is 2/3 cooked, spoon vegetable mixture over eggs. Turn heat off and transfer skillet to preheated oven. Bake until top is golden, about 10 minutes. *Cut Frittata into 6 wedges, serve immediately.*

Nutrient content per serving:

Calories	103	Cholesterol	0.3 mg
Protein	12 g	Sodium	194 mg
Carbohydrates	12 g	Potassium	260 mg
Fat	0.8 g	Iron	0.3 mg
Fiber - Dietary	0.9 g	Calcium	41 mg

7% calories from fat

Food Exchanges: 0.6 Veg., 0.2 Bread, 1.2 Meat

CHICKEN FRITTATA

Preparation time: 10 minutes   *Chef: Randa Jacobs*
Cooking time: 20-25 minutes   *Yacht: Blithe Spirit*
Serves: 4

1 cup julienne, boneless, skinless chicken breast
1 cup sliced fresh mushrooms
2 Tblsp. + 2 Tblsp. nonfat chicken broth (page 80)
1 small zucchini, julienne
1/2 green bell pepper, julienne
1/2 red bell pepper, julienne
1-1/2 cups fat-free egg substitute
2 Tblsp. nonfat skim milk
1/2 tsp. Italian herb blend
1/4 tsp. black pepper
1/4 tsp. cayenne (optional)
3 egg whites
Garnish: Tomato slices and fresh parsley sprigs

Preheat oven to 350°F. Put 2 Tblsp. chicken broth in a large nonstick ovenproof skillet, add and brown chicken and mushrooms, Add 2 more Tblsp. broth, zucchini and peppers. Cook until tender, stirring often. Beat together egg substitute, milk, Italian blend and peppers. Beat egg whites until stiff, but not dry. Fold both together and add to skillet. Bake until puffed and golden. Cut in 4 sections and serve immediately. *Garnish with tomato slices and fresh parsley sprigs.*

Note: *This also makes a great lunch served with a salad.*

Nutrient content per serving:

Calories	164	Cholesterol	48 mg
Protein	29 g	Sodium	253 mg
Carbohydrates	6 g	Potassium	395 mg
Fat	2.3 g	Iron	1.1 mg
Fiber - Dietary	1.1 g	Calcium	28 mg

13% calories from fat

Food Exchanges: 0.5 Veg., 3.8 Meat

POTATO OMELETTE

Preparation time: 15 minutes　　　　　　　　　*Chef: Beth Avore*
Cooking time: 10-15 minutes　　　　　　　　　*Yacht: Perfection*
Serves: 2

Vegetable cooking spray
1 cup cubed boiled potatoes
1/2 cup diced boiled onions
1 cup fat-free egg substitute
2 tsp. dried dill weed

Coat a small frying pan with vegetable cooking spray. Sauté potatoes and onions until golden brown on all sides. Shake the egg substitute with dill weed and pour over potatoes and onions; cover. Cook on low heat until set.

Cut in half, serve with tomato and cucumber slices sprinkled with pepper and whole wheat toast; or with fresh tomato salsa over all.

Nutrient content per serving:

Calories	193	Cholesterol	0 mg
Protein	13 g	Sodium	169 mg
Carbohydrates	33 g	Potassium	611 mg
Fat	1.0 g	Iron	1.0 mg
Fiber - Dietary	2.7 g	Calcium	33 mg

5% calories from fat

Food Exchanges: 0.5 Veg., 1.7 Bread, 1.2 Meat

Substitute 2 egg whites or 1/4 cup fat-free egg substitute for 1 whole egg.

KANSAS WHEAT BREAD

Preparation time: 1/2 hour
Resting time: 2 hours
Cooking time: 30-35 minutes
Yield: 1 Loaf - 18 slices

Chef: Donna Clark
Yacht: Domus

1 cup water
1 pkg. dry yeast
2 Tblsp. honey
2 cups white flour
1 cup wheat flour
1/2 cup wheat germ
Vegetable cooking spray

Mix together water, yeast and honey and let sit 5 minutes. Stir in remaining ingredients until too stiff to work with a spoon. Knead in remaining flour until dough is smooth and satiny, 5-8 minutes. Form dough into a ball and put in a bowl coated with vegetable spray, turn and spray top. Cover and put in a warm, draft-free place to rise until double in size, (1 hour). Punch dough down and form into a loaf. Place in a loaf pan coated with vegetable spray. Let rise until almost double in size, (1 hour). Place pan in a cool oven and turn heat to 350°F. Bake 30-35 minutes until done. Cool 5 minutes and remove from pan.

Hint: *Let cool 15 more minutes before slicing. This bread slices well for sandwiches, toasts well and keeps well. Make two loaves and give one to a friend. They'll love it!*

Note: *For a crustier bread cook in a 400°F oven.*

Note: *This bread also works very well in a bread maker.*

Nutrient content per slice:

Calories	94	Cholesterol	0 mg
Protein	3 g	Sodium	61 mg
Carbohydrates	19 g	Potassium	79 mg
Fat	0.7 g	Iron	1.2 mg
Fiber - Dietary	1.7 g	Calcium	6 mg

6% calories from fat

Food Exchanges: 1.1 Bread

Salads and Dressings

ENDIVE AND BEET SALAD

Preparation time: 15 minutes
Chilling time: 30 minutes
Serves: 4

Chef: Bobbi Fawcett
Yacht: Windwalker

2 cups chopped Belgian endives
1-1/2 cups beet slices, drained
2 green onions, finely chopped
2 Tblsp. balsamic vinegar
1/2 Tblsp. honey
1/8 tsp. Tabasco
1/8 tsp. black pepper
2 tsp. chopped fresh basil

Mix all ingredients and chill at least 30 minutes before serving.

Nutrient content per serving:

Calories	39	Cholesterol	0 mg
Protein	1 g	Sodium	179 mg
Carbohydrates	9 g	Potassium	147 mg
Fat	0.1 g	Iron	1.7 mg
Fiber - Dietary	1.1 g	Calcium	24 mg

3% calories from fat

Food Exchanges: 0.9 Veg.

Buy the whitest endive as traces of green at tips indicates the endive has been exposed to the light and will be excessively bitter.

CARROT AND SPROUT SALAD

Preparation time: 10 minutes   *Chef: Shirley King*
Serves: 6   *Yacht: Latina*

3 cups carrots, shredded
1 cup alfalfa sprouts
1/4 tsp. each of black pepper and basil
1 Tblsp. lemon juice

Combine carrots with alfalfa sprouts. Sprinkle with pepper, basil and lemon juice. *Serve with* **Latina scallops Provencale** *(page 191)* **Rice with Peas and Parsley** *(page 204) pineapple slices and sparkling water.*

Nutrient content per serving:

Calories	26	Cholesterol	0 mg
Protein	0.8 g	Sodium	20 mg
Carbohydrates	6 g	Potassium	186 mg
Fat	0.1 g	Iron	0.4 mg
Fiber - Dietary	1.9 g	Calcium	17 mg

5% calories from fat

Food Exchanges: 1.0 Veg.

CARROTS WITH YOGURT

Preparation time: 15 minutes   *Chef: Josie Gould*
Cooking time: 5 minutes   *Yacht: Amalthea of Sark*
Serves: 4

2 cups grated carrots
2 Tblsp. fat-free chicken broth (page 80) or water
1/2 cup plain nonfat yogurt
2 cloves garlic, crushed

Cook carrots in broth until just softened, 5 minutes. Set them aside to cool. Whip yogurt until smooth. Fold carrots and garlic into yogurt. *Makes a great dip, salad, or buffet accompaniment. Also a good vegetable side dish with fish and curries.*

Nutrient content per serving:

Calories	44	Cholesterol	0 mg
Protein	2 g	Sodium	61 mg
Carbohydrates	9 g	Potassium	284 mg
Fat	0.1 g	Iron	0.3 mg
Fiber - Dietary	2.0 g	Calcium	18 mg

2% calories from fat

Food Exchanges: 0.1 Milk, 1.3 Veg.

CARROT AND ORANGE SALAD

Preparation time: 15 minutes
Chilling time: 1 hour
Serves: 6

Chef: Joyce Bearse
Yacht: Ambience

3 cups finely grated carrots
2 cups oranges
1/2 cup raisins

Spicy Dressing:
1/4 cup plain nonfat yogurt
1 Tblsp. lime juice
1 tsp. ground cumin
1/2 tsp. ground cinnamon
1-1/2 Tblsp. honey
Garnish: Lime twists

Put carrots and raisins into a bowl. Cut, peel and remove pith from oranges. Remove segments and chop. Add to carrots and raisins.

Dressing: Mix all ingredients and toss with salad. Refrigerate for one hour. *Use a slotted spoon to serve. Garnish. with lime twists.*

Note: This salad is also good if you use 1/2 cup canned unsweetened crushed drained pineapple, instead of the oranges. Nice light salad for lunch or dinner.

Nutrient content per serving:

Calories	105	Cholesterol	0.2 mg
Protein	2 g	Sodium	29 mg
Carbohydrates	26 g	Potassium	384 mg
Fat	0.3 g	Iron	0.9 mg
Fiber - Dietary	3.5 g	Calcium	63 mg

2% calories from fat

Food Exchanges: 1 Veg., 0.9 Fruit

CUCUMBER–ORANGE SALAD

Preparation time: 20 minutes   *Chef: Iña Mösing*
Serves: 4   *Yacht: Relax*

1 lb. cucumber (2 large or 1 seedless)
2 cups orange segments (2 large oranges)
4 Tblsp. nonfat yogurt
1 Tblsp. raspberry vinegar
1/2 tsp. fructose
1 Tblsp. each dill weed
1 Tblsp. chopped parsley

Slice cucumbers (thin) into a bowl. Over the bowl, pare and section oranges to reserve juice. Mix remaining ingredients together (except parsley) and stir into the cucumber and orange mixture.

Garnish with chopped parsley sprinkled over the top.

Nutrient content per serving:

Calories	74	Cholesterol	0.3 mg
Protein	2 g	Sodium	89 mg
Carbohydrates	17 g	Potassium	398 mg
Fat	0.3 g	Iron	0.8 mg
Fiber - Dietary	3.0 g	Calcium	95 mg

4% calories from fat

Food Exchanges: 0.5 Veg., 0.7 Fruit

I'm tired of these ordinary Salads, let's you and I make one!!

GREEN APPLE SALAD

Preparation time: 10 minutes   *Chef: Susanne Nilsson*
Chilling time: 1 hour   *Yacht: Falcon*
Serves: 4

2/3 cup nonfat yogurt, drained
1 Tblsp. honey
1 Tblsp. grated horseradish
2 cups savoy cabbage, chopped
1-1/3 cups green apples, cored and sliced

Whisk yogurt, honey and horseradish together. Add the fine chopped savoy cabbage and sliced apples. *Chill for 1 hour before serving.*

Nutrient content per serving:

Calories	70	Cholesterol	0.7 mg
Protein	3 g	Sodium	80 mg
Carbohydrates	15 g	Potassium	233 mg
Fat	0.2 g	Iron	0.3 mg
Fiber - Dietary	1.6 g	Calcium	93 mg

3% calories from fat

Food Exchanges: 0.2 Milk, 0.3 Veg., 0.3 Fruit

CUCUMBER AND DILL SALAD

Preparation time: 15 minutes   *Chef: Bobbi Fawcett*
Chilling time: 30 minutes   *Yacht: Windwalker*
Serves: 4

2 cucumbers, finely sliced
2 Tblsp. white wine vinegar
1/2 tsp. fructose
2 Tblsp. onion, finely sliced
2 Tblsp. chopped fresh dill (or 2 tsp. dried dill weed)

Mix and chill for 30 minutes before serving.

Nutrient content per serving:

Calories	32	Cholesterol	0 mg
Protein	1 g	Sodium	153 mg
Carbohydrates	7 g	Potassium	248 mg
Fat	0.2 g	Iron	0.7 mg
Fiber - Dietary	1.6 g	Calcium	31 mg

6% calories from fat

Food Exchanges: 0.9 Veg.

DESPERADO COLE SLAW

Preparation time: 15 minutes   *Chef: Lisa Ringland*
Serves: 6
Yacht: Renegade

6 cups shredded green cabbage
1 (8 oz.) can pineapple tidbits in water, drained
1 cup raisins
4 cups grated carrots
1-1/2 cups nonfat mayonnaise
1 tsp. seasoned rice vinegar
6 pineapple rings

Add drained pineapple and raisins to cabbage. Fold in carrots. Mix rice vinegar into mayonnaise and stir into carrots.

Garnish each serving with pineapple ring.

Nutrient content per serving:

Calories	154	Cholesterol	0 mg
Protein	3 g	Sodium	77 mg
Carbohydrates	3 g	Potassium	711 mg
Fat	0.5 g	Iron	1.7 mg
Fiber - Dietary	6.2 g	Calcium	82 mg

2% calories from fat

Food Exchanges: 2.3 Veg., 1.6 Fruit

Do you have to have that cole slaw?!

TANGY TOMATO SLAW

Preparation time: 12 minutes
Cooking time: 5 minutes
Chilling time: 1 hour
Serves: 6

Chef: Jan Robinson
Yacht: Vanity

4 cups finely sliced, cored green cabbage
3 medium tomatoes, thinly sliced
1 yellow bell pepper, thinly sliced
1 onion, thinly sliced
1 jalapeño chili, seeded, minced

Sweet and Sour Dressing:
3/4 cup balsamic vinegar (or rice vinegar)
1/2 cup fructose
1/2 tsp. celery seeds
1/4 tsp. ground allspice
1/4 tsp. ground ginger
1/4 tsp. ground cinnamon
1/4 tsp. turmeric

Mix first 5 ingredients in large bowl. Combine all dressing ingredients in heavy medium saucepan. Stir over low heat until fructose dissolves and mixture is hot; do not boil. Pour dressing over cabbage and mix to coat. Let stand 1 hour. Drain slaw before serving.

Hint: *Can be prepared up to 2 days ahead. Cover and refrigerate.*

Nutrient content per serving:

Calories	128	Cholesterol	0 mg
Protein	2 g	Sodium	43 mg
Carbohydrates	30 g	Potassium	324 mg
Fat	0.4 g	Iron	2.3 mg
Fiber - Dietary	2.4 g	Calcium	37 mg

3% calories from fat

Food Exchanges: 1.4 Veg.

CABBAGE–GRAPE SALAD
WITH HONEY GINGER DRESSING

Preparation time: 15 minutes　　　　　　*Chef: Gretchen Fater*
Chilling time: 30 minutes　　　　　　　*Yacht: Maranatha*
Serves: 8

6 cups shredded green cabbage
1-1/2 cups seedless red grapes
1-1/2 cups diced tart apples, peeled, cored and
　　　　sprinkled with lemon juice

Honey-Ginger Dressing:
3/4 cup plain nonfat yogurt
3 Tblsp. nonfat mayonnaise
1-1/2 Tblsp. honey
1/2 tsp. ground ginger

Combine first three ingredients. Mix Dressing ingredients. Pour over salad and chill for 30 minutes. Toss before serving.

Note: *This cool and slightly sweet salad is a wonderful side dish with spicy Mexican or Indian food. You can also prepare it with red cabbage and green Granny Smith apples.*

Nutrient content per serving:

Calories	70	Cholesterol	0.4 mg
Protein	2 g	Sodium	76 mg
Carbohydrates	16 g	Potassium	288 mg
Fat	0.3 g	Iron	0.5 mg
Fiber - Dietary	2.2 g	Calcium	79 mg

4% calories from fat

Food Exchanges: 0.1 Milk, 0.6 Veg., 0.4 Fruit

SPINACH SALAD WITH
YOGURT–POPPY SEED DRESSING

Preparation time: 15 minutes　　　　　　　*Chef: Gretchen Fater*
Serves: 4　　　　　　　　　　　　　　　　*Yacht: Maranatha*

Salad:
1 orange
1/4 lb. spinach leaves, washed and trimmed (5 cups)
1/2 cup sliced water chestnuts
2 Tblsp. thinly sliced green onions

Yogurt Poppy Seed Dressing:
3 Tblsp. plain nonfat yogurt
2 Tblsp. nonfat mayonnaise
1 tsp. fresh lemon juice
1 Tblsp. honey
1 tsp. grated orange rind
1 tsp. poppy seeds, toasted

Peel, seed and section the orange. Place spinach leaves on serving platter. Arrange orange sections in a circular pattern on spinach. Combine water chestnuts and green onion. Place in center of salad. Top with dressing.

Hint: You can substitute romaine lettuce for spinach.

Nutrient content per serving:

Calories	72	Cholesterol	0.2 mg
Protein	2 g	Sodium	96 mg
Carbohydrates	16 g	Potassium	355 mg
Fat	0.8 g	Iron	1.0 mg
Fiber - Dietary	1.6 g	Calcium	87 mg

9% calories from fat

Food Exchanges: 0.8 Veg., 0.2 Fruit

SNOW PEA AND MANGO SALAD

Preparation time: 15 minutes   *Chef: Elaine Gregory*
Cooking time: 1 minute   *Yacht: Moorea*
Serves: 8

2 cups trimmed snow peas
2 mangoes, peeled and thinly sliced
1 cup thinly sliced red pepper

Citrus Dressing:
1/4 cup lemon juice
1/4 cup orange juice
1/4 cup honey
1 Tblsp. basalmic vinegar
1/4 tsp. black pepper

Blanch peas for one minute, drain, rinse and cool. When cooled, combine
with mangoes and peppers. Whisk together Citrus Dressing ingredients.
Toss gently with salad and grind fresh pepper over all.

Hint: *Three large nectarines or one small cantaloupe can be substituted
for the mangoes.*

Nutrient content per serving:

Calories	91	Cholesterol	0 mg
Protein	1 g	Sodium	4 mg
Carbohydrates	23 g	Potassium	201 mg
Fat	0.2 g	Iron	1.0 mg
Fiber - Dietary	2.4 g	Calcium	24 mg

2% calories from fat

Food Exchanges: 0.1 Veg., 0.6 Fruit, 0.1 Bread

*Rice will remain white when cooking by adding one
teaspoon lemon juice, or one tablespoon vinegar to
the water.*

MEXICAN MANGO SALAD

Preparation time: 12 minutes　　　　　　*Chef: Jan Robinson*
Serves: 4　　　　　　　　　　　　　　　　　*Yacht: Vanity*

2 cups (2 heads) endive leaves
1 ripe mango, peeled, sliced lengthwise
1 large grapefruit, pared, pith removed, cut in sections
1 small (1/2 lb.) jicama*, peeled and cut into 'matchsticks'
1 small bunch watercress sprigs
2 Tblsp. chopped cilantro

Arrange endive on individual salad plates. Peel mango and grapefruit over a bowl to reserve juices. Gently toss together mango, grapefruit, jicama and watercress. Arrange over the endive. Whisk cilantro into the reserved juices and pour over each salad.

***Note:** Jicama is a Mexican root vegetable available in the produce department of most supermarkets.*

*This salad goes well with **Vegetable Tacos** (page 33) or **Black Bean Burritos** (page 131).*

Nutrient content per serving:

Calories	73	Cholesterol	0 mg
Protein	2 g	Sodium	12 mg
Carbohydrates	18 g	Potassium	366 mg
Fat	0.3 g	Iron	1.1 mg
Fiber-Dietary	2.3 g	Calcium	41 mg

3% calories from fat

Food Exchanges: 0.6 Veg., 0.8 Fruit

Store garlic in a basket at room temperature. If refrigerated the garlic peel becomes moist and the head tends to dry out.

GREEN BEAN AND BABY CORN SALAD

Preparation time: 10 minutes　　　　　　*Chef: Elaine Gregory*
Cooking time: 4 minutes　　　　　　　　　*Yacht: Moorea*
Serves: 6

3-1/2 cups (1 lb.) green beans, trimmed
1 (14 oz.) can baby ears of corn
1/3 cup sliced green onions

Mustard Ginger Dressing:
2 Tblsp. rice wine vinegar
2 Tblsp. Dijon mustard
2 Tblsp. honey
2 tsp. grated ginger root
1/4 tsp. black pepper

Blanch beans for 4 minutes, drain, rinse and cool. Prepare dressing by whisking together vinegar, mustard, honey and seasonings. Chill and toss with beans, corn and onions just before serving.

Frozen whole green beans may be used if fresh are unavailable. This salad looks wonderful served on lettuce leafs and is a particularly good accompaniment to meals with an oriental flavor.

Nutrient content per serving:

Calories	97	Cholesterol	0 mg
Protein	3 g	Sodium	117 mg
Carbohydrates	23 g	Potassium	372 mg
Fat	0.6 g	Iron	1.5 mg
Fiber - Dietary	2.3 g	Calcium	47 mg

5% calories from fat

Food Exchanges: 1.1 Veg., 0.6 Bread

Vegetables can become limp during storage; freshen by cleaning and submerging in cold water and ice cubes.

TURKEY PASTA SALAD

Preparation time: 20 minutes   *Chef: Lisa Ringland*
Cooking time: 12 minutes   *Yacht: Renegade*
Serves: 6

8 oz. tri-color pasta twists
1 lb. cooked turkey breast
1 head broccoli
1 red bell pepper, chopped
1 green bell pepper, chopped
1/2 cup chopped onion

Dressing:
1 package low-fat Ranch Dressing mix
1-1/2 cups nonfat mayonnaise*

Cook pasta. Cube turkey breast and add to cooled pasta. Add broccoli, chopped peppers and onion. Mix together Ranch dressing envelope and mayonnaise.

Serve on bed of Romaine lettuce with fresh bread sticks and/or slices of fruit.

The commercial nonfat mayonnaise is very high in sodium, so if you must limit your sodium intake, substitute 1/2 the **Vegetarian Creamy Dressing recipe on page 76) (Nutrition in parenthesis for substitution.)*

Nutrient content per serving:

Calories .... (363) 382	Cholesterol .... (63) 64 mg
Protein .... (33) 31 g	Sodium ....(290) 1254 mg
Carbohydrates .... (53) 61 g	Potassium .... (580) 508 mg
Fat .... (2.5) 2.5 g	Iron .... (3.9) 3.6 mg
Fiber - Dietary .... (5.0) 4.0 g	Calcium .... (74) 52 mg

(7) 6% calories from fat

Food Exchanges: (1.1) 1 Veg., (2.7) 2.9 Bread, (3.3) 3.5 Meat

COLD CURRY TURKEY SALAD

Preparation time: 30 - 45 minutes   *Chef: Jeanne Bach*
Serves: 6   *Yacht: Iemanja*

3 cups (1 lb.) cooked cubed turkey breast
1 (16 oz). can diced pineapple in water (or fresh pineapple)
2 (8 oz.) cans sliced water chestnuts
4 long stalks celery, sliced thin crosswise
4 green onions sliced

Creamy Curry Dressing:
1 Tblsp. curry powder
2 Tblsp. water
1 cup nonfat plain yogurt, drained*
1/3 cup mango chutney
1/4 tsp. black pepper

In small pan (or use a metal measuring cup), heat curry powder in water until dissolved. Cool. Combine turkey, pineapple, water chestnuts, celery and green onions. In glass measuring cup blend yogurt, cooled curry paste and mango chutney; stir into the turkey mixture. Grind fresh pepper over all. *Chill until ready to serve.*

Serve with fruit like melon, pineapple, bananas or strawberry slices.

Hint: *Heating the curry powder eliminates the grainy texture of raw curry powder.*

Nutrient content per serving:

Calories	256	Cholesterol	53 mg
Protein	26 g	Sodium	107 mg
Carbohydrates	32 g	Potassium	579 mg
Fat	2.8 g	Iron	2.6 mg
Fiber - Dietary	2.2 g	Calcium	103 mg

10% calories from fat

Food Exchanges: 0.2 Milk, 1.6 Veg., 1.1 Fruit, 3.2 Meat

For thicker dressings - drain yogurt in a cheese cloth, a paper towel, or coffee filter lined sieve for two hours or longer.

CHICKEN CURRY SALAD
IN PINEAPPLE RINGS

Preparation time: 30 minutes   *Chef: Judy Knape*
Cooking time: 15 minutes   *Yacht: Ariel*
Serves: 6

1-1/3 lbs. boneless skinless chicken breasts
1 cup celery, chopped
2 cups apples, cored and diced
1 cup seedless grapes, halved
1 cup green pepper, diced
1 cup onion, diced
1 pineapple (cut into 6 rings, cut around leaving 1/2 inch wide
**   ring, discard core and cube remaining pineapple)**

Creamy Curry Dressing:
1 Tblsp. curry powder
2 Tblsp. water
1 cup nonfat yogurt, drained*
1/3 cup hot chutney
1/2 tsp. black pepper
1/2 tsp. paprika

Microwave chicken breasts until done (10-15 minutes) skin, cube, and chill. Heat curry and water until curry dissolved; cool. Combine with other dressing ingredients and add to chicken pieces. Add other salad ingredients including cubed pineapple cut from inside rings. To serve, mound salad inside rings, sprinkle with paprika.

Hints: *Draining yogurt in paper towel-lined sieve for 2 hours or longer produces much less watery dressing. Heating curry powder eliminates the grainy texture of raw curry powder.*

Nutrient content per serving:

Calories	279	Cholesterol	73 mg
Protein	30 g	Sodium	115 mg
Carbohydrates	32 g	Potassium	612 mg
Fat	3.8 g	Iron	1.9 mg
Fiber - Dietary	3.2 g	Calcium	120 mg

12% calories from fat

Food Exchanges: 0.2 Milk, 0.6 Veg, 1.6 Fruit, 3.7 Meat

CHICKEN SALAD WITH CURRY AND BANANA DRESSING

Preparation time: 20 minutes   *Chef: Susanne Nilsson*
Cooking time: 20 minutes   *Yacht: Falcon*
Serves: 6

1-1/2 lbs. boneless, skinless chicken breasts
1/2 tsp. tarragon
1/2 tsp. paprika
1/4 tsp. black pepper
1 head iceberg lettuce
6 tomatoes
1 large cucumber
1 small leek
1 cup frozen corn kernels (thawed)

Curry and Banana Dressing:
2 ripe bananas
1 cup nonfat yogurt, drained*
1 Tblsp. lemon juice
1-2 Tblsp. curry
1/2 tsp. black pepper

Preheat oven to 375° F. Arrange chicken breasts in single layer in baking pan, sprinkle with tarragon, paprika and pepper. Bake for 20 minutes, or until done. Chill for several hours. Tear lettuce into small pieces and slice tomato, cucumber and leek into a large salad bowl; toss everything together. Cut chicken into chunks and add to lettuce. Blend all dressing ingredients in blender for 2-3 minutes and toss with salad.

Note: Chicken may be cooked in microwave.

***Hint:** Draining yogurt in paper towel-lined sieve for 2 hours or longer produces a much less watery dressing.*

Nutrient content per serving:

Calories	294	Cholesterol	73 mg
Protein	34 g	Sodium	133 mg
Carbohydrates	33 g	Potassium	1122 mg
Fat	4.4 g	Iron	3.4 mg
Fiber - Dietary	5.3 g	Calcium	184 mg

13% calories from fat

Food Exchanges: 0.3 Milk, 2 Veg., 0.6 Fruit, 0.3 Bread, 3.7 Meat

TROPICAL CHICKEN SALAD

Preparation time: 25 minutes   *Chef: Kate Chivas*
Serves: 6   *Yacht: Tri World*

2 large head iceberg lettuce, or boston
3 cups (about 1 lb.) cooked cubed skinless chicken breasts
2 medium oranges, peeled, pith removed, and sectioned
1 cup diced fresh pineapple
1/2 cup finely diced onion
1/2 cup finely diced celery
1/2 cup diced red bell pepper
1/2 cup diced green bell pepper

Creamy Fruit Dressing:
2 cups nonfat plain yogurt
1 cup fresh strawberries (or unsweetened frozen, thawed)
1 Tblsp. fructose
1 cup fresh blueberries (or unsweetened frozen, thawed)
Garnish: Cinnamon

Wash the head of lettuce and retain the outer leaves for lettuce "bowls" in which to serve the salad. Place the outer leaves on paper towels and put in the refrigerator until needed. In a large bowl tear the remaining heads of lettuce into bite size pieces. Add the rest of the salad ingredients and toss well. Blend dressing ingredients (except blueberries) in blender.

To serve, place each lettuce "bowl" on a chilled salad plate and evenly divide the salad into them. Spoon over dressing. Sprinkle with blueberries and dash of cinnamon.

This salad is a lovely entreé for a light lunch or dinner.

Nutrient content per serving:

Calories	261	Cholesterol	66 mg
Protein	31 g	Sodium	140 mg
Carbohydrates	27 g	Potassium	901 mg
Fat	3.6 g	Iron	2.2 mg
Fiber - Dietary	5.2 g	Calcium	229 mg

12% calories from fat

Food Exchanges: 0.4 Milk, 1.1 Veg., 0.8 Fruit, 3.3 Meat

ORIENT EXPRESS SALAD WITH CREAMY BANANA–GINGER DRESSING

Preparation time: 15 minutes　　　　　　　*Chef: Jan Robinson*
Serves: 6　　　　　　　　　　　　　　　　　　*Yacht: Vanity*

3/4 lbs. cooked boneless, skinless chicken breast, julienned
1 (10-1/2 oz.) can mandarin oranges canned in juice, drained
1/2 cup sliced water chestnuts
1/2 cup chopped celery
2 Tblsp. + 2 Tblsp. chopped green onion
1 cup chopped red pepper

Creamy Banana Ginger Dressing:
1/2 cup plain nonfat yogurt, drained
1/2 cup mashed banana
3 Tblsp. honey
1 Tblsp. lemon juice
2 tsp. seasoned rice vinegar
1 Tblsp. grated fresh ginger root
1/4 cup chopped fresh cilantro
1/4 tsp. white pepper

3 cups torn romaine lettuce or dark leafy greens of choice

In mixing bowl, combine chicken, 1/2 cup orange segments, water chestnuts, celery, 2 Tblsp. green onion and red pepper. Combine yogurt, banana, honey, lemon juice, vinegar, ginger, cilantro and white pepper in blender or food processor. Purée until smooth. Pour 1/2 of the dressing over chicken, mix well and chill.

To serve, arrange romaine lettuce on serving plate, spoon chicken salad on top, surround with remaining orange segments and sprinkle remaining 2 Tblsp. green onion over all. Serve remaining dressing.

Nutrient content per serving:

Calories	189	Cholesterol	48 mg
Protein	20 g	Sodium	113 mg
Carbohydrates	22 g	Potassium	492 mg
Fat	2.3 g	Iron	1.6 mg
Fiber - Dietary	1.7 g	Calcium	77 mg

11% calories from fat

Food Exchanges: 0.1 Milk, 0.6 Veg., 0.4 Fruit, 2.5 Meat

TURKEY AND WILD RICE SALAD

Preparation time: 15 minutes   *Chef: Gretchen Fater*
Serves: 4   *Yacht: Maranatha*

2 cups cooked long grain and wild rice
1/2 lb. cooked turkey breast, cut into 1/4 inch cubes
1/2 lb. blanched snow peas
1 red pepper, seeded and chopped
1/4 cup fresh chopped parsley

Orange Vinaigrette:
2 Tblsp. red wine vinegar
1 Tblsp. low sodium prepared mustard
1-1/2 tsp. grated orange rind
1/4 tsp. black pepper
1/4 cup nonfat chicken broth (page 80) or water
1 Tblsp. honey

In a large serving bowl combine rice and next 4 ingredients. Combine vinegar, mustard, orange rind, pepper, chicken broth and honey, beat well with a wire whisk. Add *Orange Vinaigrette* to rice mixture and toss well.

Nutrient content per serving:

Calories	265	Cholesterol	43 mg
Protein	21 g	Sodium	77 mg
Carbohydrates	36 g	Potassium	443 mg
Fat	4 g	Iron	3.3 mg
Fiber - Dietary	3.2 g	Calcium	59 mg

14% calories from fat

Food Exchanges: 0.2 Veg., 1.8 Bread, 2.3 Meat, 0.1 Fat

WILD RICE - APPLE - MINT SALAD

Preparation time: 15 minutes   *Chef: Jan Robinson*
Chilling time: 1 hour   *Yacht: Vanity*
Serves: 6

2 cups cooked wild rice
2 cups cooked brown rice
1 cup diced Granny Smith apple
1 cup frozen green peas, thawed

Orange Mint Dressing:
1/2 cup orange juice
1/4 cup fresh lime juice
1/4 cup honey
1/4 cup mint jelly, heated until liquid
1/4 cup chopped fresh mint leaves
1-1/2 tsp. orange zest
1/2 tsp. freshly ground black pepper

Combine rice, apples and peas in bowl. Whisk together the dressing ingredients and pour over rice mixture. Grind fresh pepper over all and refrigerate one hour to blend flavors.

Serve over curly lettuce leaves and garnish with fresh mint leaves.

Nutrient content per serving:

Calories	249	Cholesterol	0 mg
Protein	6 g	Sodium	33 mg
Carbohydrates	56 g	Potassium	235 mg
Fat	1.0 g	Iron	1.4 mg
Fiber - Dietary	3.7 g	Calcium	25 mg

3% calories from fat

Food Exchanges: 0.3 Fruit, 1.9 Bread

Substitute whole grains for refined products, for example: brown rice instead of white rice, whole-wheat flour instead of white flour, etc.

BLACK BEAN AND WILD RICE SALAD

Preparation time: 15 minutes   *Chef: Beth Avore*
Marinating time: 1 hour to 2 days   *Yacht: Perfection*

Serves: 8
4 cups cooked black beans, or 2 [15 oz.] cans
    low sodium, drained
1 cup cooked wild rice
1 cup mexi-corn, frozen, thawed
1 red pepper, diced
1 cup scallions, chopped
1 tomato, chopped (optional)

Cilantro Dressing:
1/4 cup red wine vinegar
2 Tblsp. lime juice
2 Tblsp. honey
1 tsp. cumin
1/2 cup fresh chopped cilantro

Mix all salad ingredients together. Whip dressing together, pour over salad. Let sit for 1 hour or up to 2 days. It gets better!

Note: *More beans or rice can be added; any combination is good. Great with hot sandwiches, cold platters, rotis, fajitas, and quiches.*

Nutrient content per serving:

Calories	176	Cholesterol	0.6 mg
Protein	10 g	Sodium	65 mg
Carbohydrates	34 g	Potassium	522 mg
Fat	1.3 g	Iron	3.5 mg
Fiber - Dietary	5.1 g	Calcium	55 mg

6% calories from fat

Food Exchanges: 0.2 Veg., 1.7 Bread, 0.1 Fat

To keep lettuce fresh in the refrigerator, place lettuce in a plastic bag with a dry paper towel inside to absorb any moisture.

BLACK BEAN AND CHICK PEA SALAD

Preparation time: 15 minutes　　　　　　　*Chef: Mary Ruppert*
Marinating time: 30 minutes　　　　　　　*Yacht: Coral Sea*
Serves: 8

1 (15 oz.) can low sodium black beans, drained and rinsed
1 (15 oz.) can chick peas, drained and rinsed
1 (15 oz.) can small white beans, drained and rinsed
1 cup chopped green onions (about 4)
3/4 cup frozen green peas, thawed
1/2 cup shredded carrots
Garnish: Lettuce leaves and *Calypso Queen Hot Salsa*

Sherry Dressing:
3 cloves garlic, minced
1/3 cup sherry
1/3 cup red wine vinegar
1/4 cup honey
1/4 tsp. black pepper

Mix dressing and set aside. Combine black beans, chick peas and white beans with onions, peas, and shredded carrots. Toss with dressing. Marinate 30 minutes, mixing once or twice. *Serve on lettuce leaves with salsa over the top.*

Hint: *This salad keeps very well and actually gets better when made ahead of time.*

Nutrient content per serving:

Calories	250	Cholesterol	0 mg
Protein	10 g	Sodium	258 mg
Carbohydrates	43 g	Potassium	603 mg
Fat	1.6 g	Iron	3.5 mg
Fiber - Dietary	10.3 g	Calcium	67 mg

6% calories from fat

Food Exchanges: 0.2 Veg., 2.0 Bread

BULGUR AND ADZUKI BEAN SALAD

Preparation time: 12 minutes   *Chef: Jan Robinson*
Cooking time: 20 minutes   *Yacht: Vanity*
Chilling time: 30 minutes
Serves: 4

1-1/2 cups vegetable stock (page 81)
3/4 cup uncooked bulgur
2 Tblsp. red wine vinegar
2 Tblsp. Dijon mustard
2 Tblsp. honey
2 tsp. grated fresh ginger root
1/2 tsp. black pepper
1/2 cup chopped celery
1/2 cup chopped green pepper
3/4 cup sliced red onion
1 cup chopped tomato
1-1/2 cups cooked and drained Adzuki beans

In a medium saucepan, combine stock and bulgur. Bring to a boil, cover and cook over low heat for 20 minutes, or until bulgur is soft and stock absorbed; chill. In a bowl, mix vinegar, mustard, honey, ginger, and pepper. Transfer cooked bulgur to a serving bowl. Add vegetables and beans; toss to mix. Pour on dressing and stir well to coat. Chill for at least 30 minutes before serving.

Nutrient content per serving:

Calories	222	Cholesterol	0 mg
Protein	11 g	Sodium	205 mg
Carbohydrates	47 g	Potassium	594 mg
Fat	0.9 g	Iron	2.6 mg
Fiber - Dietary	10 g	Calcium	47 mg

3% calories from fat

Food Exchanges: 3.7 Veg, 1.3 Bread

POTATO BEAN SALAD

Preparation time: 15 minutes　　　　　　*Chef: Jan Robinson*
Cooking time: 15 minutes　　　　　　　　　*Yacht: Vanity*
Chilling time: 30 minutes
Serves: 8

8 cups (about 3 lbs.) cubed new potatoes, (peeled optional)
1 lb. fresh green beans (or 2 cups cooked red kidney beans)
1 cup chopped mushrooms
2 Tblsp. lemon juice
1/2 cup finely diced celery
1/2 cup finely diced red onion
1/4 cup chopped parsley
3/4 cup *Healthy Italian Dressing* (page 77)
Garnish: Tomato wedges

Boil new potatoes until soft, refrigerate to cool. Steam green beans, then run under cold water. Toss mushrooms with lemon juice. Mix together with the potatoes, beans, celery, onion and parsley. Add dressing and refrigerate until thoroughly chilled. *Garnish.*

Hint: *Even better the next day!*

Nutrient content per serving:

Calories	177	Cholesterol	0 mg
Protein	5 g	Sodium	10 mg
Carbohydrates	41 g	Potassium	886 mg
Fat	0.4 g	Iron	1.4 mg
Fiber - Dietary	4.1 g	Calcium	42 mg

2% calories from fat

Food Exchanges: 0.1 Veg., 2.1 Bread

Keep plastic wrap in the freezer for easy handling.

BARLEY - WHEAT BERRY - RICE SALAD

Preparation time: 15 minutes   *Chef: Jan Robinson*
Cooking time: 30 minutes   *Yacht: Vanity*
Serves: 6

2 cups cooked brown rice
2 cups cooked barley
1 cup cooked wheatberries
1 cup frozen corn, thawed
1/2 cup diced onion
1/2 cup diced celery
1 cup (1 medium) tart apple, diced
2 tsp. curry powder
1 cup *Vegetarian Creamy Dressing* (page 76)
1 Tblsp. hot chutney

Mix the rice, barley, wheatberries and corn together in large bowl.
Sauté onions, celery, apples and curry powder in 4 Tblsp. water until
onions are soft. Stir into rice mixture. Mix the chutney into the creamy
dressing and combine with the other ingredients.

*Hint: The mixture of grains can be cooked together and can be eaten by
themselves as an energy snack, or sweetened with honey and fruit as a
dessert. The mixture also tastes good hot in the morning as hot cereal.*

Note: This salad is also very good using only brown rice.

Nutrient content per serving:

Calories	251	Cholesterol	0 mg
Protein	6 g	Sodium	99 mg
Carbohydrates	56 g	Potassium	260 mg
Fat	1.6 g	Iron	1.7 mg
Fiber-Dietary	6.9 g	Calcium	43 mg

6% calories from fat

Food Exchanges: 0.2 Veg., 0.2 Fruit, 2.8 Bread

DIJON PASTA SALAD

Preparation time: 5 minutes   *Chef: Shirley King*
Serves: 6   *Yacht: Latina*

1 lb. cooked eggless pasta

***Dijon Dressing*:**
1 cup nonfat yogurt
1 Tblsp. Dijon mustard
1 Tblsp. fresh chopped tarragon (or 1 tsp. ground)
1 tsp. ground dry mustard

Mix above dressing. Add to cooked pasta. Eat hot or cold.

Serve with a spinach salad and melon slices for lunch.

Hint: *Other chefs report they use a very similar base recipe and add left over cooked vegetables, onion, celery, etc. Let your imagination be your guide.*

Nutrient content per serving:

Calories	117	Cholesterol	0.7 mg
Protein	6 g	Sodium	98 mg
Carbohydrates	22 g	Potassium	120 mg
Fat	0.9 g	Iron	1.0 mg
Fiber - Dietary	0.9 g	Calcium	83 mg

7% calories from fat

Food Exchanges: 0.2 Milk, 1.3 Bread

Substitute nonfat yogurt for sour cream.

SHRIMP ROZELLE

Preparation time: 30 minutes   *Chef: Fiona Dugdale*
Cooking time: 1 minute   *Yacht: Promenade*
Chilling time: 30 minutes
Serves: 8

2 lbs. jumbo shrimp, peeled and de-veined
1 Honeydew melon
2 cantaloupe melons
1/2 cup finely chopped green onions
1/2 cup finely chopped celery
2 Tblsp. finely chopped fresh mint
1 cup fat-free Italian dressing
1 tsp. freshly ground black pepper
Garnish: Shredded lettuce and fresh mint

Lightly cook the shrimp, approximately 1 minute, in plenty of boiling water. Do not overcook. Rinse in cold water; drain. Cut melons in half and scoop out seeds. Make melon balls using a melon baller. Cut cantaloupe shells into quarters and save. Trim remaining melon from shells and purée with dressing. Mix all ingredients (shrimp, melon balls, onions celery, mint, pepper and dressing) together and chill.

Mound the melon ball-shrimp mixture over reserved shells that have been arranged on a bed of shredded lettuce leaves. *Garnish with lime wedges. Top with fresh mint.*

Note: *Fresh mint is the key to this delightful summer salad; if not available use 1 Tblsp. mint jelly.*

Hint: *The shrimp will have more flavor if you cook them in a Court Bouillon.*

Nutrient content per serving:

Calories	295	Cholesterol	175 mg
Protein	25 g	Sodium	693 mg
Carbohydrates	47 g	Potassium	995 mg
Fat	2.4 g	Iron	3.5 mg
Fiber - Dietary	2.4 g	Calcium	109 mg

7% calories from fat

Food Exchanges: 1.2 Fruit, 3.2 Meat

CAVIAR SALAD

Preparation time: 30 minutes　　　　　*Chef: Fiona Dugdale*
Cooking time: None　　　　　　　　　　*Yacht: Promenade*
Serves: 6

3 cups finely chopped cooked potatoes (about 1 lb.)
3 cups finely chopped tomatoes (3 medium-size)
1/4 cup fresh chopped dill (or 1-1/2 Tblsp. dried dill)
1 cup finely chopped onion
1 (2 oz.) jar caviar
1 cup frozen corn, thawed
1/4 cup fresh lime juice
1/8 tsp. freshly ground black pepper
Garnish: Lettuce and lime wedges

Stir all the ingredients together and squeeze lime juice over all. Adjust the seasoning. *Serve on a bed of lettuce with lime wedges.*

Note: *Peel potatoes after cooking for better nutrition.*

Nutrient content per serving:

Calories	131	Cholesterol	31 mg
Protein	4.7 g	Sodium	95 mg
Carbohydrates	28 g	Potassium	541 mg
Fat	1.4 g	Iron	2.0 mg
Fiber - Dietary	2.8 g	Calcium	56 mg

9% calories from fat

Food Exchanges: 0.6 Veg., 0.1 Fruit, 1.3 Bread, 0.1 Meat

CAPERS AND FISH SALAD

Preparation time: 15 minutes   *Chef: Bobbi Fawcett*
Cooking time: 10 minutes   *Yacht: Windwalker*
Serves: 4

1 lb. grouper, poached or microwave
3/4 cup celery, chopped
1 red bell pepper, chopped
1/4 cup chopped green or red onion
1/2 cup alfalfa sprouts
4 cups torn Romaine lettuce
1/2 cup chopped parsley
1/4 cup capers, drained
1/2 cup *Healthy Italian Dressing* (page 77)
1/4 tsp. black pepper (or to taste)

Cut fish to bite size. Mix with rest of ingredients toss and serve with crusty bread.

Nutrient content per serving:

Calories	177	Cholesterol	53 mg
Protein	36 g	Sodium	146 mg
Carbohydrates	9 g	Potassium	815 mg
Fat	1.9 g	Iron	2.6 mg
Fiber - Dietary	2.3 g	Calcium	70 mg

9% calories from fat

Food Exchanges: 0.6 Veg., 4.7 Meat

CEVICHE

Preparation time: 40 minutes
Marinating time: 2 hours or overnight
Serves: 6

Chef: Fiona Dugdale
Yacht: Promenade

1-1/2 lb. Red Snapper-cut into 1/2" cubes
3/4 cup lime juice
1/3 cup orange juice
1 tsp. red cayenne pepper
1 tsp. freshly ground black pepper
3 Tblsp. each finely chopped cilantro, cucumber, celery, parsley,
green onion, red and green bell peppers.

Marinate the fish in the lime and orange juice for 30 minutes, turning occasionally. Stir in all the other ingredients. Serve on shredded lettuce, garnished with tomato and lime wedges. *Serve with crusty French bread.*

Hint: *Don't be put off of this wonderful dish because you have to eat raw fish. It is just as well 'cooked' by the lime as if it had been treated with heat. The fish will appear white and flaky.*

WARNING: USE ONLY VERY FRESH FISH.

Nutrient content per serving:

Calories	155	Cholesterol	42 mg
Protein	25 g	Sodium	265 mg
Carbohydrates	10 g	Potassium	810 mg
Fat	2.0 g	Iron	1.1 mg
Fiber - Dietary	1.9 g	Calcium	67 mg

11% calories from fat

Food Exchanges: 0.4 Veg., 0.3 Fruit, 3.3 Meat

SURIMI CRAB AND PESTO SALAD

Preparation time: 20 minutes   *Chef: Edna Seaman*
Cooking time: 5 minutes   *Yacht: Wahsoune*
Serves: 6

3 cups fresh broccoli florets
Water
1 cup sugar peas (or sweet peas, frozen, thawed)
3 plum (Roma) tomatoes, chopped (about 1 cup)
1 lb. Surimi crab, flaked
1 can sliced water chestnuts, drained
1 cup diced red sweet pepper
1 small red onion, sliced thin and separated
1 small head butter lettuce, separated and washed

Pesto Dressing
1 cup *Vegetarian Creamy Dressing (page 76)*
1 cup fresh basil leaves, chopped
2 cloves garlic, crushed

Cut broccoli into small florets. Bring a saucepan of water to boil, add broccoli, remove from heat. Cover and let stand for 3 minutes. Add peas and let stand for 1 minute longer. Drain and rinse in cold water to cool. Drain well. Combine broccoli, peas, tomatoes, crab, chestnuts, red pepper, and onion. Stir to mix. Serve on bed of lettuce. Combine dressing ingredients together in a blender, then toss with salad.

Nutrient content per serving:

Calories	171	Cholesterol	15.2 mg
Protein	14 g	Sodium	745 mg
Carbohydrates	27 g	Potassium	585 mg
Fat	1.8 g	Iron	2.6 mg
Fiber - Dietary	4.2 g	Calcium	89 mg

9% calories from fat

Food Exchanges: 1.9 Veg., 0.1 Bread, 1.3 Meat

DOZY GIRL DELIGHT

Preparation time: 20 minutes
Cooking time: 8-10 minutes
Chilling time: 30 minutes
Serves: 6

Chef: Jenny Meston
Yacht: Dozy Girl

8 oz. tri-color pasta twists
1 lb imitation crab meat
2 small fresh pineapple
2 cups diced tomatoes
1 cup chopped onion
1/2 cup chopped celery
1 cups *Vegetarian Creamy Dressing (page 76)*
1/4 tsp. freshly ground black pepper

Cook pasta, drain and rinse well. Flake crab meat into pasta. Halve pineapples carefully and scoop out flesh. Add to pasta, crab and juice. Also add tomatoes, celery and onion. Mix well. Fold in enough dressing to thinly coat and grind pepper over all to taste. Chill and serve piled into the 4 pineapple halves.

Hint: Use celery tops as garnish over pineapple ends.

Note: If fresh pineapple is not available, use canned pineapple pieces, drained and serve on lettuce leaves..

Nutrient content per serving:

Calories	273	Cholesterol	11 mg
Protein	13 g	Sodium	592 mg
Carbohydrates	51 g	Potassium	426 mg
Fat	2.1 g	Iron	1.0 mg
Fiber - Dietary	2.4 g	Calcium	38 mg

7% calories from fat

Food Exchanges: 0.7 Veg., 0.4 Fruit, 0.8 Bread, 1.0 Meat

SEAFOOD PASTA SALAD

Preparation time: 10 minutes   *Chef: Judy Garry*
Cooking time: 2-3 minutes   *Yacht: Sloopy*
Serves: 4

6 oz. rock shrimp, peeled and de-veined
6 oz. imitation crabmeat
1/2 cup chopped canned artichoke hearts
2 scallions, chopped
3/4 cup *Vegetarian Creamy Dressing* (page 76)
1 tsp. lemon pepper
1 Tblsp. fresh chopped dill, or 1 tsp. dill weed
4 cups cooked pasta
Garnish: Cherry tomatoes, lemon wedges and parsley

Cook rock shrimp 2-3 minutes in boiling water. Mix all remaining ingredients. Add shrimp. Better after refrigerating over night.

Garnish with Cherry tomatoes, lemon wedges and parsley. Serve on big bed of leafy lettuce. Delicious served with hot fat-free whole wheat bread.

Nutrient content per serving:

Calories	505	Cholesterol	184 mg
Protein	30 g	Sodium	589 mg
Carbohydrates	85 g	Potassium	358 mg
Fat	4.4 g	Iron	5.6 mg
Fiber - Dietary	1.0 g	Calcium	77 mg

8% calories from fat

Food Exchanges: 0.6 Veg., 4.8 Bread, 2.0 Meat, 0.6

SINFUL SEAFOOD SALAD

Preparation time: 15 minutes　　　　　　　*Chef: Shirley King*
Cooking time: 3 minutes　　　　　　　　　*Yacht: Latina*
Serves: 8

8 radishes
2 red bell peppers
1 green bell pepper
1 yellow bell pepper
3 plum tomatoes
1 lb. sea scallops
Vegetable cooking spray
1 lb. cooked shrimp, shelled and de-veined
1/2 cup sliced water chestnuts
1/2 head chicory
1 small head (1/4 lb.) Romaine lettuce
1 small head (1/4 lb.) Boston lettuce
1 (4 oz.) pkg. alfalfa sprouts
1/2 cup cooked black beans

Caribbean Dressing:
1/4 cup fresh lime juice
1/4 cup honey
1/4 cup chopped, fresh cilantro
1/2 tsp. each ground cumin and red pepper flakes
1/2 tsp. freshly ground black pepper

In a nonstick skillet sauté scallops in a little vegetable spray. Slice or chop vegetables. Tear lettuce into bite size pieces. Combine all ingredients and toss. Blend dressing ingredients and toss with salad.

Nutrient content per serving:

Calories	197	Cholesterol	106 mg
Protein	24 g	Sodium	206 mg
Carbohydrates	21 g	Potassium	764 mg
Fat	1.9 g	Iron	3.1 mg
Fiber - Dietary	3.2 g	Calcium	117 mg

9% calories from fat

Food Exchanges: 1.3 Veg., 0.1 Bread, 2.9 Meat

VEGETARIAN CREAMY DRESSING

Preparation time: 10 minutes   *Chef: Jan Robinson*
Chilling time: 30 minutes   *Yacht: Vanity*
Yield: 2 cups

1/2 cup water
2 Tblsp. arrowroot
8 oz. low fat tofu, chopped
4 cloves garlic, chopped
1 Tblsp. low sodium prepared mustard
1/4 cup lemon juice
1 Tblsp. seasoned rice vinegar
2 Tblsp. less salt soy sauce
2 Tblsp. honey
2 Tblsp. chopped green onion
3 Tblsp. chopped parsley
1/4 tsp. black pepper

Dissolve arrowroot in 2 Tblsp. water. Boil remaining water and add
arrowroot mixture to boiling water. Place in freezer to cool
(approximately 10 minutes). In blender or food processor, combine all
ingredients and blend until smooth.

Nutrient content per 1/4 cup serving:

Calories	51	Cholesterol	0 mg
Protein	3 g	Sodium	136 mg
Carbohydrates	8 g	Potassium	70 mg
Fat	1.1 g	Iron	1.5 mg
Fiber - Dietary	0.2 g	Calcium	30 mg

18% calories from fat

Food Exchanges: 0.1 Veg., 0.1 Bread, 0.2 Meat

HEALTHY ITALIAN DRESSING

Preparation time: 10 minutes　　　　　　　*Chef: Jan Robinson*
Chilling time: 30 minutes　　　　　　　　　*Yacht: Vanity*
Makes: 2 cups

1/4 cup cider vinegar
1/4 cup finely chopped onion
1 cup apple juice
1/4 cup fresh lemon juice
4 cloves garlic, chopped
2 Tblsp. honey
1 tsp. dried sweet basil
1/2 tsp. dried oregano
1/2 tsp. dried rosemary
1/4 tsp. dried marjoram
1 tsp. black pepper
1 (13-1/2 oz.) can artichoke hearts, packed in water
　　　rinsed and drained (6 - 8 hearts)

Combine all ingredients in blender or food processor and purée until smooth. Chill for 15 minutes or so before serving.

Hint: Store remaining dressing in a covered container in the refrigerator.

Nutrient content per serving: 2 Tblsp.

Calories	34	Cholesterol	0 mg
Protein	0.6 g	Sodium	15 mg
Carbohydrates	8.6 g	Potassium	84 mg
Fat	0.07 g	Iron	0.4 mg
Fiber - Dietary	0.2 g	Calcium	13 mg

2% calories from fat

Food Exchanges: 0.3 Veg, 0.1 Fruit

Health Conscious...

TOFU MAYONNAISE

Preparation time: 10 minutes   *Chef: Jan Robinson*
Makes: 1 cup   *Yacht: Vanity*

8 oz. low fat tofu
2 cloves garlic, minced
1 Tblsp. low sodium prepared mustard
1 Tblsp. rice wine vinegar (or white vinegar)
1/4 cup fresh lemon juice
2 Tblsp. coarsely chopped parsley
2 Tblsp. coarsely chopped green onion
1 tsp. brown rice syrup

Combine all ingredients in a food processor and purée until smooth.

Hint: *Store in a covered container in the refrigerator.*

Nutrient content per 1 Tblsp.

Calories	16	Cholesterol	0 mg
Protein	1 g	Sodium	20 mg
Carbohydrates	1 g	Potassium	12 mg
Fat	0.6 g	Iron	0.1 mg
Fiber - Dietary	0.3 g	Calcium	2.7 mg

34% calories from fat

Food Exchanges: 0

    Tofu *may be used effectively in recipes when you wish to boost the whole-protein content without changing the taste. Tofu, often called soybean curd, is a derivative of coagulated soy milk, rich in calcium, iron, potassium and above all rich in protein. Although tofu is relatively high in unsaturated fat it contains no cholesterol.*
    Tofu is available in low fat and regular. Low fat comes only in a firm form. Regular may be obtained in three forms; soft, firm, and extra-firm. Soft is best used in recipes being blended or mashed with other ingredients. The firm type is best for dishes that call for sliced or cubed tofu, and the extra-firm for stir-fries.
    Tofu is available vacuum packed with water. Once opened it will keep about a week if covered with water that is changed daily. It may be kept for approximately three months if frozen, but the texture will change.

Soups and Sandwiches

CHICKEN BROTH (STOCK)

Preparation time: 5 minutes   *Chef: Jan Robinson*
Cooking time: 2 hours   *Yacht: Vanity*
Yield: About 3 cups

**3 lbs. chicken, bones and scraps cut into pieces (either raw or
     cooked or combination)**
6 cups water
1 small onion, halved and stuck with 2 cloves
1 carrot, cut in three
1 stalk celery including leaves, halved
2 bay leaves
1 leek, white part only, cut in half
3 sprigs parsley
1/4 tsp. each crushed dried basil, thyme and peppercorns

In a large soup pot put chicken pieces and water. Bring to boil, reduce
heat and skim off particles that rise to the surface. Add remaining
ingredients and simmer gently for 2 hours leaving the pot uncovered.
Strain broth through a fine sieve. Discard vegetables. Let broth cool at
room temperature until lukewarm, then remove fat from the surface
by drawing paper towels over it. Refrigerate for several hours or
overnight. Before using, skim off all the fat that has risen to the
surface.

*Hint: Use within 3 days or freeze. To freeze, pour into containers with
airtight lids or use small ziplock bags. Freeze up to 3 months.*

*Variation: Add 1 heaping Tblsp. light miso to recipe. This will make
stock cloudy but adds extra zest.*

*Note: A quick way is in the microwave. Cut the ingredients into small
pieces. Microwave on high for 40 minutes, stirring occasionally. Let
stand for 30 minutes, strain. Chill. Skim off fat before using.*

*If you do not have time to make your own broth /
stock, check our Stocking A Healthy Kitchen (page
252) for fat free chicken broths that you can buy.*

VEGETABLE STOCK (BROTH)

Preparation time: 10 minutes　　　　　　　*Chef: Jan Robinson*
Cooking time: 1 hour　　　　　　　　　　　*Yacht: Vanity*
Yield: 12 cups

3 qts. water
4 cups assorted vegetables parts: skins, peels, stems, leftovers
1 medium-size whole onion studded with 2 cloves
3 bay leaves
1 Tblsp. peppercorns

Place water and other ingredients in a large pot. Bring to a boil, reduce heat, cover and simmer over medium-low heat for about 1 hour. Strain and discard the vegetables.

Hint: *I freeze in 1 cup containers and just defrost the amount needed for the recipe I am making. Some vegetables that are particularly good in the stock are onions, carrots, potatoes, potato peels, garlic, green peppers, zucchini, green onion tops, corncobs, old vegetables that are going soft. You can also use this as a base for a large variety of soups.*

SPICY TROPICAL SOUP

Preparation time: 15 minutes   *Chef: Jan Robinson*
Cooking time: 25 minutes   *Yacht: Vanity*
Serves: 4

4 cups vegetable stock (page 81)
1 cup sliced mushrooms
3/4 cup chopped celery
1/2 cup diced tomatoes
1/2 cup diced red or green pepper
1/4 cup thinly chopped green onion
2 cloves garlic, minced
1/2 tsp. crushed dried oregano
1/2 tsp. ground thyme
1/2 tsp. crushed dried basil
1/2 tsp. crushed dried tarragon
1/2 tsp. ground cumin
1/8 tsp. cayenne pepper
1 Tblsp. finely chopped fresh cilantro
1 cup fresh or frozen whole kernel corn
1 Tblsp. fresh lemon juice

In a soup pot, combine stock, all vegetables and seasonings except cilantro, corn, and lemon juice. Bring to boil. Cover, reduce heat and simmer 20 minutes. Add corn and cilantro, cover and cook about 2 minutes, until heated through. Stir in lemon juice and serve.

Serve with a green salad and warm corn tortillas.

Nutrient content per serving:

Calories 68	Cholesterol ....0 mg
Protein ....5 g	Sodium ....477 mg
Carbohydrates .... 13 g	Potassium ....366 mg
Fat ....0.3 g	Iron ....1 mg
Fiber - Dietary .... 1.7 g	Calcium ....25 mg

4% calories from fat

Food Exchanges: 0.5 Veg, 0.5 Bread

TOMATO AND ORANGE SOUP

Preparation time: 5 minutes　　　　　*Chef: Penny Knowles*
Cooking time: 3 minutes　　　　　　*Yacht: Golden Skye*
Chilling time: 30 minutes
Serves: 6

3/4 cup orange juice
5 cups low sodium tomato juice
1/4 cup fresh lemon juice
1/4 tsp. black pepper
1 orange
Garnish: chopped fresh parsley and strips of orange peel

Combine orange juice, tomato juice, and lemon juice. Season with pepper. Cover and refrigerate for at least 30 minutes. Cut orange peel, (save orange) into matchstick-size strips, blanch in boiling water for 3 minutes. Drain and chill. Squeeze the juice from the orange and add to the soup before serving.

Pour soup into chilled bowls. Sprinkle with a few orange strips and some chopped parsley. Serve chilled.

Nutrient content per serving:

Calories	65	Cholesterol	0 mg
Protein	2 g	Sodium	21 mg
Carbohydrates	16 g	Potassium	577 mg
Fat	0.2 g	Iron	1.3 mg
Fiber - Dietary	3.1 g	Calcium	33 mg

2% calories from fat

Food Exchanges: 1.4 Veg, 0.4 Fruit

To remove the white membrane from oranges easily, soak them in boiling water for a few minutes before you peel them.

CHILLED TOMATO SOUP

Preparation time: 10 minutes   *Chef: Ann Glenn*
Chilling time: 4-6 hours   *Yacht: Encore*
Serves: 10

9 cups (72 oz.) low sodium tomato juice
1/4 cup + 2 Tblsp. low sodium tomato paste
1 Tblsp. grated zest of lime
1/4 cup + 2 Tblsp. lime juice
6 small green onions, minced
3/4 tsp. fructose
2 tsp. curry powder
1 tsp. ground thyme
1/4 tsp. hot sauce
1-3/4 cups plain nonfat yogurt
Garnish: 1/4 cup plain nonfat yogurt and 2 Tblsp.
      fresh chopped parsley

Combine all ingredients, except yogurt, in a large pitcher or punch bowl. Stir well. Chill 4-6 hours or overnight. Add 1-3/4 cups yogurt to tomato mixture, beating with a wire whisk until well blended.

Serve in individual chilled soup bowls. Garnish each serving with a dollop of yogurt and a sprinkle of parsley.

Nutrient content per serving:

Calories	76	Cholesterol	0 mg
Protein	5 g	Sodium	68 mg
Carbohydrates	16 g	Potassium	716 mg
Fat	0.3 g	Iron	1.9 mg
Fiber - Dietary	3.2 g	Calcium	31 mg

3% calories from fat

Food Exchanges: 0.2 Milk, 1.8 Veg

NICK'S GAZPACHO

Preparation Time: 10 minutes   *Chef: Jill Christiansen*
Chilling Time: 4-6 hours   *Yacht: Emerald Zephyr*
Serves: 6

4 cucumbers peeled, seeded, and cut in chunks
2 green peppers, cut in chunks
2 red peppers, cut in chunks, or local island sweet peppers
2 cups chopped onion
1 (28 oz.) can low sodium tomatoes
1 (24 oz) can V-8 juice
1/8 tsp. Tabasco sauce, or local island hot sauce
1 tsp. Worcestershire sauce
1 Tblsp. chopped fresh cilantro, or parsley
1/4 tsp. each of dried basil, thyme and oregano
1/2 tsp. freshly ground black pepper
Garnish: Finely chopped cucumber, peppers and onions

Put first 5 ingredients through a meat grinder or food processor until finely chopped. Add V-8 juice and seasonings. Chill for 4-6 hours (or in a freezer until very cold). Taste, if too *spicy* hot, add more chopped cucumber and V-8 juice.

Hint: *If you have a mate, significant other, or hubby (like mine) who can chop veggies quicker and more evenly than a food processor, disregard the first sentence of the method!*

Tip: *The V-8 juice is crucial to the taste of this South American style gazpacho.*

Nutrient content per serving:

Calories	101	Cholesterol	0 mg
Protein	3 g	Sodium	58 mg
Carbohydrates	23 g	Potassium	1042 mg
Fat	0.5 g	Iron	2.7 mg
Fiber - Dietary	6.3 g	Calcium	76 mg

4% calories from fat

Food Exchanges: 3.9 Veg

BOUNTIFUL BORSCHT

Preparation time: 15 minutes　　　　　　*Chef: Jan Robinson*
Cooking time: 1 hour and 10 minutes　　　　*Yacht: Vanity*
Chilling time: 1 hour
Serves: 6

Vegetable cooking spray
1 cup finely chopped onion
4 cups vegetable stock (page 81) or water
2 cups peeled fresh beets, julienned
2 cups peeled red potatoes, julienned
1-1/2 Tblsp. brown rice syrup
1 tsp. dried dill weed
1/2 tsp. black pepper
2 Tblsp. red wine vinegar
Garnish: 6 tsp. plain nonfat yogurt and
**　　　　finely chopped green onion.**

Coat a large saucepan with cooking spray. Place over medium heat. When hot, add onion. Cover and cook until softened. Add stock or water and next 6 ingredients. Stir well. Bring to a boil. Cover, reduce heat, simmer 1 hour or until beets are tender. Pour into a large bowl. Cover and chill. *To serve, ladle into individual soup bowls, top with a swirl of yogurt and finely chopped green onion.*

Nutrient content per serving:

Calories 76	Cholesterol ....0.08 mg
Protein.....................................2 g	Sodium ....40 mg
Carbohydrates ....17 g	Potassium ....371 mg
Fat ....0.3 g	Iron ....0.8 mg
Fiber - Dietary ....1.6 g	Calcium ....34 mg

3% calories from fat

Food Exchanges: 0.4 Milk 0.9 Veg, 0.4 Bread

CARROT SOUP WITH SPICY YOGURT

Preparation time: 10 minutes   *Chef: Josie Gould*
Cooking time: 40 minutes   *Yacht: Amalthea of Sark*
Chilling time: 15 minutes
Serves: 6

1/2 cup + 4 cups vegetable stock (page 81)
2 cups finely chopped onions
4 garlic cloves, minced
1/4 cup dry white wine
3 lb. carrots, chopped (12 - 15 medium carrots)
1/2 tsp. ground black pepper
Garnish: 1/2 tsp. cumin, 1/8 tsp. cayenne pepper,
          1/4 tsp. tumeric, 1 cup plain nonfat yogurt

Over medium heat in a large pan put 1/2 cup vegetable stock, add onions and garlic. Cover and cook until onions are translucent, but not brown. Add wine, cook 5 minutes. Add carrots and 4 cups vegetable stock. Bring to a boil. Reduce heat and cook covered until soft, about 15 minutes. Pureé in blender. Season with pepper.

Garnish: Toast spices in small dry skillet 1 minute, shaking well. Cool. Mix into yogurt. Chill.

Hint: *Spicy yogurt garnish can be topped with finely grated carrot. It also makes a dip for fresh vegetables or chips.*

Nutrient content per serving:

Calories	165	Cholesterol	0 mg
Protein	5 g	Sodium	765 mg
Carbohydrates	34 g	Potassium	942 mg
Fat	1.5 g	Iron	1.6 mg
Fiber - Dietary	8.1 g	Calcium	88 mg

8% calories from fat

Food Exchanges: 0.1 Milk, 5.5 Veg

VEGETABLE - BASIL - BEAN SOUP

Preparation time: 15 minutes　　　　　　　　*Chef: Jan Robinson*
Cooking time: 20 minutes　　　　　　　　　　*Yacht: Vanity*
Serves: 8

1 cup diced potatoes
2 cups diced carrots
2 cups diced onions
1-1/2 quarts vegetable stock (page 81)
1-1/2 quarts water
2 cups cut fresh green beans
1 cup uncooked macaroni twists
1/2 cup low sodium tomato paste
1/4 tsp. cayenne pepper
1/2 tsp. black pepper
4 cloves garlic, minced
1/4 cup fresh chopped basil (or 1-1/2 Tblsp. dried basil leaves)
1 (16 oz.) can low sodium white beans, drained and rinsed

Boil potatoes, carrots and onions in the 3 quarts of stock and water,
about 10 minutes. Add green beans and macaroni. Cook until tender.
In separate bowl, combine tomato paste, cayenne, black pepper, garlic
and basil. Add slowly, about 2 cups of the hot soup to the tomato paste
mixture, stirring continuously. Pour mixture back into soup pot and
mix well. Add white beans. *Serve hot.*

Nutrient content per serving:

Calories	190	Cholesterol	0 mg
Protein	2 g	Sodium	401 mg
Carbohydrates	38 g	Potassium	760 mg
Fat	0.7 g	Iron	3 mg
Fiber - Dietary	3.7 g	Calcium	82 mg

3% calories from fat

Food Exchanges: 2.2 Veg, 1.5 Bread, 0.2 Meat

CREAM OF BROCCOLI SOUP

Preparation time: 15 minutes
Cooking time: 15 minutes
Serves: 6

Chef: Davis Bailey
Yacht: Maverick

2 Tblsp. + 2-1/2 cups vegetable stock (page 81)
1/2 large yellow onion, chopped
5 cups broccoli (1 large head) peel and chop stalks,
break head into florets
1-1/2 cups nonfat skim milk mixed with 1 Tblsp. arrowroot
1/2 tsp. black pepper
1/4 cup low fat grated Parmesan cheese
1/2 tsp. Tabasco, or to taste
Garnish: Matchstick strips of red and yellow bell peppers

Using a soup pot cook onions in 2 Tblsp. stock until softened. Add 2-1/2 cups stock and broccoli and simmer until tender. Add milk and arrowroot mixture and bring to quick boil, stirring frequently. Allow to cool. Puree in small batches in blender to desired texture. Return to pot on low heat. Gradually stir in Parmesan cheese and pepper. Tabasco adds final zing to soup. Do **not** boil.

Very filling soup. I usually serve it with a light salad and bread.

Nutrient content per serving:

Calories	76	Cholesterol	6 mg
Protein	7 g	Sodium	326 mg
Carbohydrates	10 g	Potassium	383 mg
Fat	1.4 g	Iron	0.7 mg
Fiber - Dietary	2 g	Calcium	108 mg

15% calories from fat

Food Exchanges: 0.2 Milk, 0.8 Veg

Run cold water in the sink while you pour hot water from vegetables, it prevents the steam from scalding your hands..

PUMPKIN SOUP

Preparation time: 15 minutes   *Chef: Edna Beaman*
Cooking time: 45 minutes   *Yacht: Wahsoune*
Serves: 4

2 Tblsp. + 3 cups vegetable stock (page 81)
1/3 cup chopped onion
2 small stalks celery, diced
1 tsp. arrowroot (or 1 Tblsp. flour)
2 cloves garlic, pressed
1/8 tsp. ground ginger
1/8 tsp. ground nutmeg
1/8 tsp. ground cloves (optional)
1 (16 oz.) can pumpkin
2 tsp. cider vinegar
1 cup nonfat skim milk
Garnish: Chopped scallions

Sauté onion and celery in saucepan with 2 Tblsp. stock until golden.
Blend in flour and seasonings. Add broth and pumpkin. Simmer 30
minutes. Purée in blender. Add vinegar and milk and reheat. *Garnish
with chopped scallions.*

Nutrient content per serving:

Calories	91	Cholesterol	1 mg
Protein	6.3 g	Sodium	423 mg
Carbohydrates	17 g	Potassium	535 mg
Fat	0.5 g	Iron	1.9 mg
Fiber - Dietary	2.9 g	Calcium	121 mg

5% calories from fat

Food Exchanges: 0.2 Milk, 0.3 Veg, 0.6 Bread

SWEET POTATO SOUP

Preparation time: 12 minutes　　　　　　*Chef: Beverly Grant*
Cooking time: 45 minutes　　　　　　*Yacht: Safe Conduct II*
Serves: 4

2 Tblsp. + 6 cups vegetable stock (page 81)
1 small onion, finely chopped
1-1/2 lbs. sweet potatoes, peeled and chopped
1/8 tsp. each of cinnamon and nutmeg
1-1/2 cups fresh or frozen corn kernels
2 tsp. finely chopped jalapeño
1/2 cup nonfat skim milk
1/2 tsp. cider vinegar
1/2 tsp. black pepper, or to taste
Garnish: 4 tsp. nonfat plain yogurt

Heat 2 Tblsp. stock in saucepan and cook onions until tender. Add potatoes, cinnamon, nutmeg and 6 cups stock. Bring to a boil. Reduce heat, cover and simmer for 30 minutes. Strain soup. Return stock to saucepan. Transfer potatoes to processor and puree. Return purée to stock. Add corn, vinegar and jalapeño, simmer for 5 minutes, then add milk and pepper. *Garnish each serving with a dollop of yogurt.*

Nutrient content per serving:

Calories	201	Cholesterol	0.5 mg
Protein	10 g	Sodium	781 mg
Carbohydrates	42 g	Potassium	876 mg
Fat	0.2 g	Iron	1 mg
Fiber - Dietary	6.2 g	Calcium	72 mg

1% calories from fat

Food Exchanges: 0.1 Milk, 0.5 Veg, 1.9 Bread

The difference bettween us... I'm
Sweet you're fried or chips!

EASY BLACK BEAN SOUP

Preparation time: 10 minutes   *Chef: Jan Robinson*
Cooking time: 30 minutes   *Yacht: Vanity*
Serves: 4

1/4 cup vegetable stock (page 81) or water
1 cup finely chopped onion
1/2 cup finely chopped celery
4 cloves garlic, crushed
2 (15 oz.) cans very low sodium black beans,
1 tsp. pepper
1/4 tsp. ground cumin
1 Tblsp. dried oregano
1/2 tsp. cider vinegar
1/4 tsp. Tabasco, (or Sunny Caribbee Hot Sauce)
Garnish: 2 finely chopped green onions
         1-1/3 cups cooked rice (brown or white) and

Sauté onion, celery and garlic in 1/4 cup stock, or water over medium heat. Cook a few minutes before adding the black beans. Mix thoroughly and simmer for 15 minutes. Stir in pepper, cumin, oregano, vinegar and Tabasco. Serve soup in individual bowls with a garnish of green onions. In a separate bowl place the cooked rice for your guests to help themselves.

This makes a good quick lunch served with a green salad.

Nutrient content per serving:

Calories	243	Cholesterol	0 mg
Protein	10 g	Sodium	80 mg
Carbohydrates	38 g	Potassium	715 mg
Fat	1.4 g	Iron	1.5 mg
Fiber - Dietary	14.2 g	Calcium	53 mg

6% calories from fat

Food Exchanges: 0.7 Veg., 1.9 Bread

CUCUMBER AND SHRIMP SOUP

Preparation time: 5 minutes   *Chef: Candice Carson*
Chilling time: 1 hour   *Yacht: Freight Train II*
Serves: 4

1-1/2 cups buttermilk
3 medium cucumbers, peeled
1/2 cup nonfat sour cream
1 Tblsp. fresh lemon juice
1 garlic clove, minced
1 Tblsp. fresh chopped dill (or 1 tsp. dried dill)
1/2 tsp. black pepper
1/4 lb. cooked shrimp
Garnish: Thin cucumber slices and dill sprigs

Put ingredients (except shrimp) in food processor; or blender. Season with salt and pepper. Cover and refrigerate until well chilled. Add shrimp, garnish, serve.

Nutrient content per serving:

Calories	102	Cholesterol	47 mg
Protein	10 g	Sodium	146 mg
Carbohydrates	12 g	Potassium	550 mg
Fat	1.6 g	Iron	1.6 mg
Fiber - Dietary	2.4 g	Calcium	2.4 mg

14% calories from fat

Food Exchanges: 0.3 Milk, 1.3 Veg, 0.8 Meat, 0.1 Fat

What you
Let's make a band
instead of a soup!

MARYLAND SHE–CRAB SOUP

Preparation time: 12 minutes   *Chef: Beverly Grant*
Cooking time: 45 minutes   *Yacht: Safe Conduct II*
Serves: 4

1/4 cup vegetable stock (page 81)
1/2 cup chopped celery
1/2 cup chopped scallions
1 Tblsp. arrowroot
6 cups nonfat skim milk
2 tsp. less salt soy sauce
2 tsp. Worcestershire sauce
1/4 cup sherry
1/2 tsp. white pepper
1/4 tsp. thyme
1 whole bay leaf
1/4 tsp. cayenne pepper or to taste
2 cups crabmeat
Garnish: Chopped parsley

Heat stock in saucepan over medium heat. Cook celery and scallions until softened. Add arrowroot and blend well. Add milk 1 cup at a time, stirring constantly until blended. Add soy sauce and Worcestershire, sherry and spices. Simmer, covered for 45 minutes. Stir in crabmeat and cook until hot. *Garnish with chopped parsley.*

Nutrient content per serving:

Calories	261	Cholesterol	54 mg
Protein	34 g	Sodium	1264 mg
Carbohydrates	23 g	Potassium	957 mg
Fat	1.5 g	Iron	1.4 mg
Fiber - Dietary	0.6 g	Calcium	525 mg

5% calories from fat

Food Exchanges: 1.3 Milk, 0.3 Veg, 2.8 Meat

CHILLED BANANA SOUP

Preparation time: 5 minutes　　　　　　　*Chef: Sharon Perry*
Chilling time: 1 hour　　　　　　　　　　*Yacht: Redhead*
Serves: 4

3 ripe bananas
2 cups nonfat plain yogurt
1 Tblsp. fructose
1 tsp. ground cinnamon
1 tsp. ground nutmeg
1 Tblp. fresh lemon or lime juice
Nonfat skim Milk (optional)
Garnish: Freshly grated nutmeg

Put bananas, yogurt, sugar, cinnamon, and nutmeg in blender. Blend. (Add milk if necessary to thin to consistency desired). Chill. *Grate fresh nutmeg on top just before serving.*

Hint: *Serve with old fashioned cinnamon toasts. Great cold soup to use up over-ripe bananas or in place of salad when produce runs low.*

Note: *Elaine Gregory from yacht Moorea uses 29 oz. can of peaches in instead of bananas and adds 1 tsp. vanilla*

Nutrient content per serving: 3/4 cup

Calories	157	Cholesterol	0 mg
Protein	7 g	Sodium	96 mg
Carbohydrates	33 g	Potassium	633 mg
Fat	0.6 g	Iron	0.5 mg
Fiber - Dietary	1.4 g	Calcium	13 mg

3% calories from fat

Food Exchanges: 0.6 Milk, 1.3 Fruit, 0.1 Bread

SMOKED TURKEY SALAD SANDWICH

Preparation time: 12 minutes   *Chef: Edna Beaman*
Serves: 4   *Yacht: Wahsoune*

1/2 cup chopped onion, or green onion
3/4 lb. smoked turkey chunks
1/2 tsp. coarse ground black pepper
1/2 tsp. rice wine vinegar
1/4 cup fat-free mayonnaise
8 slices rye bread
1 tomato thinly sliced
2 cups alfalfa sprouts

Combine onions, turkey, pepper, vinegar and mayonnaise. Top 4 slices of bread with tomato, turkey salad, sprouts and top with bread. Cut diagonally. *Serve with fruit.*

Note: *Pumpernickel bread usually has less fat than whole wheat or rye. If you substitute regular turkey and add spices, sodium would be 528 mg.*

Nutrient content per serving:

Calories	252	Cholesterol	35 mg
Protein	22 g	Sodium	1082 mg
Carbohydrates	31 g	Potassium	402 mg
Fat	2.6 g	Iron	2.3 mg
Fiber - Dietary	4.2 g	Calcium	55 mg

10% calories from fat

Food Exchanges: 0.5 Veg., 1.5 Bread, 2.1 Meat, 0.4 Fat

Smoked
Turkey

Non-smoked
Turkey

GREEK-STYLE TURKEY BURGER
IN PITA BREAD

Preparation time: 15-20 minutes　　　*Chef: Randa Jacobs*
Cooking time: 5-10 minutes　　　　　*Yacht: Blithe Spirit*
Serves: 6

1 lb. ground turkey, fat removed
1/4 cup whole wheat bread crumbs
1 small onion, minced (about 1/2 cup)
2 cloves garlic, minced
2 Tblsp. chopped, fresh mint leaves
2 tsp. black pepper
1 Tblsp. paprika
1 Tblsp. chopped fresh parsley
6 whole wheat pita bread halves
1 cup torn lettuce
1 tomato cubed

Yogurt Sauce:
1 cup plain yogurt
1 clove garlic, crushed
1 tsp. fresh chopped mint leaves
1 tsp. black pepper

Combine turkey, bread crumbs, onion, garlic, mint leaves, parsley, paprika, and pepper. Mix well. Form into oval patties. Broil or pan fry without fat until browned on both sides and cooked. Combine ingredients for yogurt sauce. Serve in pockets of pita bread stuffed with lettuce and tomatoes. Top with yogurt sauce.

Note: *This recipe also makes a tasty appetizer* **Turkey Patties**. *Form into small patties brown on both sides until cooked. Serve with* **Yogurt Sauce** *for dipping.*

Nutrient content per serving:

Calories	252	Cholesterol	63 mg
Protein	30 g	Sodium	312 mg
Carbohydrates	28 g	Potassium	444 mg
Fat	1.3 g	Iron	2.6 mg
Fiber - Dietary	1.2 g	Calcium	124 mg

5% calories of fat

Food Exchanges: 0.2 Milk, 0.2 Veg,, 1.5 Bread, 3.2 Meat

PARADISE PITAS

Preparation time: 15 minutes   *Chef: Diane Delorey*
Cooking time: 2 minutes   *Yacht: September Morn*
Serves: 10

3 cups diced turkey ham
1 cup shredded fat-free cheddar cheese
1 cucumber-peeled and diced (2 cups)
1 bunch green onions, chopped (1 cup)
1 cup diced tomato
1 cup fat-free Italian dressing
1/4 tsp. ground pepper
10 whole wheat pita breads
2 cups alfalfa sprouts

Mix together first eight ingredients and marinate. Warm pita bread until pita "puffs" in microwave oven (about 10 seconds). Split and stuff with 1/2 cup mixture and sprouts.

Hint: *Substitute low sodium turkey breast for turkey ham to lower sodium content.*

Nutrient content per serving:

Calories	286	Cholesterol	33 mg
Protein	26 g	Sodium	1368 mg
Carbohydrates	36 g	Potassium	331 mg
Fat	2.5 g	Iron	1.7 mg
Fiber - Dietary	5.0 g	Calcium	15 mg

8% calories from fat

Food Exchanges: 0.4 Veg,, 1.8 Bread, 2.3 Meat

TUNA PITA POCKETS

Preparation time: 30 minutes   *Chef: Tabatha Gardner*
Cooking time: 5-10 minutes
Serves: 4

4 whole wheat pita bread pockets (8 halves)
1 (6-1/4 oz.) can white tuna in spring water (drained)
1/2 cup red onion, chopped
1/2 cup diced cucumber (or zucchini)
1 large tomato, diced (1 cup)
1 green pepper, diced
2 Tblsp. fat-free mayonnaise
2 tsp. lemon juice
1/4 tsp. black pepper
1/8 tsp. of Tabasco
Garnish: Alfalfa sprouts

Preheat oven to 350°F. To form pockets cut each pita bread in half. In a bowl flake tuna; mix in all other ingredients and spoon into pita pockets. Place pockets on a baking sheet and bake until crispy (about 5-10 minutes). *Garnish.*

Note: *These can also be heated in the microwave.*

Nutrient content per serving:

Calories	191	Cholesterol	19 mg
Protein	17 g	Sodium	456 mg
Carbohydrates	27 g	Potassium	327 mg
Fat	1.8 g	Iron	1.5 mg
Fiber - Dietary	1.8 g	Calcium	42 mg

9% calories from fat

Food Exchanges: 0.7 Veg., 1.4 Bread, 1.6 Meat

HOT PITA POCKETS

Preparation time: 45 minutes   *Chef: Jeanne Bach*
Cooking time: 15 minutes   *Yacht: Iemanja*
Serves: 6

2 (6-1/8 oz.) cans Albacore tuna in spring water, draind
1/4 cup onion, diced
2 (8 oz.) cans sliced water chestnuts, drained and chopped
1/2 cup fat-free Mozzarella cheese
6 whole wheat pita bread halves
1/8 tsp. paprika
1/2 tsp. garlic powder
1/2 tsp. pepper
1/2 cup fat-free mayonnaise (or tofu mayonnaise page 78)

Marmalade Dressing:
1/2 cup low-sugar orange marmalade (or ginger marmalade)
2 Tblsp. low sodium ketchup
2 Tblsp. cider vinegar
3 Tblsp. water
1 tsp. ground ginger (if not able to find ginger marmalade)

Preheat oven to 350°F. Combine and mix drained tuna, onion, paprika, water chestnuts, pepper and mayonnaise. Put slice of cheese into each 1/2 pocket. Then equally portion filling into each pita pocket. Heat in oven for 10-15 minutes until cheese melts slightly. Marmalade **Dressing:** Combine the ingredients and shake well. *Serve with a green salad.*

Nutrient content per serving:

Calories	244	Cholesterol	28 mg
Protein	24 g	Sodium	666 mg
Carbohydrates	34 g	Potassium	327 mg
Fat	1.8 g	Iron	1.6 mg
Fiber - Dietary	0.7 g	Calcium	24 mg

6% calories from fat

Food Exchanges: 1.6 Veg,, 0.7 Bread, 2.7 Meat

Sips, Dips
and Appetizers

TROPICAL LASSI

Preparation time: 5 minutes   *Chef: Joyce Pfaff*
Serves: 1   *Yacht: Flash Vert*

1/3 cup orange juice
1/3 cup plain nonfat yogurt
1 very ripe banana
2 ice cubes

Combine ingredients in a blender and process until smooth.

Hint: *Use your imagination; try a flavored yogurt or different fruit.*

Nutrient content per serving:

Calories	185	Cholesterol	1 mg
Protein	6 g	Sodium	60 mg
Carbohydrates	41 g	Potassium	801 mg
Fat	0.7 g	Iron	0.5 mg
Fiber - Dietary	2 g	Calcium	165 mg

3% calories from fat

Food Exchanges: 0.4 Milk, 2.4 Fruit

SHARK ATTACK

Preparation time: 10 minutes   *Chef: Sheila Kruse Boyce*
Serves: 4   *Yacht: Victorious*

2/3 cup grapefruit juice, frozen concentrate
1/3 cup cranberry juice, bottled
1/3 cup water
1 cup rum (optional)
1-1/2 tsp. fructose
Juice of 1 lime

Place all ingredients in blender, and blend at high speed until well blended. If too thin, pour some out and add ice. Blend until slightly thickened .

This is not a sweet drink, but is very refreshing on a hot, sunny afternoon.

Nutrient content per serving:

Calories	199	Cholesterol	0 mg
Protein	0.8 g	Sodium	3 mg
Carbohydrates	18 g	Potassium	189 mg
Fat	0.2 g	Iron	0.4 mg
Fiber - dietary	0.2 g	Calcium	16 mg

1% calories from fat

Food Exchanges: 1.0 Fruit

MANGO-BANANA MANIA

Preparation time: 5 minutes   *Chef: Jan Robinson*
Serves: 2   *Yacht: Vanity*

1/2 cup peel, diced fresh mango chunks
1 fresh ripe banana
4 oz. unsweetened apple juice
4 oz. fresh orange juice
2 oz. fresh lime juice
2 tsp. honey
6 ice cubes
Garnish: Mint leaves

In a blender combine all ingredients. Blend for 30 seconds or until smooth. Pour into two fluted glasses and garnish with fresh mint leaves.

Note: *A little rum added to this goes well, but remember to adjust the nutrients.*

Nutrient content per serving:

Calories	169	Cholesterol	0 mg
Protein	1 g	Sodium	3.9 mg
Carbohydrates	44 g	Potassium	517 mg
Fat	0.4 g	Iron	0.5 mg
Fiber - Dietary	2.1 g	Calcium	12 mg

2% calories from fat

Food Exchanges: 2.4 Fruit

HUMMUS PARTY DIP

Preparation time: 5 minutes · *Chef: Jan Robinson*
Chilling time: 1 hour · *Yacht: Vanity*
Serves: 6

1 (16 oz.) can garbanzo beans, drained, liquid reserved
2 Tblsp. fresh lemon juice
5 garlic cloves, minced
2 Tblsp. fincly chopped onion
1 tsp. paprika
1/2 tsp. white pepper
1 tsp. tahini
Garnish: 1 red cabbage

In a blender or food processor fitted with the metal blade, combine 1/2 cup reserved bean liquid and remaining ingredients. Process until mixture is a smooth paste. Add more liquid if needed to make desired consistency. Cover and refrigerate until chilled. *Hollow out cabbage, fill with Hummus and serve.*

Serve with fat-free chips or pita bread. Use as a dip for cruditiés, or use to stuff celery.

Nutrient content per serving: 1/4 Cup

Calories 58	Cholesterol .... 0 mg
Protein .... 3 g	Sodium .... 6 mg
Carbohydrates .... 10 g	Potassium .... 143 mg
Fat .... 1.1 g	Iron .... 0.2 mg
Fiber - Dietary .... 2.1 g	Calcium .... 7 mg

15% calories from fat

Food Exchanges: 1.8 Veg, 0.1 Fat

BLACK BEAN DIP

Preparation time: 5 minutes　　　　　　　*Chef: Bobbi Fawcett*
Cooking time: 10 minutes　　　　　　　*Yacht: Windwalker*
Serves: 6

**1/4 cup chopped onion
6 cloves garlic, chopped
2 Tblsp. fat-free chicken broth (page 80) or water
1 (15 oz.) can low sodium black beans
1 Tblsp. Worcestershire sauce
1/4 tsp. cumin
2 tsp. lemon juice
1 Tblsp. chopped fresh cilantro
1/2 tsp. Tabasco or cayenne pepper**

In a medium size saucepan cook onion and garlic in 2 Tblsp. chicken broth for a few minutes, until softened. Add black beans, Worcestershire, and cumin. Simmer, stir occasionally. Stir in cilantro and hot stuff last. Whirl in a blender. *Serve hot or cold with vegetable crudités.*

Nutrient content per serving:

Calories	87	Cholesterol	0 mg
Protein	8 g	Sodium	144 mg
Carbohydrates	20 g	Potassium	353 mg
Fat	1.1 g	Iron	0.3 mg
Fiber - Dietary	6.5 g	Calcium	11 mg

8% calories from fat

Food Exchanges: 3.7 Veg,

SPICY BLACK BEAN DIP

Preparation time: 5 minutes   *Chef: Ann Glenn*
Serves: 8   *Yacht: Encore*

2 cups cooked black beans, drained, reserve 1/2 cup liquid
1 Tblsp. no salt added tomato paste
1 Tblsp. plain nonfat yogurt
1 Tblsp. fresh lime juice
1 green onion, minced
3 large clove of garlic, minced
1/2 tsp. ground cumin
1 tsp. coriander
1 Tblsp. finely chopped jalapeño
Garnish: Minced green onion

Combine all ingredients, including liquid in a blender or food processor. Blend until smooth. Transfer to a serving bowl.

Garnish with minced green onion, including the green part and / or a dollop of yogurt.

Hint: *Serve hot salsa on the side with tortilla chips. Great fiber too!*

Nutrient content per serving:

Calories	64	Cholesterol	0 mg
Protein	4 g	Sodium	19 mg
Carbohydrates	12 g	Potassium	193 mg
Fat	0.3 g	Iron	1.1 mg
Fiber - Dietary	1.9 g	Calcium	18 mg

4% calories from fat

Food Exchanges: 0.1 Veg, 0.6 Bread

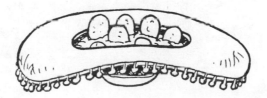

TASTY BEAN DIP

Preparation time: 5 minutes   *Chef: Jan Robinson*
Cooking time: 15 minutes   *Yacht: Vanity*
Serves: 16

1/4 cup diced green chilies
1/4 cup salsa (hot or mild, to taste)
4 green onions, chopped
1/2 tsp. cumin
4 cloves garlic, minced
2 (16 oz.) cans vegetarian fat-free refried beans

Combine chilies, salsa, onions and seasonings in a saucepan and cook over medium heat, until onions are tender. Add beans and cook about 10 minutes. *Serve either hot or cold with warm flour tortillas or low fat tortilla chips.*

Nutrient content per serving: 1/4 cup

Calories	47	Cholesterol	0 mg
Protein	3 g	Sodium	232 mg
Carbohydrates	9 g	Potassium	207 mg
Fat	0.05 g	Iron	0.2 mg
Fiber - Dietary	1.4 g	Calcium	3 mg

1% calories from fat

Food Exchanges: 0.4 Bread

BLOODY CAESAR CLAM DIP

Preparation time: 5 minutes   *Chef: Gwen Hamlin*
Serves: 4   *Yacht: Whisper*

1 (8 oz.) pkg. fat-free cream cheese, softened
1/2 cup hot salsa (or to taste)
3 Tblsp. prepared horseradish sauce
1 (6-1/2 oz.) can minced clams, drained
1/2 tsp. Worcestershire sauce

Combine all ingredients in a bowl. *Serve with fat-free tortilla chips or vegetables.*

Nutrient content per serving:

Calories	50	Cholesterol	8.6 mg
Protein	9 g	Sodium	283 mg
Carbohydrates	4 g	Potassium	103 mg
Fat	0.1 g	Iron	0.9 mg
Fiber - Dietary	0.3 g	Calcium	0.6 mg

2% calories from fat

Food Exchanges: 0.1 Veg, 0.9 Meat

CREAMY CRAB DIP

Preparation time: 10 minutes　　　　　*Chef: Shirley Keahey*
Cooking time: 12 minutes　　　　　　　*Yacht: Capricious*
Serves: 6

1 (8 oz.) pkg. fat-free cream cheese, softened
1/4 cup nonfat skim milk
1/4 cup nonfat mayonnaise
1/4 cup chopped green onions
1/4 tsp. Worcestershire sauce
6 water chestnuts, chopped
1/8 tsp. chili sauce (or to taste)
1/2 tsp. paprika
1/4 lb. chopped imitation crabmeat (surimi)

Preheat oven to 350°F. Mix softened cream cheese, milk and mayonnaise until smooth. Add remaining ingredients. Put in a small attractive baking dish and sprinkle top with paprika. Bake for 12 minutes.

Serve hot with wheat thins; or vegetables.

Nutrient content per serving:

Calories	73	Cholesterol	11 mg
Protein	11 g	Sodium	436 mg
Carbohydrates	8 g	Potassium	121 mg
Fat	0.3 g	Iron	0.4 mg
Fiber - Dietary	0.2 g	Calcium	22 mg

4% calories from fat

Food Exchanges: 0.2 Veg., 1.1 Meat

Reduce cholesterol intake by using tofu instead of yogurt and other milk products; however, tofu has a higher fat content than nonfat yogurt.

HOT ARTICHOKE DIP

Preparation time: 10 minutes　　　　　　　　*Chef: Jan Robinson*
Cooking time: 30 minutes　　　　　　　　　　　*Yacht: Vanity*
Serves: 8

1 (15 oz.) can artichokes, drained and chopped
1 (4 oz.) can mild green chilies, drained and chopped
1/4 cup nonfat mayonnaise
1/4 tsp. Tabasco
1/4 tsp. black pepper

Preheat oven to 350°F. Mix all ingredients together. Bake until warm (about 30 minutes) stirring occasionally. *Serve warm with fat-free crackers or fresh vegetables.*

Note: This may also be heated in the microwave.

Nutrient content per serving:

Calories	37	Cholesterol	0 mg
Protein	2 g	Sodium	311 mg
Carbohydrates	9 g	Potassium	217 mg
Fat	0.2 g	Iron	0.8 mg
Fiber - Dietary	0.2 g	Calcium	27 mg

4% calories from fat

Food Exchanges: 1.2 Veg

Fat
Potato
Chip

You're not supose to
be in this recipe

ARTICHOKE ARIEL

Preparation time: 15 minutes   *Chef: Judy Knape*
Waiting time: 30 minutes   *Yacht: Ariel*
Serves: 6

1 cup plain nonfat yogurt
2 (15 oz.) cans artichoke hearts, drained
1 shallot, finely minced
1 jalapeño, minced (or to taste)
1 Tblsp. lemon juice
2 Tblsp. fresh cilantro, chopped
1 medium tomato, diced
1/2 tsp. pepper

Drain yogurt in paper towel-lined sieve for 30 minutes or more. Set aside. Chop artichokes. Blend all ingredients.

Serve with chips.

Nutrient content per serving:

Calories	100	Cholesterol	0 mg
Protein	7 g	Sodium	170 mg
Carbohydrates	21 g	Potassium	684 mg
Fat	0.6 g	Iron	2.2 mg
Fiber - Dietary	0.3 g	Calcium	74 mg

4% calories from fat

Food Exchanges: 0.2 Milk, 3.0 Veg

TOFU CURRY DIP
(OR DRESSING)

Preparation time: 12 minutes　　　　　　*Chef: Jan Robinson*
Yield: 2 cups　　　　　　　　　　　　　　　*Yacht: Vanity*

10 oz. low fat firm tofu
2 Tblsp. less salt soy sauce
1 Tblsp. hot chutney
2 garlic cloves, crushed
1 Tblsp. curry powder
2 Tblsp. seasoned rice vinegar
2 Tblsp. honey
1/4 cup fresh lemon juice

Place all ingredients in blender. Blend until smooth. *Serve with fresh vegetables or pita breads or use as a dressing on* **Lentils, Barley and Rice** *(page 126)*

Hint: Make ahead, as it will keep in refrigerator for a week.

Nutrient content per serving: 1/4 cup

Calories	152	Cholesterol	0 mg
Protein	6 g	Sodium	222 mg
Carbohydrates	27 g	Potassium	372 mg
Fat	2.8 g	Iron	2.3 mg
Fiber - Dietary	6.7 g	Calcium	132 mg

16% calories from fat

Food Exchanges: 0.1 Fruit, 0.6 Meat, 0.2 Fat

Healthy Food!

TROPICAL SALSA

Preparation time: 12 minutes   *Chef: Jan Robinson*
Cooking time: 20 minutes   *Yacht: Vanity*
Serves: 4

**2 cups finely chopped fresh pineapple (or 1 (20 oz.) can
      pineapple chunks, drained)**
1 cup finely chopped tomato
1/2 cup diced red onion
1/2 jalapeño pepper, minced or finely chopped
1/2 tsp. cumin powder
1/2 tsp. coriander powder

Combine all ingredients in a saucepan. Cover and cook over
low heat until reduced to desired consistency, about 15 to 20
minutes.

*Serve with enchiladas, corn chips, frittatas and anything else
you would like to spice up.*

Nutrient content per serving:

Calories	60	Cholesterol	0 mg
Protein	1 g	Sodium	23 mg
Carbohydrates	14 g	Potassium	262 mg
Fat	0.7 g	Iron	1.0 mg
Fiber - Dietary	2 g	Calcium	19 mg

8% calories from fat

Food Exchanges: 0.6 Veg, 0.6 Fruit

STUFFED MUSHROOMS

Preparation time: 15 minutes   *Chef: Jan Robinson*
Cooking time: 30 minutes   *Yacht: Vanity*
Serves: 6

1/4 cup vegetable stock (page 81) or water
12 mushrooms, remove stems and put aside
1 (10 oz.) pkg. frozen chopped spinach, thawed
1/2 cup fat-free Ricotta cheese
1/2 cup fat-free mozzarella cheese
2 cloves garlic, crushed
1/2 tsp. black pepper
Garnish: Paprika

Preheat oven to 350°F. Heat vegetable stock or water in skillet. Cook mushroom caps just until they lose their raw effect. Chop stems finely, and mix with spinach, cheeses, garlic and pepper. Stuff mushroom caps. *Sprinkle with paprika. Bake for 20 minutes.*

This recipe was given to me from a friend Jayne Thylan, as we walked to the "bus stop" in Utah!

Nutrient content per serving: 1/4 cup

Calories	65	Cholesterol	5 mg
Protein	11 g	Sodium	186 mg
Carbohydrates	7 g	Potassium	305 mg
Fat	0.3 g	Iron	1.3 mg
Fiber - Dietary	1.6 g	Calcium	74 mg

3% calories from fat

Food Exchanges: 0.3 Milk 0.9 Veg, 0.6 Meat

No thanks.
I'm stuffed

MUSHROOM SPREAD

Preparation time: 12 minutes   *Chef: Jan Robinson*
Cooking time: 15 minutes   *Yacht:Vanity*
Serves: 6

1/4 cup fat-free chicken broth (page 80) or water
1/3 cup chopped onion
3 garlic cloves, crushed
1 cup chopped mushrooms
1 tsp. dried thyme leaves (or 1 Tblsp. chopped fresh)
1 tsp. lemon zest
3 Tblsp. low fat grated Romano cheese
1 Tblsp. fresh lemon juice
3 Tblsp. chopped fresh parsley
1/2 tsp. black pepper

Heat the chicken broth, or water in large skillet over medium-low heat. Add onion and garlic and sauté for about 5 minutes, until softened. Add mushrooms, thyme and zest to skillet. Stir then cover and cook for another 5 minutes, until mushrooms are tender. Uncover, increase heat and cook another 5 minutes, until mushrooms begin to brown. Transfer mushroom mixture to processor. Add cheese and lemon juice. Use on/off to finely chop mixture. Stir in parsley and pepper. Transfer to a serving bowl. *Serve with crackers.*

Hint: *This can be made a few hours ahead of time.*

Nutrient content per serving: 1/4 cup

Calories 26
Protein ....2 g
Carbohydrates ....3 g
Fat ....0.8 g
Fiber - Dietary ....0.4 g

Cholesterol.......................4 mg
Sodium ....64 mg
Potassium ....81 mg
Iron ....0.4 mg
Calcium.........................10 mg

27% calories from fat

Food Exchanges: 0.3 Veg

SARDINE DOLMADES

Preparation time: 10 minutes　　　　　　　*Chef: Bobbi Fawcett*
Cooking time: 25 minutes　　　　　　　　*Yacht: Windwalker*
Serves: 8

1/2 tsp. fructose
2 Tblsp. white vinegar (or rice vinegar)
1/2 cup cooked rice (or kasha)
1 (3-3/4 oz.) can water packed sardines, drained
2 green onions sliced
20 grape vine leaves
Garnish: 3 Tblsp. low sodium mustard

Dissolve fructose in vinegar stir into rice (or kasha). On each leaf place a teaspoon of rice (or kasha). Top with a piece of sardine and a little green onion. Roll and serve with mustard.

Note: Blanched spinach or romaine leaves may be used instead of grape leaves.

Nutrient content per serving:

Calories	107	Cholesterol	20 mg
Protein	7 g	Sodium	114 mg
Carbohydrates	16 g	Potassium	364 mg
Fat	1.5 g	Iron	3.1 mg
Fiber - Dietary	1.7 g	Calcium	146 mg

13% calories from fat

Food Exchanges: 0.4 Veg., 0.6 Bread, 0.4 Meat

STUFFED BABY POTATOES

Preparation time: 15 minutes   *Chef: Jan Robinson*
Cooking time: 10 minutes (microwave)   *Yacht: Vanity*
Serves: 8

1 lb. small red potatoes, scrubbed and halved
1 cup low-fat cottage cheese
2 tsp. prepared horseradish
1 Tblsp. minced chives
2 tsp. fresh finely cut dill weed (or 1/2 tsp dried)
1/4 tsp. black pepper

Gently prick the potato skins in several places with a fork. Arrange half of the potatoes on a microwave-safe pan, preferably a ring pan. Microwave on high for 3 to 4 minutes, or until fork-tender. Transfer to a plate. Repeat with the remaining potatoes. Let stand until cool enough to handle. Using a tiny melon scoop or spoon, hollow out each potato, leaving a sturdy shell. Purée the cottage cheese in a food processor until smooth. Transfer to a small bowl. Stir in horseradish, chives, dill and pepper. Spoon into the potato shells. *Serve warm or chilled.*

Hint: *As an alternative vary the filling by using different herbs. Or you may replace the horseradish with about 1/4 cup minced pimentos, salsa, chopped cooked spinach or pesto sauce.*

Note: *If you don't have a microwave, steam the potatoes until tender, about 15-20 minutes.*

Nutrient content per serving:

Calories	66	Cholesterol	1.3 mg
Protein	4 g	Sodium	19 mg
Carbohydrates	12 g	Potassium	228 mg
Fat	0.1 g	Iron	0.3 mg
Fiber - Dietary	0.9 g	Calcium	11 mg

2% calories from fat

Food Exchanges: 0.7 Bread, 0.4 Meat

Meatless Main Dishes...

COOKING TIMES

Per 1/2 Cup Uncooked	Liquid(cups)	Cooking Times	Yield(cups)
RICE:			
Brown, long grain	1	25 to 30 minutes	1-1/2
Brown, short grain	1	40 minutes	1-1/2
Brown, instant	1/2	5 minutes	3/4
Brown, quick	3/4	10 minutes	1
White, long grain	1	20 minutes	1-3/4
White, instant	1/2	5 mimutes (stand 5 mins.)	1
Converted	1-1/3	31 minutes	2
Arborio	3/4	15 minutes	1-1/2
Basmati, white	1/2	15 minutes	2
Jasmine	1	15 to 20 minutes	1-3/4
Texmati, long grain, brown	1(plus 2 Tblsp.)	40 minutes	2
Texmati, long grain, white	3/4(plus 2 Tblsp.)	15 minutes	1-1/4
Wehani	1	40 minutes	1-1/4
Wild	2	50 minutes	2
Wild pecan	1	20 minutes	1-1/2

LEGUMES:

(for each cup of beans add 3 cups of liquid and soak overnight before cooking)

Per 1/2 Cup Uncooked	Liquid(cups)	Cooking Times	Yield(cups)
Adzuki beans	2	40 minutes	1-1/2
Black beans	2	1 hour 20 minutes	1-1/3
Black-eyed peas	2	1 hour	1-1/2
Cannellini beans	1-1/2	1 hour 35 minutes	1-1/2
Chick-peas (Garbanzo)	2	1 hour 5 minutes	1-1/2
Cranberry beans	2	1 hour 5 minutes	1-1/2
Fava beans	2	30 to 40 minutes	1
Flageolet beans	2	1 hour 10 minutes	1-1/2
Great Northern beans (white)	2	1 hour	1-1/2
Kidney beans	2	55 minutes	1-1/2
Lentils, green (whole)	1-1/2	35 minutes	1-1/2
Lentils, orange (whole)	1-1/2	20 minutes	1-1/3
Lima bans	2-2/3	45 minutes	1-1/3
Mung beans	2	35 to 45 minutes	2
Navy beans (small, white)	2	1 hour	1-1/2
Pinto beans	2	1 hour	1-1/2
Red beans	1-1/2	45 minutes	1-1/2
Soybeans	2	2 hours 25 minutes	1-1/3
Split peas	2	30 to 35 minutes	1

GRAINS: (Per 1 cup dry)

	Liquid(cups)	Cooking Times	Yield(cups)
Amaranth	3	25 minutes	2-1/2
Barley (whole)	3	1 hour 15 minutes	3-1/2
Bulgur Wheat (cracked wheat)	2	15 to 20 minutes	2-1/2
Cornmeal (course)	4	25 minutes	3
Oats (flaked, rolled, oatmeal)	3	30 minutes	2-1/2

PASTA: (Dry)

			Yield(cups)
Spaghetti	2 ounces		1
	1 pound		8
Elbows	1/2 cup = (2 ounces)		1
	1 cup = (3-1/2 ounces)		1-3/4
Orzo	1/2 cup = (3 ounces)		1-1/2
	2-1/2 cups = (1 pound)		6-1/2
Fresh pasta	3 ounces		1

SWEET AND SOUR VEGETABLES WITH GINGER AND TOFU

Preparation time: 20 minutes
Cooking time: 15 minutes
Serves: 6

Chef: Jan Robinson
Yacht: Vanity

1/3 cup rice wine vinegar
4 tsp. arrowroot
1/4 cup brown rice syrup
2 Tblsp. less salt soy sauce
1-1/2 tsp. freshly grated ginger root
1 (16 oz.) can pineapple bits, with juice
6 Tblsp. vegetable stock (page 81)
2 cloves garlic, minced
1 cup onion, in thin lengthwise slices
1 large green pepper, sliced
1 cup sliced mushrooms
1 (8 oz.) can sliced water chestnuts, drained
1 cup fresh pea pods (10 oz. pkg. frozen)
8 oz. low fat firm tofu, cubed in 1/4 inch cubes
2 cups quartered tomatoes

Prepare sauce by mixing together vinegar and arrowroot. Cook over medium heat, adding brown rice syrup, soy sauce, ginger and pineapple; simmer until thick and set aside. Heat broth, add garlic and next five ingredients. Stir fry until vegetables are crisp tender. Gently stir into sauce and tofu; add tomatoes and heat through.

*Serve over **Brown Rice** (page 205) or **Fresh Pasta** (page 135).*

Nutrient content per serving:

Calories	150	Cholesterol	0 mg
Protein	7 g	Sodium	201 mg
Carbohydrates	29 g	Potassium	558 mg
Fat	2 g	Iron	1.9 mg
Fiber - Dietary	3.5 g	Calcium	52 mg

11% calories from fat

Food Exchanges: 2.6 Veg., 0.4 Fruit, 0.2 Bread, 0.2 Fat

STUFFED PEPPERS

Preparation time: 20 minutes　　　　　　　*Chef: Jan Robinson*
Cooking time: 40 minutes　　　　　　　　　*Yacht: Vanity*
Serves: 4

4 medium red or yellow peppers
2 oz. sun-dried tomatoes
5 oz. low fat firm tofu, drained
1/2 cup chopped onion
4 cloves garlic, chopped
1 tsp. crushed, dried oregano
1 tsp. crushed, dried basil
1/4 cup chopped fresh mint leaves
2 cups cooked brown rice
1/4 cup raisins
1 cup + 1/4 cup no salt added tomato sauce
1 Tblsp. + 2 tsp. brown rice syrup
1/8 tsp. cayenne pepper

Preheat oven to 350° F. Cut tops from peppers, remove seeds and inner ribs and steam 4 minutes to soften slightly. Remove peppers from steamer and invert to drain. Place tomatoes in boiling water in steamer base and blanch 2 minutes. Drain and chop. Crumble tofu and combine in skillet with onion and garlic. Sauté over medium heat until tofu is dry. Remove from heat and add sundried tomatoes, oregano, basil, mint, brown rice, raisins, 1 cup tomato sauce and 1 Tblsp.rice syrup. Mix well. Fill peppers with tofu-rice mixture and stand upright in a baking pan. Mix remaining 1/4 cup tomato sauce with remaining 2 tsp. rice syrup and cayenne pepper. Spoon sauce on top of each pepper. Pour hot water around peppers to a depth of about 1 inch and bake for 40 minutes, or until peppers are tender and sauce on top is thick.

Nutrient content per serving:

Calories	272	Cholesterol	0 mg
Protein	10 g	Sodium	50 mg
Carbohydrates	55 g	Potassium	572 mg
Fat	2.7 g	Iron	2.2 mg
Fiber - Dietary	6.4 g	Calcium	70 mg

8% calories from fat

Food Exchanges: 2.4 Veg., 0.4 Fruit, 1.5 Bread, 0.2 Fat

MEDITERRANEAN EGGPLANTS

Preparation time: 25 minutes
Cooking time: 50 minutes
Serves: 2

Chef: Dena Edwards
Yacht: Majestic Lady

2 eggplants
1/4 cup vegetable stock (page 81)
1/2 cup onion, finely chopped
2 cloves garlic, minced
2 medium size tomatoes
1 cup cooked long grain rice
3 Tblsp. fresh chopped marjoram (3 tsp. dried)
1/8 tsp. cinnamon
1/4 tsp. freshly ground black pepper

Garnish:
2 Tblsp. finely chopped parsley

Preheat oven to 350°F. Wrap eggplants in foil and bake 20 minutes to soften, allow to cool. Cut eggplants in half, carefully scoop out pulp, leaving a 3/8-inch border. In a pan heat broth. Cook onion and garlic until soft. Finely chop eggplant pulp, stir into onion mixture, cover and cook about 5 minutes. Cut a small cross in the skin of tomatoes, plunge it into boiling water for 30 seconds, then peel. Quarter the tomatoes and remove the pips, chop tomato flesh, stir into onion mixture, along with rice, marjoram, cinnamon, and pepper. Pile rice mixture into eggplant shells, cover with aluminium foil and bake for 30 minutes.

Sprinkle with parsley. Serve accompanied with a tomato and onion salad, and a crusty loaf of bread.

Note: *This also makes a wonderful side dish for 4 people.*

Nutrient content per serving:

Calories	237	Cholesterol	0 mg
Protein	6.3 g	Sodium	23 mg
Carbohydrates	53 g	Potassium	903 mg
Fat	1.3 g	Iron	3.6 mg
Fiber - Dietary	8.9 g	Calcium	68 mg

5% calories from fat

Food Exchanges: 3.6 Veg., 1.8 Bread

DIRTY RICE AND BEANS

Preparation time: 15 minutes   *Chef: Jan Robinson*
Cooking time: 40 minutes   *Yacht: Vanity*
Serves: 6

1/4 cup + 3-1/2 cups vegetable stock (page 81)
2 cups uncooked brown rice
1-1/2 cups chopped onion
3 garlic cloves, crushed
1 cup finely diced carrots
1/2 cup chopped celery
1 Tblsp. jalapeño chili, seeded and minced
1 Tblsp. each: ground cumin, ground coriander, chili powder
1 cup no salt added tomato juice
1-1/2 cups cooked kidney beans
1-1/2 cups chopped tomatoes
1/2 cup fresh or frozen corn kernels
1/4 cup chopped cilantro

In a large saucepan put 1/4 cup vegetable stock, the next nine ingredients and sauté over medium heat for 3-5 minutes; stir constantly to keep from sticking. When browned add 3-1/2 cups stock and tomato juice to mixture; bring to boil over high heat. Cover, lower heat to the lowest setting and simmer for 15 minutes. Add the beans, tomatoes and corn, stir, cover, and simmer for 20 more minutes, or until the rice is cooked. Remove from the heat and add the cilantro. Serve.

Garnish with fresh cilantro leaves and tomato slices.

Nutrient content per serving:

Calories	344	Cholesterol	0 mg
Protein	11 g	Sodium	43 mg
Carbohydrates	71 g	Potassium	686 mg
Fat	2.6 g	Iron	3.5 mg
Fiber - Dietary	6.7 g	Calcium	69 mg

7% calories from fat

Food Exchanges: 1.5 Veg., 3.9 Bread, 0.2 Meat

CARIBBEAN BLACK BEANS AND RICE

Preparation time: 10 minutes   *Chef: Jan Robinson*
Cooking time: 1-1/4 hours   *Yacht: Vanity*
Serves: 6

Beans:
1-1/2 cups uncooked black beans* or 2 (15 oz.) cans, drained
5 cups + 1/4 cup water
1 medium onion, peeled and stuck with 6 whole cloves
1 cup chopped onion
2 cloves garlic, minced
1/4 tsp. black pepper
2 tsp. dried oregano leaves

Rice:
1-1/2 cups long-grain brown or white rice(5 cups cooked)

Red and Gold Salsa:
2 tomatoes, finely chopped
1 yellow bell pepper, finely chopped
3 scallions, sliced
1 Tblsp. chopped fresh cilantro
2 Tblsp. lemon juice
1 Tblsp. finely chopped jalapeño

*Soak beans overnight. Next day *Prepare Salsa*: In a bowl mix all ingredients, cover and refrigerate. Drain beans, add fresh water and bring beans to a boil. Add clove-studded onion; reduce heat to low. Cook 1 hour. In a small pan, heat 1/4 cup water, add chopped onion, garlic, pepper and oregano. Cook until onion is transparent and water is evaporated, then add to beans. Cook for 30 minutes longer. Beans should be tender but not mushy. Discard clove-studded onion. As Beans are cooking, cook rice according to package instructions.

Serve black beans over cooked rice and top with salsa.

Nutrient content per serving:

Calories	361	Cholesterol	0 mg
Protein	11 g	Sodium	50 mg
Carbohydrates	70 g	Potassium	670 mg
Fat	1.1 g	Iron	2.5 mg
Fiber - Dietary	11.1 g	Calcium	46 mg

3% calories from fat

Food Exchanges: 1.9 Veg., 3.7 Bread

LENTILS, BARLEY AND RICE

Preparation time: 15 minutes   *Chef: Jan Robinson*
Cooking time: 35 minutes   *Yacht: Vanity*
Serves: 6

1 cup diced onion
2 cloves minced garlic
4 cups vegetable stock (page 81)
1/2 cup red lentils
1/4 cup yellow lentils
1/4 cup green lentils
1/2 cup sliced green onions
2 Tblsp. chili powder
1 Tblsp. ground coriander
2 tsp. ground turmeric
1/3 cup lime juice
1-1/4 cups cooked barley
1-1/4 cups cooked long-grain brown rice

In a stock pot heat 4 Tblsp. water and sauté onion and garlic until soft, over medium heat. Add next eight ingredients; stir well and bring to a boil. Cover and reduce heat and simmer 35 minutes or until lentils are tender; drain any remaining fluid. Stir in lime juice and add barley and brown rice to mixture.

Serve hot with steamed vegetables of your choice and spicy chutney. It is also very good cold: stir in blanched pea pods and **Tofu Curry Dip** *(page 113).*

Nutrient content per serving:

Calories	238	Cholesterol	0 mg
Protein	12 g	Sodium	41 mg
Carbohydrates	47 g	Potassium	640 mg
Fat	1.5 g	Iron	5.0 mg
Fiber - Dietary	9.5 g	Calcium	58 mg

5% calories from fat

Food Exchanges: 0.7 Veg., 2.5 Bread

STUFFED CHILIES
WITH BLACK BEAN SAUCE

Preparation time: 15 minutes   *Chef: Jan Robinson*
Cooking time: 20 minutes   *Yacht: Vanity*
Serves: 4

Vegetable cooking spray
1-1/2 cups cooked brown rice
1/2 cup diced red pepper
1 Tblsp. roasted + 1 tsp. ground cumin
1 Tblsp. roasted + 1 tsp. ground coriander
1/2 tsp. ground pepper
1 Tblsp. + 1 Tblsp. freshly chopped cilantro
8 whole green chilies, freshly roasted or canned
1/4 cup vegetable stock (page 81)
3 Tblsp. minced red onion
1 clove garlic, crushed
1/2 tsp. chili powder
1 Tblsp. sherry
2 Tblsp. tomato paste
1 tsp. minced jalapeño
1-1/2 cups cooked black beans

Spray baking sheet with Vegetable cooking spray. Combine the next
six ingredients. Slice chilies lengthwise and stuff with rice mixture.
Place chilies on prepared baking sheet and warm in 350°oven for 10-15
minutes. Combine next five ingredients plus 1 tsp. each cumin and
coriander in sauce pan and cook 3 minutes. Add tomato paste, 1 Tblsp.
cilantro, jalapeño and beans and cook for 5 more minutes. Put bean
mixture in blender or food processor and blend until smooth and
creamy. Add more stock or water if mixture is too thick.

To serve, place black bean sauce on plates, set two chilies on each plate.
Garnish with chopped fresh cilantro and tomatoes sprinkled over all.

Nutrient content per serving:

Calories	238	Cholesterol	0 mg
Protein	10 g	Sodium	32 mg
Carbohydrates	47 g	Potassium	694 mg
Fat	2.0 g	Iron	4.4 mg
Fiber - Dietary	6.1 g	Calcium	74 mg

7% calories from fat

Food Exchanges: 2.4 Veg., 2 Bread

THE GREAT BEAN STROGANOFF

Preparation time: 15 minutes   *Chef: Jan Robinson*
Cooking time: 15 minutes   *Yacht: Vanity*
Serves: 6

1/4 cup + 3/4 cup vegetable stock (page 81)
2 cups chopped onions
2 clove garlic, minced
3 cups chopped mushrooms
2 Tblsp. arrowroot + 2 Tblsp. water
1/4 cup dry sherry
1-1/2 Tblsp. Worcestershire sauce
1/4 tsp. dried marjoram leaves
1/4 tsp. chili powder
1/4 tsp. dried thyme leaves
1/8 tsp. nutmeg
3 cups cooked pinto beans *or* 2 (16 oz.) cans
      low sodium beans, drained and rinsed
2 tsp. fresh lemon juice
1-1/2 cups plain nonfat yogurt

In a large skillet, heat 1/4 cup broth, add onions, garlic and mushrooms, cook until tender. Mix arrowroot with water and add to skillet with 3/4 cup broth, sherry, Worcestershire sauce and spices. Cook until thickened. Add beans, cook over low heat until heated through. Remove from heat, stir in lemon juice and yogurt. *Serve over cooked brown rice, bulgur, or egglesss noodles.*

Nutrient content per serving:

Calories 207	Cholesterol .... 0 mg
Protein .... 12 g	Sodium .... 157 mg
Carbohydrates .... 37 g	Potassium .... 817 mg
Fat .... 0.7 g	Iron .... 3.1 mg
Fiber - Dietary .... 1.4 g	Calcium .... 62 mg

3% calories from fat

Food Exchanges: 0.3 Milk, 1.0 Veg., 1.6 Bread, 0.3 Meat

VEGETARIAN CHILI

Preparation time: 25 minutes   *Chef: Jan Robinson*
Cooking time: 35 minutes   *Yacht: Vanity*
Serves: 6

1 cup + 2 Tblsp. Vegetable Stock (page 81)
3/4 cup diced carrots
1 cup (each) diced: onions, green & red bell peppers, celery
2 cloves garlic, crushed
1 tsp. each: dried oregano, dried thyme, ground cumin
1/2 tsp. each: ground coriander, chili powder
1 Tblsp. minced canned jalapeño (or to taste)
2 cups chopped tomatoes
3 cups cooked kidney beans
1 cup fresh (or frozen, thawed) corn kernels
1-1/2 Tblsp. no salt added tomato paste
1 Tblsp. lime juice
1 tsp. red wine vinegar
1 tsp. freshly ground black pepper
1/2 cup chopped fresh cilantro

In a large stock pot with 2 Tblsp. vegetable stock, sauté carrots, onions, peppers, and celery for 4-5 minutes. Add the spices, jalapeño, tomatoes, beans, and remaining vegetable stock. Bring to a boil, reduce the heat, and simmer for 20 minutes. Add the corn kernels and simmer for 7 minutes. In small bowl, combine tomato paste, lemon juice and vinegar until blended. Stir into the chili. Season with freshly ground pepper and top with fresh cilantro.

Nutrient content per serving:

Calories	189	Cholesterol	0 mg
Protein	10 g	Sodium	88 mg
Carbohydrates	38 g	Potassium	805 mg
Fat	1.1 g	Iron	4.7 mg
Fiber - Dietary	3.9 g	Calcium	79 mg

5% calories from fat

Food Exchanges: 1.7 Veg., 1.6 Bread, 0.4 Meat

UPSIDE-DOWN VEGETARIAN CHILI PIE

Preparation time: 15 minutes   *Chef: Jan Robinson*
Cooking time: 35 minutes   *Yacht: Vanity*
Serves: 4

Pie:
**2 (15 oz.) cans fat-free vegetarian chili with black beans, spicy
      (or mild according to taste)**
1 cup frozen corn kernels
1/2 cup chopped onion
2 garlic cloves, minced
1 tsp. ground cumin

Topping:
1/2 cup whole wheat pastry flour
3/4 cup cornmeal
2 tsp. no sodium baking powder
1/4 cup honey
1/2 cup water
1/4 cup fat-free egg substitute
2 Tblsp. finely chopped red bell pepper
2 Tblsp. finely chopped onion
1 Tblsp. finely chopped jalapeño

Preheat oven to 375°F. Combine all Pie ingredients in a 10-inch diameter ovenproof casserole. Mix all dry ingredients together in one bowl. Mix honey, water, egg substitute, pepper, onion and jalapeño in cup measure. Add all at once to dry ingredients, mixing just to moisten. Pour on top of chili pie. Bake for 35 minutes.

Nutrient content per serving:

Calories	254	Cholesterol	0 mg
Protein	6 g	Sodium	65 mg
Carbohydrates	58 g	Potassium	273 mg
Fat	1.1 g	Iron	2.5 mg
Fiber - Dietary	17.5 g	Calcium	22 mg

4% calories from fat

Food Exchanges: 0.5 Veg., 2.3 Bread, 0.1 Meat

BLACK BEAN BURRITOS

Preparation time: 10 minutes   *Chef: Jan Robinson*
Cooking time: 15 minutes (microwave)   *Yacht: Vanity*
Serves: 4

1/4 cup water
1-1/2 cups chopped onion
2 cloves garlic, minced
2 cups cooked black beans
1-1/2 cups chopped unpeeled tomato
1 Tblsp. lime juice
1-1/2 tsp. ground cumin
2 Tblsp. jalapeño chilies, chopped
2 Tblsp. chopped fresh cilantro
8 (6-inch) corn tortillas

In a 2-quart casserole combine 1/4 cup water, onion and garlic. Cover and microwave on HIGH 5 minutes, until softened, stirring once or twice. Mash beans. Add beans, tomato, lime juice, cumin and chilies to onion mixture; stir well. Microwave on HIGH 10 minutes, or until thickened, stirring every 5 minutes. Add cilantro, let stand a few minutes while heating tortillas. Wrap tortillas in damp paper towels; microwave on HIGH 45 seconds to heat. Divide mixture evenly between tortillas. Spoon down center of each and roll up.

Serve immediately. Good served with **Red and Gold Salsa** *(page 133)*

Nutrient content per serving:

Calories	246	Cholesterol	0 mg
Protein	9 g	Sodium	131 mg
Carbohydrates	43 g	Potassium	612 mg
Fat	3.0 g	Iron	2.2 mg
Fiber - Dietary	11.0 g	Calcium	112 mg

11% calories from fat

Food Exchanges: 1.2 Veg., 1.9 Bread, 1 Meat, 0.4 Fat

VEGETARIAN ROTI

Preparation time: 40 minutes   *Chef: Gwen Hamlin*
Cooking time: 20 minutes   *Yacht: Whisper*
Serves: 8

1/4 cup + 1 cup vegetable stock (page 81)
1 cup finely chopped onion
4 cloves garlic, minced
3 Tblsp. curry powder
1/2 tsp. each: *XXX Calypso hot sauce* and *Caribbean hot sauce**
1 cup nonfat milk
1 Tblsp. coconut flavoring
2 cups cauliflower (1/2 head), broken in small pieces
1 cup sliced carrots (2 large)
1 cup chopped celery (2 stalks)
3 chopped scallions
2 boiled, diced potatoes
1 cup cooked lentils
1 (10 oz.) pkg. frozen green peas, thawed
2 tsp. arrowroot
8 large flour tortillas

In a large saucepan sauté onion, garlic and curry in 1/4 cup vegetable stock, until softened. Add 1 cup vegetable stock, stirring constantly; add hot sauces, milk, and coconut flavoring. Add cauliflower, carrots, celery and scallions. Cook 10 minutes. Remove vegetables and thicken sauce with arrowroot mixed with 2 Tblsp. water. Sir in potatoes, lentils and green peas. Return vegetables to pan. Heat through. In nonstick skillet, heat tortillas on both sides until blistered. Or wrap tortillas in paper towels and microwave 10-30 seconds.

To serve, place filling down center of tortillas, fold left and right side over. Place on serving plate seam side down. Very good with a variety of fruit chutneys and salsas.
*Check **Stocking a Healthy Kitchen** *page 254 for availability.*

Nutrient content per serving:

Calories	229	Cholesterol	0.5 mg
Protein	10 g	Sodium	79 mg
Carbohydrates	44 g	Potassium	597 mg
Fat	2.5 g	Iron	3.7 mg
Fiber - Dietary	6.4 g	Calcium	139 mg

10% calories from fat
Food Exchanges: 0.1 Milk, 1.1 Veg., 2.1Bread, 0.2 Fat

VEGETABLE TACOS WITH SALSA

Preparation time: 15 minutes   *Chef: Jan Robinson*
Cooking time: 16 minutes   *Yacht: Vanity*
Serves: 6

Red and Gold Salsa:
2 tomatoes, finely chopped
1 yellow bell pepper, finely diced
3 scallions, sliced
1 Tblsp. finely chopped cilantro
2 Tblsp. lemon juice
1 Tblsp. finely chopped jalapeño

Tacos:
1/4 cup vegetable stock (page 81)
1 large zucchini, quartered lengthwise and sliced
1-1/2 cup finely chopped onion
1 cup fresh or frozen corn kernels
1 red bell pepper, finely diced
2 Tblsp. finely chopped jalapeño pepper
2 Tblsp. Mexican Spice
1 (8oz.) pkg. frozen winter squash, thawed
12 corn tortillas
3 cups shredded lettuce

Mix together all ingredients for salsa, cover and chill. Put vegetable stock in large skillet with zucchini, onion, corn, red pepper and jalapeño. Sauté until soft (10-12 minutes). Mix in mexican spice and winter squash. Warm through. Microwave tortillas wrapped in paper towels for 30 seconds. Roll vegetables in tortillas and serve immediately.

To serve: Place two tacos on shredded lettuce, top with 1/2 cup salsa.

Nutrient content per serving:

Calories	221	Cholesterol	0 mg
Protein	7 g	Sodium	181 mg
Carbohydrates	46 g	Potassium	650 mg
Fat	3.0 g	Iron	2.4 mg
Fiber - Dietary	6.6 g	Calcium	120 mg

11% calories from fat

Food Exchanges: 2 Veg., 1.9 Bread, 0.4 Fat

RATATOUILLE STRUDEL

Preparation time: 15 minutes   *Chef: Gillian Pfister*
Cooking time: 45 minutes   *Yacht: Effects*
Serves: 8

2 cloves garlic, crushed
2 cups (1 small) eggplant, peeled and chopped
1 cup (1 medium) zucchini, chopped
1 cup no salt added tomatoes, drained and chopped
1 cup chopped onion
1 red pepper, diced
1 cup sliced mushrooms
2 Tblsp. no salt added tomato paste
2 Tblsp. chopped parsley
1 tsp. thyme leaves
1 tsp. black pepper
10 sheets filo (phyllo) pastry
Butter-flavored vegetable cooking spray

Preheat oven to 350° F. In a large skillet heat 1/2 cup water, sauté garlic and chopped vegetables for 15 minutes or until soft. Stir in tomato paste, parsley, thyme and pepper. Set aside. Layer sheets of pastry on top of each other spraying with vegetable spray between each layer. Spoon vegetable mixture down long edge, leaving 2 inches at each end. Roll up and tuck under ends. Place on sprayed oven tray and spray top. Bake until lightly browned (25-30 minutes).

Nutrient content per serving:

Calories	130	Cholesterol	0 mg
Protein	4 g	Sodium	147 mg
Carbohydrates	23 g	Potassium	388 mg
Fat	2.9 g	Iron	2.1 mg
Fiber - Dietary	2.2 g	Calcium	28 mg

19% calories from fat

Food Exchanges: 1.4 Veg., 0.8 Bread, 0.2 Fat

FRESH PASTA

Preparation time: 20 minutes
Resting time: 1/2 to 2 hours
Cooking time: 5-7 minutes
Serves: 6

Chef: Beth Avore
Yacht: Perfection

3 cups flour
1 cup fat-free egg substitute

Mix flour and egg substitute together in a bowl or on the counter until a soft dough forms. Let rest for 1/2 to 2 hours. If you don't have a pasta roller: roll dough with wooden pin on floured surface until very thin, cut into strips. If you have a pasta machine; follow general directions for dough and make into six thin sheets. Cut with noodle cutter. Cook in boiling water 5-7 minutes before serving with your favorite sauce.

Hint: *This recipe is good for all pasta dishes: spaghetti, lasagna, ravioli, tortellini, etc. You can experiment to make many different colors and flavors of fresh pasta; see following page for some ideas and the nutrition on each.*

Nutrient content per serving:

Calories	244	Cholesterol	0 mg
Protein	10 g	Sodium	54 mg
Carbohydrates	48 g	Potassium	67 mg
Fat	0.6 g	Iron	2.9 mg
Fiber - Dietary	1.7 g	Calcium	9 mg

2% calories from fat

Food Exchanges: 3.2 Bread, 0.4 Meat

Cook extra pasta, brown rice, and beans. Place in ziplock bags, seal, label with contents and date, then refrigerate or freeze. These are are great to use when you're in a hurry.

FRESH PASTA - VARIATIONS

See previous page for basic method and timing.

PUMPKIN   Serves 8
5 cups flour
3/4 cup fat-free egg substitute
1 cup canned pumpkin

Nutrient content per serving:

Calories	304	Cholesterol	0 mg
Protein	10 g	Sodium	33 mg
Carbohydrates	62 g	Potassium	147 mg
Fat	0.8 g	Iron	4.1 mg
Fiber - Dietary	2.7 g	Calcium	19 mg

3% calories from fat
Food Exchanges: 4.1 Bread, 0.2 Meat

TOMATO   Serves 6
3 cups flour
3/4 cup fat-free egg substitute
1/4 cup no-salt-added tomato paste

Nutrient content per serving:

Calories	249	Cholesterol	0 mg
Protein	9 g	Sodium	48 mg
Carbohydrates	50 g	Potassium	169 mg
Fat	0.7 g	Iron	3.2 mg
Fiber - Dietary	2.2 g	Calcium	13 mg

3% calories from fat
Food Exchanges: 0.4 Veg., 3.2 Bread, 0.3 Meat

SPINACH   Serves 6
3 cups flour
3/4 cup fat-free egg substitute
1 (8 oz.) pkg. frozen, chopped spinach, thawed and squeezed dry

Nutrient content per serving:

Calories	250	Cholesterol	0 mg
Protein	10 g	Sodium	70 mg
Carbohydrates	50 g	Potassium	169 mg
Fat	0.7 g	Iron	3.4 mg
Fiber - Dietary	2.4 g	Calcium	59 mg

2% calories from fat
Food Exchanges: 0.3 Veg., 3.2 Bread, 0.3 Meat

PEPPERS AND PASTA

Preparation time: 15 minutes   *Chef: Jan Robinson*
Cooking time: 15 minutes   *Yacht: Vanity*
Serves: 4

2/3 cup Vegetable stock (page 81)
1 each: yellow, green and red bell peppers, cut in thin strips
8 cups Swiss chard, washed well and cut into thin strips
**   (substitutes: kale or escarole)**
2 Tblsp. grated lemon peel
4 cloves of garlic, crushed
2 cups cooked white beans
1 tsp. ground black pepper
1/4 cup lemon juice
8 oz. dry penne and farfalle pasta (4 oz. each)

Heat the vegetable stock to a simmer in large sauté pan over moderate
heat. Add the pepper strips and simmer for 5-8 minutes. Then add the
greens, lemon peel and garlic, stirring until greens are wilted, 3-4
minutes (longer if using kale). Add beans to mixture and warm through.
Season to taste with pepper and lemon juice. Meanwhile, cook the
pasta according to package directions and drain. Toss with beans and
vegetables.

Nutrient content per serving:

Calories	378	Cholesterol	0 mg
Protein	18 g	Sodium	169 mg
Carbohydrates	75 g	Potassium	1216 mg
Fat	1.5 g	Iron	5.5 mg
Fiber - Dietary	2.4 g	Calcium	142 mg

4% calories from fat

Food Exchanges: 1.3 Veg., 2.7 Bread, 0.6 Meat

MIGHTY MEATLESS LASAGNA

Preparation time: 30 minutes　　　　　　　　*Chef: Jan Robinson*
Cooking time: 1-1/2 hours　　　　　　　　　　*Yacht:Vanity*
Serves: 6

1/4 cup + 1/2 cup vegetable stock (page 81)
2 cups chopped onions
4 cloves garlic, minced
3/4 lb. mushrooms, sliced
1/2 tsp. black pepper
2 tsp. oregano leaves
2 tsp. basil leaves
1 (16 oz.) can low sodium kidney beans, drained and rinsed
1/4 cup no salt added tomato paste
2 (14.5 oz.) cans no salt added tomatoes, drained and chopped
1 (8 oz.) pkg. uncooked lasagna noodles
3 cups nonfat ricotta cheese
1/4 cup chopped fresh parsley
1/2 cup (4 oz.) fat-free mozzarella cheese, grated
1/2 tsp. paprika

In a nonstick skillet heat 1/4 cup stock, onions, and garlic; cook for 3 minutes. Add mushrooms, pepper, oregano, basil, and 1/4 cup stock. Sauté for 5-10 minutes, until vegetables are soft and stock has evaporated. Stir in beans, tomato paste and tomatoes. Cover pan and simmer for about 30 minutes, stirring occasionally, until thickened. Preheat oven to 375°F. Cook lasagna noodles just until softened. Whip parsley into ricotta cheese. Assemble lasagna in a 9x13-inch baking dish. Spread 1/2 cup sauce over bottom of dish. Make two layers starting with 3 noodles, 1 cup tomato sauce, 1/2 ricotta mixture and 2 Tblsp. mozzarella. End with a layer of 3 noodles, 1 cup tomato sauce and mozarella. Sprinkle a little paprika on top. Bake 30 minutes covered. Uncover and cook 30 min. more. Cool 10 minutes before serving.

Nutrient content per serving:

Calories	389	Cholesterol	15 mg
Protein	35 g	Sodium	222 mg
Carbohydrates	65 g	Potassium	951 mg
Fat	1.6 g	Iron	5.5 mg
Fiber - Dietary	2.8 g	Calcium	88 mg

4% calories from fat

Food Exchanges: 2 Milk, 2.4 Veg., 2.7 Bread, 0.9 Meat

SPINACH LASAGNA

Preparation time: 25 minutes   *Chef: Jan Robinson*
Cooking time: 1-1/2 to 2 hours   *Yacht: Vanity*
Serves: 6

1 cup chopped onion
4 cloves garlic, chopped
1/4 cup water
2 cups sliced mushrooms
3 cans (15 oz. each) no salt added tomato sauce
1 can (13-3/4 oz.) artichoke hearts, chopped
3 Tblsp. honey
2 tsp. crushed dried oregano
1 tsp. each: crushed dried basil, thyme leaves, crushed rosemary
1/4 tsp. black pepper
1 (10 oz. pkg.) frozen chopped spinach, thawed and squeezed
2 cups nonfat ricotta cheese
4 egg whites, lightly beaten
1 tsp. fresh grated nutmeg
1/4 cup fresh chopped parsley
1 (8 oz.) pkg. lasagna noodles, uncooked

Bring a large, covered pot of water to boiling. Preheat oven to 350° F. In medium saucepan, over medium heat, cook onion and garlic in water for 3 minutes, until softened and beginning to color. Add mushrooms and cook, stirring constantly, until they soften. Add tomato sauce, artichokes, honey, oregano, basil, thyme, rosemary and pepper. Bring to a boil, simmer gently 5-10 minutes to blend flavors. Combine spinach with ricotta cheese, nutmeg, egg whites and parsley. Cook lasagne noodles in boiling water until just soft. Spread 1/2 cup tomato sauce over bottom of an 8 inch baking pan. Cover with 1/3 of the noodles, 1-1/4 cups sauce and 1/2 the ricotta cheese mixture. Repeat this layering with noodles, 1-1/4 cups sauce and remaining ricotta cheese. Top with remaining noodles. Spread remaining sauce (about 1 cup) over top of lasagna. Cover pan and bake for 1 hour. Remove cover and bake 15-30 minutes longer until pasta is tender.

Nutrient content per serving:

Calories	388	Cholesterol	8 mg
Protein	26 g	Sodium	238 mg
Carbohydrates	73 g	Potassium	596 mg
Fat	1.2 g	Iron	4.0 mg
Fiber - Dietary	5.0 g	Calcium	132 mg

3 % calories from fat
Food Exchanges: 1.3 Milk, 5.6 Veg., 1.8 Bread, 0.3 Meat

PASTA PRIMAVERA

Preparation time: 15 minutes   *Chef: Jan Robinson*
Cooking time: 20 minutes   *Yacht: Vanity*
Serves: 6

1 cup chopped onion
4 cloves garlic, crushed
1/4 cup + 2 Tblsp. vegetable stock (page 81)
2 (15 oz.) cans no salt added tomato sauce
2 Tblsp. honey
2 tsp. each: crushed dried oregano and crushed dried basil
1/2 tsp. black pepper
1 large red pepper, cut in 1-inch strips
1-1/2 cups each: sliced mushrooms, broccoli florets
1-1/2 cups each: zucchini (or yellow summer squash), and carrots
      cut in thin sticks 1-1/2 inches long
2 Tblsp. + 1 Tblsp. balsamic vinegar
1 (10 oz.) pkg. frozen asparagus tips, thawed
1 (12 oz.) pkg. Rainbow Rotini pasta (tri-color twists), cooked

In large saucepan, over medium heat, cook onion and garlic in 1/4 cup. stock until softened. Add tomato sauce, honey, oregano, basil and pepper. Bring to a boil, reduce heat and simmer gently for 20 minutes. In a skillet, combine red pepper, mushrooms, squash, carrots, broccoli and 2 Tblsp. each broth and vinegar. Stir-fry over medium heat until crisp tender, about 10 minutes; add asparagus and stir-fry 2 more minutes, set aside. Add 1 Tblsp. vinegar to sauce and cook for 5 minutes. Reserve 1 cup sauce to serve at the table; pour remaining sauce over cooked pasta and stir fried vegetables and toss thoroughly.

Garnish: Sprinkle 1/4 cup chopped green onion and chopped parsley over top and serve immediately.

Nutrient content per serving:

Calories	318	Cholestrol	0 mg
Protein	12 g	Sodium	101 mg
Carbohydrates	66 g	Potassium	484 mg
Fat	1.2 g	Iron	3.5 mg
Fiber - Dietary	5.6 g	Calcium	63 mg

3% calories from fat

Food Exchanges: 4.2 Veg., 2.2 Bread

RIGELETTO SAUCE DARK HORSE WITH PASTA

Preparation time: 15 minutes   *Chef: Dawn Barrington*
Cooking time: 30 minutes   *Yacht: Dark Horse*
Serves: 6

1 (12 oz.) can no salt added whole tomatoes
2 (8 oz.) cans no salt added tomato sauce
1 (10 oz.) pkg. frozen spinach, thawed and drained
3 canned artichoke hearts, chopped
6 pitted green olives, chopped
6 pitted black olives, chopped
1 cup chopped fresh mushrooms
2 tsp. oregano leaves
2 tsp. basil leaves
1/2 tsp. thyme leaves
1 (12 oz.) pkg. vermicelli pasta
Garnish: 1/4 cup fresh chopped parsley
           1/4 cup low fat grated Parmesan cheese

Combine all ingredients, except parsley, grated cheese and pasta, in large saucepan. Stir together and let simmer for 30 minutes. Prepare pasta according to package directions (omitting oil) and serve sauce on top.

Garnish with fresh parsley and grated cheese.

Nutrient content per serving:

Calories	297	Cholesterol	5 mg
Protein	13 g	Sodium	248 mg
Carbohydrates	56 g	Potassium	474 mg
Fat	3 g	Iron	4.5 mg
Fiber - Dietary	1.9 g	Calcium	90 mg

9% calories from fat

Food Exchanges: 2.2 Veg., 2.8 Bread

VEGETABLES OOH LA LA!

Preparation time: 20 minutes   *Chef: Jan Robinson*
Cooking time: 7 minutes   *Yacht: Vanity*
Serves: 4

Vegetable cooking spray
5 cups sliced zucchini
4 cloves garlic, crushed
1 cup sliced sweet peppers (green or red)
1-1/2 cups sliced onions
1 Tblsp. sliced fresh ginger root
1 Tblsp. fresh dill, chopped
1 cup chopped fresh tomatoes
1 (12 oz.) pkg. fresh eggless fettuccine (or recipe page 135)
1 Tblsp. plain nonfat yogurt
1 tsp. black pepper
2 Tblsp. each of fresh lemon and lime juice
2 Tblsp. each: grated low fat Parmesan, chopped fresh parsley

Fill large saucepan with water and bring to a boil. Spray large skillet with cooking spray, add garlic and zucchini, stir fry 2 minutes. Add sweet pepper, onions and ginger root for 2 minutes. Add dill and tomatoes, cook just until warmed through and toss gently. While stir frying the vegetables, add pasta to boiling water and cook 4 minutes, or according to directions. Toss the pasta with yogurt and black pepper.

To serve, place pasta in the center of a plate, cover with the vegetables, sprinkle with lemon/lime juice, grated Parmesan and fresh parsley.

Note: *This recipe was created by Barb Lawrence in between her editing!*

Nutrient content per serving:

Calories	293	Cholesterol	4 mg
Protein	13 g	Sodium	82mg
Carbohydrates	61 g	Potassium	933 mg
Fat	2.8 g	Iron	3.1 mg
Fiber - Dietary	7.2 g	Calcium	94 mg

8% calories from fat

Food Exchanges: 4.0 Veg., 2.5 Bread

PASTA WITH ZUCCHINI AND TOMATOES

Preparation time: 15 minutes   *Chef: Edna Beaman*
Cooking time: 25 minutes   *Yacht: Wahsoune*
Serves: 4

2 medium sized zucchini
1/4 cup water
1 cup chopped onion
2 Tblsp. no salt added tomato paste
2 clove garlic, minced
2 cups chopped mushrooms
2 (14-1/2 oz.) cans no salt added tomatoes, chopped
1 tsp. dried oregano
1 tsp. pepper
1 tsp. basil
2 Tblsp. chopped fresh parsley
1 (8 oz.) pkg. spaghetti

Fill large pot with water, cover and heat to boiling. Cut zucchini into quarters lengthwise and then slice. Put 1/4 cup water in saucepan and cook onion over medium heat until softened. Stir in tomato paste, zucchini, garlic and mushrooms. Cook 3 minutes. Add tomatoes and seasonings. Simmer for 20 minutes. Put spaghetti in boiling water and cook according to package directions; drain and top with sauce.

Nutrient content per serving:

Calories	296	Cholesterol	0 mg
Protein	11 g	Sodium	68 mg
Carbohydrates	61 g	Potassium	1084 mg
Fat	2.0 g	Iron	2.9 mg
Fiber - Dietary	4.1 g	Calcium	97 mg

6% calories from fat

Food Exchanges: 3.3 Veg., 1.2 Bread

SUN-DRIED TOMATOES AND BASIL PASTA

Preparation time: 30 minutes   *Chef: Joyce Pfaff*
Cooking time: 15 minutes   *Yacht: Flash Vert*
Serves: 8

1 (16 oz.) pkg. spinach linguini
1 cup + 1 cup *Vegetarian Creamy Dressing* **(page76)**
1/2 cup water
1 (3oz.) pkg. sun dried tomatoes, chopped
2 cups onions, sliced lengthwise
1 large red pepper, sliced
2 large green pepper, sliced
1/4 cup fresh basil, chopped
1/4 cup fresh parsley, chopped
1 tsp. black pepper

If you don't already have some dressing made up, do that first. Cook and drain linguini, mix with 1 cup of the dressing and keep warm. In a sauté pan, cook tomatoes and onions in 1/2 cup water for two minutes. Add red and green peppers, basil, parsley and black pepper. Cook until onion is translucent and peppers are still crunchy (add more water as needed). Just before serving, mix *Vegetarian Creamy Dressing* with pasta and toss together with pepper mixture.

Works well served with **Green Bean and Baby Corn Salad** *(page 53) and whole grain rolls.*

Nutrient content per serving:

Calories	309	Cholesterol	0 mg
Protein	10 g	Sodium	169 mg
Carbohydrates	64 g	Potassium	552 mg
Fat	1.6 g	Iron	1.4 mg
Fiber - Dietary	3.0 g	Calcium	55 mg

5% calories from fat

Food Exchanges: 0.8 Veg., 1.3 Bread

When adding fresh herbs to cooked dishes, do so late in the cooking process so they retain their freshness. Overexposure to heat dissipates the essential oils that give herbs their unique flavor.

VEGETABLE SPAGHETTI

Preparation time: 30 minutes　　　　　　　　*Chef: Beth Avore*
Cooking time: 45 minutes　　　　　　　　　*Yacht: Perfection*
Serves: 6

1 (8 oz.) pkg. dry pasta (or fresh pasta page 135)
Vegetable cooking spray
3 carrots, julienned
1-1/2 cups zucchini, julienned
1-1/2 cups yellow squash, julienned
2 cloves garlic, minced
2 Tblsp. fresh chopped basil
1/4 cup chopped green onion tops

Garnish:
1 Tblsp. fresh grated low fat Parmesan per serving (optional)

Cook pasta per package directions; keep warm. Spray a large skillet with vegetable cooking spray. Sauté garlic and carrots until crisp (about 10 minutes). Add squash. Sauté until all vegetables are done (about 5 minutes). Add spaghetti and spices. Cook 5 minutes.

To serve, sprinkle with Parmesan. (Nutrition below is shown with 1 Tblsp. parmesan per person--fat is substantially decreased without the cheese.) Serve with loaf of French bread and green leaf salad with tomato wedges.

Hint: *Try squeezing lemon juice over all and a generous grind of fresh black pepper.*

Nutrient content per serving:

Calories	204	Cholesterol	8 mg
Protein	9 g	Sodium	138 mg
Carbohydrates	37 g	Potassium	376 mg
Fat	2.5 g	Iron	2.1 mg
Fiber - Dietary	2.5 g	Calcium	41 mg

11% calories from fat

Food Exchanges: 0.9 Veg., 1.9 Bread

SUMMER SPAGHETTI

Preparation time: 30 minutes
Cooking time: 15 minutes
Draining time: 1 hour
Serves: 4

Chef: Joyce Pfaff
Yacht: Flash Vert

6 medium very ripe tomatoes
10 fresh basil leaves, chopped
2 Tblsp. fresh parsley, chopped
1/4 cup lemon juice
1/4 cup Tofu Mayonnaise (page 78)
1/2 tsp. black pepper
1 (12 oz.) pkg. spaghetti (spinach linguini also works well)

Score tomatoes and dip in boiling water, for 30 seconds, remove, peel and chop. Drain in colander for 1 hour. Combine drained tomatoes, parsley, basil, lemon juice, tofu mayonnaise and pepper in large bowl. Cook and drain pasta. Toss half the sauce (cold) with warm pasta. Place dollops of remaining sauce on individual servings.

The flavor and uniqueness of this recipe is in the fresh basil. If fresh basil is unavailable, substitute another fresh herb--maybe tarragon or oregano--dried herbs don't work.

Nutrient content per serving:

Calories	367	Cholesterol	0 mg
Protein	13 g	Sodium	86 mg
Carbohydrates	76 g	Potassium	712 mg
Fat	1.6 g	Iron	4.9 mg
Fiber - Dietary	2.8 g	Calcium	56 mg

4% calories from fat

Food Exchanges: 1.3 Veg., 4.2 Bread

ARTICHOKE–MUSHROOM MARINARA SAUCE ON PASTA

Preparation time: 10 minutes   *Chef: Jan Robinson*
Cooking time: 25 minutes   *Yacht: Vanity*
Serves: 6

1 cup chopped onion
4 cloves garlic, chopped
2 cups sliced mushrooms
1 (13-3/4 oz.) can artichoke hearts, drained and chopped
2 cans (15 oz.) no salt added tomato sauce
3 Tblsp. honey
2 tsp. crushed dried oregano
2 tsp. crushed dried basil
1/4 tsp. black pepper
1/4 cup red wine
1 (12 oz.) pkg. whole grain pasta, cooked

Garnish:
3 Tblsp. chopped green onion

In medium saucepan, cook onion, garlic and mushroom in water 5-7 minutes or until softened, over medium high heat. Add artichokes, tomato sauce, honey, oregano, basil and pepper. Bring to a boil, reduce heat and simmer gently for 20 minutes. Add red wine and simmer for additional 5 minutes. Pour the sauce over cooked pasta and toss thoroughly.

Sprinkle green onion over top and serve immediately.

Nutrient content per serving:

Calories	321	Cholesterol	0 mg
Protein	13 g	Sodium	102 mg
Carbohydrates	68 g	Potassium	441 mg
Fat	1.2 g	Iron	3.4 mg
Fiber - Dietary	2.9 g	Calcium	81 mg

3% calories from fat

Food Exchanges: 4.0 Veg., 2.5 Bread

VEGETABLE FETTUCINE

Preparation time: 10 minutes   *Chef: Jan Robinson*
Cooking time: 7 minutes (microwave)   *Yacht: Vanity*
Serves: 2

1 cup sliced celery
1 cup sliced onion
2 cloves garlic, crushed
1/4 cup water
1-1/2 cups sliced mushrooms
1 cup broccoli pieces
2 green onions, chopped
2 tomatoes, chopped
1 Tblsp. dried Italian Blend herb
1/2 tsp. pepper
6 oz. raw fettucine
Garnish: Paprika

Combine celery and onion in a dish with garlic and water. Cook covered, HIGH power 3 minutes. Add mushrooms, broccoli, green onion and tomatoes. Cook uncovered HIGH power, 4 minutes. Set aside. Cook fettucine according to package directions. Place fettucine on plate and spoon vegetable mixture on top. *Sprinkle with paprika.*

Note: This recipe is easily doubled for four, or halved for one. Although I usually make the whole portion and keep half for the next day.

Nutrient content per serving:

Calories	426	Cholesterol	0 mg
Protein	17 g	Sodium	91 mg
Carbohydrates	87 g	Potassium	1216 mg
Fat	2.6 g	Iron	6.2 mg
Fiber - Dietary	6.5 g	Calcium	119 mg

5% calories from fat

Food Exchanges: 3.7 Veg., 4.1 Bread

Poultry

APRICOT CHICKEN ON BULGUR

Preparation time: 20 minutes   *Chef: Jan Robinson*
Cooking time: 40 minutes   *Yacht: Vanity*
Serves: 6

3/4 cup uncooked bulgur
1/2 cup + 1/3 cup chopped onion
1/3 cup chopped dates
1-1/4 cups + 1/4 cup fat-free chicken broth (page 80)
1 cup canned apricots in juice, diced (drain, reserve 1/4 cup)
3/4 cup fruit juice sweetened apricot preserves
3 Tblsp. low sodium tomato paste
3 Tblsp. apple cider vinegar
2 Tblsp. lemon juice
2 cloves + 2 cloves garlic, chopped
1/2 tsp. black pepper
1-1/2 tsp. prepared mustard, spicy or Dijon
l lb. boneless skinless chicken breast filets, cut in 2-inch cubes

Preheat oven to 350°F. In small saucepan, combine bulgur, 1/2 cup onion, dates, and 1-1/4 cups broth. Bring to boil, cover and cook for 20 minutes. Remove bulgur mixture from heat and stir in 1 cup diced apricots. Transfer mixture to shallow 2-quart baking dish. In small saucepan, combine preserves, tomato paste, vinegar, lemon juice, 2 cloves chopped garlic, pepper and mustard, and cook over medium heat for 10 minutes to blend flavors. Heat 1/4 cup broth in a large skillet over medium-high heat. Stir-fry chicken, 2 cloves chopped garlic and onion for about 10 minutes, until chicken is no longer pink inside. Place chicken pieces on bulgur and spoon preserve mixture over all. Bake for 15 minutes. Arrange remaining apricot pieces around chicken. Bake uncovered 5 minutes longer, or until apricots are heated. *Serve with a fresh garden salad. This recipe takes awhile, but is worth it! It was given to me by a special friend Sandra Hall "Sis."*

Nutrient content per serving:

Calories	343	Cholesterol	64 mg
Protein	28 g	Sodium	713 mg
Carbohydrates	46 g	Potassium	566 mg
Fat	4.7 g	Iron	2 mg
Fiber - Dietary	6.3 g	Calcium	45 mg

12% calories from fat

Food Exchanges: 0.7 Veg., 0.5 Fruit, 1.4 Bread, 3.3 Meat

HERBED SHERRY CHICKEN

Preparation time: 12 minutes *Chef: Jeanne Bach*
Cooking time: 20 minutes *Yacht: Iemanja*
Serves: 6

Vegetable cooking spray (optional)
6 (4 oz.) boneless, skinless chicken breasts
1/2 cup sliced onion
1/4 cup + 3/4 cup fat-free chicken broth (page 80)
1 Tblsp. basil flakes, crumbled
1 tsp. dried thyme
1 tsp. dried marjoram
1 tsp. black pepper
1/2 lb. sliced mushrooms (approx. 4 cups sliced)
1/2 cup dry sherry

Brown chicken in a nonstick Dutch oven or deep fry pan (if not a non-stick pan, spray with vegetable cooking spray). Remove chicken after 2-3 minutes on each side. Over medium heat, sauté onions in 1/4 cup broth until transparent. Reduce heat to low and return chicken to pan. Add 3/4 cup chicken broth, then sprinkle basil flakes onto chicken. Combine thyme, marjoram and pepper; sprinkle over chicken. Cover and cook for 5 more minutes. Then turn chicken parts, add mushrooms and sherry. Stir a little. Finish cooking 5-10 minutes, or until completely cooked.

Serve over **Pepper Pressure Cooker Rice** *(page 202).*

Nutrient content per serving:

Calories	211	Cholesterol	84 mg
Protein	32 g	Sodium	154 mg
Carbohydrates	5 g	Potassium	467 mg
Fat	3.9 g	Iron	2.1 mg
Fiber - Dietary	0.8 g	Calcium	34 mg

17% calories from fat

Food Exchanges: 0.5 Veg., 4.3 Meat

SPICE CHICKEN STIR FRY

Preparation time: 15 minutes   *Chef: Tabatha Gardner*
Cooking time: 15 minutes
Serves: 4

4 (4 oz.) boneless, skinless chicken breasts
3 Tblsp. + 3 Tblsp. fat-free chicken broth (page 80)
1 cup sliced zucchini
1 red bell pepper, sliced
4 scallions, sliced
1 cup fresh mushrooms, sliced
1 carrot, sliced
2 tsp. ground ginger
2 cloves garlic, crushed
1/2 tsp. black pepper
2 Tblsp. lite soy sauce

Slice chicken into long, thin pieces. Heat 3 Tblsp. broth in a nonstick skillet or wok over medium heat. Add chicken and stir until lightly brown. Remove chicken from skillet. Add the other 3 Tblsp. broth and rest of ingredients, except soy sauce. Stir fry until crunchy (2-3 minutes). Return chicken, sprinkle with soy sauce, stir and *serve over a bed of brown rice.*

Nutrient content per serving:

Calories	204	Cholesterol	84 mg
Protein	33 g	Sodium	404 mg
Carbohydrates	8 g	Potassium	570 mg
Fat	3.9 g	Iron	2.1 mg
Fiber - Dietary	2.1 g	Calcium	42 mg

16% calories from fat

Food Exchanges: 1.2 Veg. 4.3 Meat

When buying soy sauce read and compare labels, as there is a wide variation in the sodium content. All are very high, so use sparingly, or pour the contents into a larger bottle and add an equal amount of water.

CHICKEN RATATOUILLE

Preparation time: 12 minutes   *Chef: Edna Beaman*
Cooking time: 20 minutes   *Yacht: Wahsoune*
Serves: 4

4 (4 oz.) boneless, skinless chicken breasts
1/4 cup + 3 Tblsp. fat-free chicken broth (page 80)
3/4 cup chopped onion
1 green pepper, cut into rings
2 cups sliced zucchini
2 medium-size tomatoes, peeled and cut into wedges
2 cloves garlic, minced
1 tsp. black pepper
2 tsp. oregano
1-1/2 tsp. dried basil
2 Tblsp. fresh lemon juice

Cut chicken into crosswise strips. Sauté onion and pepper rings in 1/4 cup broth, over medium heat until soft (about 3 minutes). Add zucchini and cook until it begins to brown (3 - 4 minutes). Add tomatoes and cook until soft (about 3 minutes). Push veggies aside, add 3 more Tblsp. broth and cook chicken, stirring until it starts to brown. Stir in garlic, pepper, herbs and cook until chicken is done and liquid evaporates (about 5 minutes). Add lemon juice before serving.

Serve with a big bowl of rice or pasta.

Nutrient content per serving:

Calories	190	Cholesterol	73 mg
Protein	29 g	Sodium	102 mg
Carbohydrates	11 g	Potassium	652 mg
Fat	3.6 g	Iron	2.2 mg
Fiber - Dietary	2.7 g	Calcium	58 mg

17% calories from fat

Food Exchanges: 1.5 Veg., 3.8 Meat

To easily peel a tomato cut an X-mark on the top then drop it in boiling water for 30 seconds, remove and peel.

LIMEY CHICKEN

Preparation time: 10 minutes   *Chef: Evelyn Rogers*
Cooking time: 15 minutes   *Yacht: Anne Marie 2*
Serves: 4

4 (4 oz.) boneless, skinless chicken breasts
3/4 cup lime juice
2 cloves garlic, chopped
1 cup fresh sliced mushrooms
1 tsp. oregano
1 tsp. black pepper

Slice chicken into 1 inch strips. Sauté chicken and garlic in lime juice until chicken is tender. Add mushrooms, oregano and pepper. Brown chicken lightly.

*Serve over **Brown Rice** (page 205.) I usually add chopped mango for color and flavor. Serve with a crisp green salad and French bread.*

Nutrient content per serving:

Calories	185	Cholesterol	84 mg
Protein	32 g	Sodium	74 mg
Carbohydrates	6 g	Potassium	385 mg
Fat	3.7 g	Iron	1.5 mg
Fiber - Dietary	0.4 g	Calcium	28 mg

18% calories from fat

Food Exchanges: 0.2 Veg., 0.2 Fruit, 4.3 Meat

Eliminate oil from your cooking by using nonstick cookware.

SELF SAUTÉED CHICKEN

Preparation time: 5 minutes   *Chef: Gwen Hamlin*
Cooking time: 20 minutes   *Yacht: Whisper*
Serves: 4

Vegetable cooking spray
4 chicken breasts, boneless *with* skin
2 medium onions, sliced thin
1 tsp. basil
1 tsp. oregano
1 garlic clove, crushed
1 tsp. arrowroot
1/4 cup sweet vermouth

Lightly coat frying pan with cooking spray. Remove chicken skin from breasts (this helps prevent temptation later!) Lay skin in pan and place chicken breasts on top. Cover with sliced onions and sprinkle with herbs. Cover pan and cook over low heat, just until juices run clear. Remove breasts to serving platter. *Discard* chicken skins. Mix arrowroot with vermouth, then stir back into pan to heat and thicken. Pour onion sauce over breasts. *Serve with steamed green beans, carrots and little red potatoes.*

Nutrient content per serving:

Calories	213	Cholesterol	84 mg
Protein	32 g	Sodium	76 mg
Carbohydrates	9 g	Potassium	403 mg
Fat	4.0 g	Iron	1.6 mg
Fiber - Dietary	1.3 g	Calcium	50 mg

17% calories from fat

Food Exchanges: 1.0 Veg., 4.3 Meat

Don't bother I'm self Sautéed Chicken

CHICKEN TAHINI

Preparation time: 30 minutes   *Chef: Gretchen Fater*
Cooking time: 40 minutes   *Yacht: Maranatha*
Serves: 4

2 Tblsp. tahini
3 Tblsp. chopped parsley
2 garlic cloves, chopped
1 tsp. lemon juice
1/2 tsp. cayenne pepper
4 boneless, skinless chicken breasts
2 Tblsp. plain nonfat yogurt
1/2 cup fat-free cracker crumbs

Sauce:
1 Tblsp. thinly sliced shallot (or green onion)
2 Tblsp. + 1 cup fat-free chicken broth (page 80)
1/4 cup sherry
4 tsp. arrowroot, mixed with 2 Tblsp. water
1 tomato peeled, the outer flesh cut into strips
1/2 tsp. black pepper

Preheat oven to 350°F. Combine tahini, parsley, garlic, lemon juice and cayenne. Cut a pocket in each chicken breast; stuff with mixture. To bread the chicken, coat the pieces in yogurt and then in cracker crumbs. Place chicken in a baking dish and bake in oven until cooked, about 30 minutes.

Sauce: Sauté shallot in 2 Tblsp. of chicken broth, add sherry, and cook to reduce mixture to 1 Tblsp. Pour in the rest of the chicken broth and bring liquid to simmer. Stir in arrowroot mixture and cook 2 minutes. Add tomato strips and pepper. Pour sauce over stuffed breasts. *Serve with rice and a green vegetable.*

Nutrient content per serving:

Calories	283	Cholesterol	96 mg
Protein	45 g	Sodium	270 mg
Carbohydrates	13 g	Potassium	472 mg
Fat	6.3 g	Iron	1.6 mg
Fiber - Dietary	0.4 g	Calcium	29 mg

19% calories from fat

Food Exchanges: 0.3 Veg., 0.5 Bread, 5.0 Meat, 0.4 Fat

CARIBBEAN CHICKEN

Preparation time: 10 minutes   *Chef: Elaine Gregory*
Cooking time: 25-30 minutes   *Yacht: Moorea*
Serves: 6

6 (4 oz.) boneless, skinless chicken breasts
1/2 cup brown rice syrup
1/4 cup rum
1 (6-1/4 oz.) can pineapple chunks (or slices), in water
2 tsp. arrowroot

Preheat oven to 350°F. Brown chicken breasts quickly in a nonstick skillet, then transfer to a roasting pan. Combine remaining ingredients (including juice from pineapple) and pour over chicken. Bake for 25-30 minutes. Thicken sauce with arrowroot and a little water. *Serve with sauce and pineapple topped on chicken.*

Serve over rice. Any sauce mixture remaining can be served on the side.

Nutrient content per serving:

Calories	187	Cholesterol	84 mg
Protein	31 g	Sodium	74 mg
Carbohydrates	5.3 g	Potassium	283mg
Fat	3.6 g	Iron	1.2 mg
Fiber - Dietary	0.5 g	Calcium	18 mg

18% calories from fat

Food Exchanges: 0.2 Fruit, 4.3 Meat

SHREDDED POTATO SKINNED CHICKEN

Preparation time: 15 minutes   *Chef: Beth Avore*
Cooking time: 30 - 45 minutes   *Yacht: Perfection*
Serves: 6

2 cups peeled and grated potatoes
1/4 cup chopped onion
6 Tblsp. Dijon mustard
2 cloves garlic, minced
1/2 tsp. ground thyme
1 tsp. black pepper
6 (4 oz.) boneless, skinless chicken breasts
Vegetable cooking spray
1 tsp. dried rosemary

Preheat oven to 425°F. Put grated potatoes in bowl of ice water for 5 minutes. Soften onion in the microwave or in 1 Tblsp water in skillet. Mix onion together with mustard, garlic, thyme and pepper. Rinse chicken well. Dry and spread each breast with an equal share of mustard mix on one side. Place on baking sheet sprayed with vegetable spray. Drain, squeeze and dry potatoes. Divide into 6 portions and layer on top of mustard on chicken. Sprinkle with rosemary. Bake until chicken is no longer pink and potatoes are golden. Brown under broiler if necessary.

Serve with a large veggie stir fry and fresh dinner rolls.

Nutrient content per serving:

Calories	213	Cholesterol	84 mg
Protein	32 g	Sodium	113 mg
Carbohydrates	10 g	Potassium	425 mg
Fat	4.0 g	Iron	1.5 mg
Fiber - Dietary	0.7 g	Calcium	28 mg

18% calories from fat

Food Exchanges: 0.1 Veg., 0.5 Bread, 4.3 Meat

Crush dried rosemary leaves before using to release the aroma and flavor.

CHICKEN PICCATA

Preparation time: 10 minutes   *Chef: Paulette C. Hadley*
Cooking time: 15 minutes   *Yacht: Chardonnay*
Serves: 6

6 (4 oz.) boneless, skinless chicken breasts
1/2 tsp. white pepper
1/4 cup chopped parsley
1/3 cup fat-free chicken broth (page 80) or water
2 Tblsp. lemon juice
1 Tblsp. arrowroot
1/3 cup white wine
1 lemon, sliced thin
Garnish: fresh parsley

Dry chicken and flatten between wax paper to 1/4 inch thick. Sprinkle pepper and parsley over both sides of chicken. Heat chicken broth in a nonstick skillet, place over medium heat, add chicken and cook 4 to 5 minutes on each side. (Add a little more broth or water if necessary) Remove chicken to a platter or individual plates and keep warm. Mix lemon juice with arrowroot and add with wine and lemon slices to pan. Cook until heated, scraping bottom of the pan and stirring. Pour over chicken. *Garnish with parsley and serve.*

Holds for an hour or more when kept covered in warm oven. Stir sauce at last minute.

Nutrient content per serving:

Calories	198	Cholesterol	96 mg
Protein	36 g	Sodium	110 mg
Carbohydrates	2 g	Potassium	329 mg
Fat	4.1 g	Iron	1.5 mg
Fiber - Dietary	0.3 g	Calcium	24 mg

19% calories from fat

Food Exchanges: 5.0 Meat

VERY HEALTHY CHICKEN

Preparation time: 45 minutes　　　　　　*Chef: Vanessa Owen*
Cooking time: 30 minutes　　　　　　　　*Yacht: Dream On*
Serves: 4

1/2 Christophene, julienned
1 carrot, julienned
4 (4 oz.) boneless, skinless chicken breasts
1/2 tsp. black pepper

Sauce:
1/2 cup chopped onion
Vegetable cooking spray
2 tomatoes, peeled and seeded
1 sweet red pepper, julienned
1 garlic clove
1/4 + 1/4 cup water
1/2 tsp. black pepper

Mix Christophene and carrot strips, sprinkle with pepper. Lay out breasts, cover with plastic wrap and pound until thin (the bottom of a large saucepan is great for this!) Place vegetables in center of each breast, fold in edges and roll. Wrap tightly in plastic wrap* and poach in 1/4 cup water for 15 minutes. Spray pan with cooking spray and cook onion until softened. Add tomatoes, red pepper, garlic and rest of the water. Cover and cook 15 minutes. Strain the sauce, taste and season.

To serve: Spoon a wide arc of sauce onto plate. Remove plastic wrap, slice chicken on diagonal, about 1/2 inch thick. Arrange slices overlapping in center of sauce. Looks delicious!

***Reminder:** Don't forget to remove the plastic wrap before serving!*

Nutrient content per serving:

Calories	205	Cholesterol	84 mg
Protein	32 g	Sodium	93 mg
Carbohydrates	9 g	Potassium	543 mg
Fat	4.0 g	Iron	1.8 mg
Fiber - Dietary	2.3 g	Calcium	36 mg

18% calories from fat

Food Exchanges: 1.3 Veg., 4.3 Meat

MARINATED CHICKEN BREASTS

Preparation time: 10 minutes
Cooking time: 25 minutes
Marinating time: 2 hours
Serves: 8

Chef: Bobbi Fawcett
Yacht: Windwalker

8 (4 oz.) boneless, skinless chicken breasts
1 cup plain nonfat yogurt
2 Tblsp. Worcestershire sauce
1 Tblsp. lemon (or lime juice)
1 tsp. celery salt
3 cloves garlic, chopped
1/2 tsp. black pepper
1/2 tsp. paprika
3/4 cup fat-free cracker crumbs (or Amaranth flakes, crushed)
Garnish: lemon twists and parsley sprigs

Place chicken in a flat non-metallic baking dish. Mix next seven ingredients. Spread over chicken. Marinate 2 hours or more, turning chicken once or twice. Preheat oven to 350°F. Sprinkle crumbs over breasts before putting in oven. Bake about 25 minutes, or until cooked.

Garnish with a lemon twist and parsley sprig on each chicken breast.

Nutrient content per serving:

Calories	202	Cholesterol	84 mg
Protein	38 g	Sodium	173 mg
Carbohydrates	8 g	Potassium	371 mg
Fat	3.6 g	Iron	1.4 mg
Fiber - Dietary	0.04 g	Calcium	24 mg

15% calories from fat

Food Exchanges: 0.1 Milk, 0.2 Bread, 4.3 Meat

CITRUS BREAST OF CHICKEN

Preparation time: 15 minutes   *Chef: Julie Simpson*
Cooking time: 30 minutes   *Yacht: Adela*
Marinating time: 1 hour or more
Serves: 6

Citrus Marinade:
1 Tblsp. orange zest
1 Tblsp. lemon zest
1-1/2 cups orange juice
1/2 cup lemon juice
1 Tblsp. lite soy sauce
1/2 tsp. rosemary, crushed
1/4 tsp. garlic powder
1/4 tsp. dried parsley

6 (5 oz.) chicken breasts, with skin and fat removed
1-1/2 cups each of cooked brown and wild rice
Garnish: 12 orange slices and watercress

Combine first eight ingredients. Pour marinade into a plastic bag with chicken breasts. Marinate 1 hour or more. Preheat oven to 350°F. Place chicken, bone side up, in a 3-quart rectangular baking pan. Pour half of marinade over chicken (enough so meat side sits in marinade). Bake for 30 minutes, or until cooked. Remove and keep warm. Pour remaining marinade in pan; boil to thicken.

Place chicken on brown and wild rice and pour marinade over. Garnish with two orange slices and watercress.

Nutrient content per serving:

Calories	311	Cholesterol	84 mg
Protein	35 g	Sodium	167 mg
Carbohydrates	33 g	Potassium	541 mg
Fat	4.2 g	Iron	1.6 mg
Fiber - Dietary	2.5 g	Calcium	49 mg

12% calories from fat

Food Exchanges: 0.7 Fruit, 1.3 Bread, 4.3 Meat

WHISPER CHICKEN ROTI

Preparation time: 30 minutes   *Chef: Gwen Hamlin*
Cooking time: 15 minutes   *Yacht: Whisper*
Marinating time: 2 hours
Serves: 6

6 (4 oz.) boneless, skinless chicken breasts, cut in 1" pieces
1 medium onion, diced
2 garlic cloves, minced
1 scallion, finely chopped
1 tsp. *Sunny Caribbee Yellow Hot Sauce* (or hot sauce of choice)
1-1/2 tsp. *XXX Calypso Hot Sauce* (optional)
3 Tblsp. curry powder
1 Tblsp. cumin
1/8 tsp. each ground ginger and chili powder
1/2 Tblsp. ground black pepper
1/2 cup plain nonfat yogurt
1 potato, boiled and diced
Vegetable cooking spray
1/3 cup water
6 large flour tortillas

Combine all ingredients in a bowl (except cooking spray, water and tortillas.) Marinate 2 hours or overnight. Spray skillet. Stir-fry chicken over medium heat for 5 minutes, add water. Continue cooking until chicken is no longer pink inside. Heat tortillas either in a skillet or in microwave. *Fold chicken into warm tortillas and serve seam-side down.*

Hint: *Serve with selection of chutney, especially mango-ginger. Also great is Sunny Caribbee Kulchela (see page 252). Served with rice and peas; this becomes a nice West Indian dinner.*

Nutrient content per serving:

Calories	310	Cholesterol	84 mg
Protein	36 g	Sodium	105 mg
Carbohydrates	27 g	Potassium	475 mg
Fat	6.1 g	Iron	3.9 mg
Fiber - Dietary	2.3 g	Calcium	98 mg

18% calories from fat

Food Exchanges: 0.2 Veg., 1.3 Bread, 4.3 Meat, 0.2 Fat

MARGARITA CHICKEN

Preparation time: 30 minutes   *Chef: Glenn Altshuler*
Cooking time: 20 minutes   *Yacht: Whisper*
Marinating time: 1 hour
Serves: 4

Note: The original Margarita Chicken entreé won 3rd prize in 1992 Grand Marnier Cookoff. Where the recipe has been modified (to decrease the fat, calories and cholesterol) the ingredients are shown in parenthesis.

6 (4 oz.) boneless, skinless chicken breasts
2 tsp. minced onion
4 tsp. finely chopped garlic
1 tsp. each of oregano and paprika
2 tsp. cumin
4 tsp. chili powder
1-1/2 tsp. cayenne pepper (optional)
1/2 tsp. black pepper (1 tsp. salt)
3 Tblsp. low sodium catsup (8 tsp. BBQ sauce)
2 tsp. red wine vinegar
2 tsp. honey
2 tsp. tequila
1 tsp. Grand Marnier
1/2 lime, squeezed
6 warmed flour tortillas
Garnish: 2 cups shredded lettuce, 4 Tblsp. (nonfat) sour cream,
**   and 8 Tblsp. salsa**

Cut chicken into 1-inch pieces. Combine all other ingredients (except flour tortillas and garnish). Marinate chicken in this for 1 hour or longer. Then pour into a saucepan and simmer for 20 minutes. *Serve in tortillas with garnish.*

Hint: *You can nuke tortillas in their package - about 1 minute to warm.*

Nutrient content per serving:

Calories	321	Cholesterol	84 mg
Protein	36 g	Sodium	162 mg
Carbohydrates	30 g	Potassium	485 mg
Fat	6.3 g	Iron	3.6 mg
Fiber - Dietary	2.3 g	Calcium	99 mg

18% calories from fat

Food Exchanges: 0.3 Veg., 1.1 Bread, 4.3 Meat, 0.2 Fat

CARIBBEAN CHICKEN K-BOBS

Preparation time: 20 minutes *Chef: Diane Delorey*
Marinating time: 3 hours *Yacht: September Morn*
Cooking time: 10 minutes (grill)
Serves: 8

8 (4 oz.) boneless skinless chicken breasts
1 cup fat-free Italian Dressing
2 cups small fresh mushroom caps
2-1/2 cups pineapple chunks (in own juice)
2 medium onions, cut in large chunks
1/2 each of red, yellow and green peppers, seeded
      and cut into wide strips
8 cherry tomatoes

Cut chicken breasts in 1-1/2-inch cubes. Marinate for at least 3 hours in Italian Dressing, stirring occasionally. Alternate chicken on 8 skewers with mushrooms, pineapple, onion, and peppers (leave room at end for tomato.*) Brush leftover marinade over entire k-bob. Grill over hot fire, or broil 4 inches from heat for about 10 minutes, turning to brown evenly. *Serve over **Caribbean Rice** (page 202)*

* Hint: *To prevent tomatoes from falling into the fire,* thread all the tomatoes on one skewer. Put on grill at the last minute and cook briefly. Remove from grill, then remove tomatoes and add one to each of the other skewers.

Hint: *Presoaking bamboo skewers in water prevents them from burning when broiling or grilling k-bobs.*

Nutrient content per serving:

Calories	216	Cholesterol	84 mg
Protein	32 g	Sodium	188 mg
Carbohydrates	13 g	Potassium	522 mg
Fat	4.0 g	Iron	1.7 mg
Fiber - Dietary	2.0 g	Calcium	27 mg

17% calories from fat

Food Exchanges: 0.9 Veg., 0.3 Fruit, 4.3 Meat

TOMBSTONE CHICKEN

Preparation time: 10 minutes　　　　　　　*Chef: Darrel Goss*
Marinating time: 2 hours　　　　　　　*Yacht: Champagne Lady*
Cooking time: 5-10 minutes (grill)
Serves: 4

4 (4 oz.) boneless, skinless chicken breasts
1/4 cup white wine
1/4 cup water
2 Tblsp. Worcestershire sauce
2 garlic cloves, minced
1 tsp. each of oregano and basil
1-1/2 tsp. each rosemary, sage, black pepper
1 tsp. *Caribbee Hot Sauce* (or hot sauce of your choice)

Combine all ingredients (except chicken) in a bowl. Mix well. Place chicken in a large Ziplock bag, add marinade and marinate a minimum of 2 hours (maximum 24 hours) turning often. Chicken is best grilled on charcoal grill, or can be sautéed on the stove top or baked at 350°F until done, basting frequently.

Serve with roasted potatoes, **Amaretto Carrots** *(page 216) cut in Tombstone shapes; tossed salad, hot rolls and Angel Cake garnished with flower petals. Suggested wine: dry white.*

Nutrient content per serving:

Calories	183	Cholesterol	84 mg
Protein	31 g	Sodium	116 mg
Carbohydrates	2 g	Potassium	326 mg
Fat	3.6 g	Iron	1.8 mg
Fiber - Dietary	0.1 g	Calcium	41 mg

19% calories from fat

Food Exchanges: 0.1 Veg., 4.3 Meat

WHERE "TOMBSTONE CHICKEN" ORIGINATED

*It was a beautiful day in the Caribbean. Capt. Chef Darrel was preparing for a charter and, as often happens to yacht chefs, there was no fresh chicken to be found. The same day Capt. Darrel was having a minor welding repair made and casually mentioned his plight to the young welder, who promptly went to the door of his shed and yelled across the dirt road to his wife, telling her to catch a couple of chickens from the graveyard. The young welder then turned and said "Skipper, get the fire and brimstone ready." Chef Darrel tested various marinades and came up with his own mixture of spices and Caribbean hot sauce. The specific hot sauce listed in his recipe is Sunny Caribbee and can be purchased by calling **toll free** to **1-800-338-6072**.*

CHICKEN FREIGHT TRAIN

Preparation time: 10 minutes   *Chef: Candice Carson*
Cooking time: 15 - 20 minutes (grill)   *Yacht: Freight Train II*
Serves: 6

Herb Baste:
1/4 cup nonfat mayonnaise
1-1/2 Tblsp. Dijon mustard
1 shallot, minced
1 Tblsp. chopped parsley
1 tsp. each chervil and chives

6 leeks
2 large onions, peeled and quartered
6 (4 oz.) boneless, skinless chicken breasts, pounded thin

In a mixing bowl or food processor combine herb baste ingredients. Set
aside at room temperature. In a saucepan put enough water to cover
the leeks. Bring to a boil and poach leeks over medium heat for 10
minutes. Put leeks and onions on hot grill and brush with herb baste.
Grill chicken over hot coals quickly and brush with herb baste.

Nutrient content per serving:

Calories	311	Cholesterol	84 mg
Protein	34 g	Sodium	203 mg
Carbohydrates	36 g	Potassium	601 mg
Fat	4.1 g	Iron	4.1 mg
Fiber - Dietary	3.5 g	Calcium	108 mg

12% calories from fat

Food Exchanges: 3.4 Veg., 4.3 Meat

CHICKEN APRICOT GINGER

Preparation time: 5 minutes
Cooking time: 10 minutes (grill or broiler)
Serves: 8

Chef: Penny Knowles
Yacht: Golden Skye

8 (4 oz.) boneless, skinless chicken breasts
1 (10 oz.) can apricots in water, mashed
1 Tblsp. lite soy sauce
1 Tblsp. grated fresh ginger
2 tsp. arrowroot
Garnish: 2 chopped scallions, parsley, orange twists

Grill or broil chicken. While chicken is cooking, combine apricots, soy sauce and ginger in a small pan. Cook together, about 5 minutes, to allow flavors to blend. Dissolve arrowroot in a little water and add to fruit mix; cook gently until thickened. Spoon over chicken and garnish.

Hint: Use a little of the sauce to baste the chicken while it is cooking.

Nutrient content per serving:

Calories	175	Cholesterol	84 mg
Protein	31 g	Sodium	143 mg
Carbohydrates	2.8 g	Potassium	316 mg
Fat	3.6 g	Iron	1.2 mg
Fiber - Dietary	0.6 g	Calcium	22 mg

19% calories from fat

Food Exchanges: 4.3 Meat

Use arrowroot to thicken a sauce instead of flour or cornstarch. Substitute 1 tsp. arrowroot for 1 Tblsp. flour; 2 tsp. arrowroot for 1 Tblsp. cornstarch.

DIJON CHICKEN BREASTS

Preparation time: 10 minutes
Cooking time: 20 minutes (Broiler)
Serves: 4

Chef: Bobbi Fawcett
Yacht: Windwalker

2 whole chicken breasts, halved and skinned
1 Tblsp. lemon juice
2 green onions, chopped
2 Tblsp. Dijon mustard
1/4 tsp. black pepper
1/4 cup nonfat cracker crumbs

Preheat broiler. Broil breasts 5 minutes on each side. Mix lemon juice, onion, Dijon and pepper together. Spread over chicken; sprinkle with cracker crumbs. Broil until cooked and browned, about 10 minutes.

Nutrient content per serving:

Calories	177	Cholesterol	84 mg
Protein	35 g	Sodium	117 mg
Carbohydrates	3 g	Potassium	265 mg
Fat	3.6 g	Iron	1.1 mg
Fiber - Dietary	0.1 g	Calcium	17 mg

18% calories from fat

Food Exchanges: 0.1 Bread, 4.3 Meat

If your herbs come from the supermarket rather than your own garden, store them properly. Wrap in a damp paper towel, enclose in plastic and refrigerate. Check each day or two for browning or wilting leaves and remove them.

TURKEY BALSAMICO

Preparation time: 15 minutes
Cooking time: 12 minutes
Serves: 4

Chef: Bobbi Fawcett
Yacht: Windwalker

3 Tblsp. flour
1/4 tsp. black pepper
14 oz. turkey breast, sliced
Vegetable cooking spray
1/2 cup fat-free chicken broth (page 80)
3 cloves garlic, minced
2 large red peppers, sliced in rings
1/4 cup fresh basil (or 1 tsp. dried)
3 Tblsp. balsamic vinegar

Mix flour and pepper then coat turkey slices. Spray skillet with vegetable cooking spray and sauté turkey until light brown on both sides. Remove turkey. Pour chicken broth in pan with garlic and red peppers and reduce heat to low setting. Cover and cook for 3 minutes, stirring twice. Add basil, vinegar and turkey. Raise heat, stirring for a minute or two. Serve immediately.

Nutrient content per serving:

Calories	203	Cholesterol	69 mg
Protein	31 g	Sodium	96 mg
Carbohydrates	10 g	Potassium	407 mg
Fat	3.3 g	Iron	2.4 mg
Fiber - Dietary	0.8 g	Calcium	35 mg

15% calories from fat

Food Exchanges: 0.6 Veg., 0.2 Bread, 3.1 Meat

The less you handle fresh herbs, the better you protect their essential oils. If they're not dirty, don't wash them. If it is necessary to rinse them, do so quickly under cool water, then gently pat dry.

SWEET AND SOUR TURKEY MEATBALLS

Preparation time: 20 minutes
Chilling time: 30 minutes
Cooking time: 35 minutes
Serves: 4

Chef: Dena Edwards
Yacht: Majestic Lady

1/4 cup fat-free chicken broth (page 80)
1/2 cup chopped onion
14 oz. ground turkey breast, ground without fat
1 clove garlic, minced
2-1/2 Tblsp. chopped fresh parsley
1/2 tsp. black pepper
1/4 tsp. ground ginger
1-1/4 Tblsp. chopped seedless raisins
1/4 cup fat-free cracker crumbs
2 egg whites, beaten
4 green onions, chopped
1-1/4 cups low-sodium tomato juice
2-1/2 Tblsp. low-sodium tomato paste
Juice of 1/2 lemon
1-1/4 Tblsp. honey
1 green chili, seeded and thinly sliced
2 slices fresh pineapple, chopped
1 medium sweet pepper, cut in thin strips
2 carrots, peeled and coarsely grated

Soften onions in chicken broth. Mix turkey with garlic, parsley, pepper, ginger, raisins, crackers and egg whites. Stir in cooked onions. Mix well. Divide mixture into 16 and shape into balls. Chill. Put remaining ingredients into a shallow pan and bring to a boil. Cover and simmer 10 minutes, stirring occasionally. Drop chilled meatballs into sauce. Cover and simmer for a further 20 minutes, or until meatballs are completely cooked. If sauce starts to evaporate, add a little more broth or water. *Serve with brown rice or whole wheat pasta.*

Nutrient content per serving:

Calories	253	Cholesterol	68 mg
Protein	35 g	Sodium	138 mg
Carbohydrates	22 g	Potassium	773 mg
Fat	3.6 g	Iron	2.9 mg
Fiber - Dietary	3.0 g	Calcium	33 mg

12% calories from fat

Food Exchanges: 1.6 Veg., 0.3 Fruit, 0.3 Bread, 26.1 Meat

OVER THIRTY TURKEY

Preparation time: 20 minutes   *Chef: Jan Robinson*
Cooking time: 1 hour   *Yacht: Vanity*
Serves: 4

1 turkey breast, cut in 4 pieces and skinned (about 1-1/4 lbs.)
39 garlic cloves, peeled
1/3 cup dry white wine
2/3 cup fat-free chicken broth (page 80)
1 tsp. dried oregano
1 tsp. dried basil
2 Tblsp. freshly chopped parsley
1/8 tsp. cayenne pepper
1/8 tsp. black pepper
1 lemon
4 ribs celery, cut in 2 inch pieces

Preheat oven to 375° F. Place turkey pieces in a shallow baking pan, bone side down. Pour white wine and broth over turkey, then sprinkle with oregano, basil, parsley, cayenne, and black pepper. Imbed a garlic or two into each piece of turkey, then place the remainder of garlic on top and around. Squeeze lemon juice over all; cut lemon rind into pieces and arrange around the chicken along with the celery. Cover with foil and bake for 45 minutes. Remove foil and bake an additional 15 minutes. Baste once or twice during cooking.

Note: 4 (5 oz.) chicken breasts may be substituted for the turkey breast.

Nutrient content per serving:

Calories	284	Cholesterol	98 mg
Protein	45 g	Sodium	142 mg
Carbohydrates	15 g	Potassium	751 mg
Fat	5 g	Iron	3.4 mg
Fiber - Dietary	1 g	Calcium	110 mg

15% calories from fat

Food Exchanges: 2.1 Veg., 0.1 Fruit, 35.4 Meat

Fish and Shellfish

NUTRITIVE AND CALORIC VALUE

TYPE OF FISH	CALORIES	PROTEIN	FAT	CARBOHY-DRATES	CHOLES-TEROL
(3.0 oz. or 84 gms)		(gms.)	(gms.)	(gms.)	(gms.)
Cod, Pacific	70	15.2	0.5	0	31
Flounder, Sole	68	14.9	0.5	0	n.a.x.
Haddock	74	16.1	0.6	0	49
Pike, Northern	75	16.4	0.6	0	33
Dolphin fish	73	15.7	0.6	0	62
Scallops	75	14.3	0.6	2.0	28
Pollock, Walleye	68	14.6	0.7	0	61
Lobster, Northern	77	16.5	0.8	0	81
Perch	77	16.5	0.8	0	76
Surimi	84	12.9	0.8	5.8	25
Tuna, Yellowfin	92	19.9	0.8	0	38
Grouper	78	16.5	0.9	0	31
Tuna, Skipjack	88	18.7	0.9	0	40
Flatfish	78	16.0	1.0	0	41
Snapper	85	17.4	1.1	0	31
Whiting	77	15.6	1.1	0	57
Lobster, Spiny	95	17.5	1.3	2.1	60
Shrimp	90	17.3	1.5	0.8	130
Clams, Canned	126	21.0	1.7	4.4	57
Mussels, Blue	73	10.1	1.9	3.1	24
Halibut	93	17.7	2.0	0	27
Oysters, Pacific	69	8.0	2.0	4.2	46
Oysters, Eastern	58	5.9	2.1	3.3	46
Salmon, Pink	99	17.0	2.9	0	44
Salmon, Chum	102	17.1	3.2	0	63
Swordfish	103	16.8	3.4	0	33
Bluefish	105	17.0	3.6	0	50
Tuna, Bluefin	122	19.8	4.2	0	42
Whitefish	114	16.2	5.0	0	51
Salmon, Coho	124	18.4	5.1	0	33
Salmon, Atlantic	121	16.9	5.4	0	47
Orange Roughy	107	12.5	6.0	0	17
Salmon, Sockeye	143	18.1	7.3	0	53
Pompano, Florida	140	15.7	8.1	0	43
Salmon, Chinook	153	17.1	8.9	0	56
Mackerel, Atlantic	174	15.8	11.8	0	60

SNAPPER VERA CRUZ

Preparation time: 10 minutes   *Chef: Doris Bailey*
Cooking time: 20 minutes   *Yacht: Maverick*
Serves: 8

2 lbs. red snapper fillets
1/4 cup lime juice
Vegetable cooking spray
1 cup chopped onion
2 (15 oz.) cans low-sodium tomatoes, chopped and drained
1 Tblsp. chopped jalapeño pepper, or to taste
1 tsp. black pepper
1 Tblsp. low-sodium tomato paste
1/2 cup sliced green olives
1/4 cup chopped fresh cilantro, or parsley
4 cups cooked basmati rice
Garnish: fresh parsley sprigs

Sprinkle fillets with lime juice and set aside. In a large nonstick skillet sauté onions in cooking spray until softened. Stir in tomatoes, jalapeño, pepper and tomato paste together in large skillet. Cover skillet and cook about 7 minutes. Add fillets in single layer. Cover and simmer about 10 minutes, or until fish is opaque and flakes easily with a fork. Remove and keep warm. Add olives and cilantro to sauce and bring to a boil. Stir 2 to 3 minutes until thickened. Place fillets on a bed of rice. Spoon sauce over fish. *Garnish with parsley.*

Note: If snapper is not available use grouper, or check **Fish Chart** *(page 174) to find a fish of similar nutritional value.*

Sweet corn and diced red bell peppers or glazed matchstick carrots add cool contrast and color as an accompaniment.

Nutrient content per serving:

Calories	324	Cholesterol	53 mg
Protein	34 g	Sodium	384 mg
Carbohydrates	36 g	Potassium	932 mg
Fat	4.3 g	Iron	2.5 mg
Fiber - Dietary	2.7 g	Calcium	99 mg

12% calories from fat

Food Exchanges: 1.1 Veg., 1.8 Bread, 4.1 Meat

SZECHUAN FISH

Preparation time: 20 minutes
Cooking time: 20 minutes
Serves: 8

Chef: Fiona Dugdale
Yacht: Promenade

8 (4 oz.) red snapper fillets, skinned
1/3 cup less salt soy sauce
1/4 cup dry sherry
2 Tblsp. honey
6 garlic cloves, crushed
2 Tblsp. fresh ginger root, finely chopped
1/4 cup lemon juice
Vegetable cooking spray
1/4 tsp. + 1 tsp. chili powder
3 large tomatoes, finely chopped
6 green onions, finely chopped

Preheat oven to 375°F. Place fillets side by side in baking dish large enough to hold fish in a single layer. Meanwhile, mix together the soy sauce, sherry and honey with 1/2 of the garlic, ginger, chili and lemon juice. Pour over fish and bake for about 20-25 minutes, depending on thickness of fillets. Spray a skillet and sauté the remaining garlic and ginger with the chili for 1 minute. Add the tomatoes, onion, and lemon juice and sauté for 3 more minutes. Remove fish from baking dish when cooked, place on serving dish. Add the soy sauce mixture to the skillet and reduce by half. *Spoon the sauce over the fish and serve hot with rice and snow peas.*

Note: *Use any variety of fresh fish that is available, but check* **fish chart** *Page 174) for fat content.*

Nutrient content per serving:

Calories	139	Cholesterol	32 mg
Protein	20 g	Sodium	619 mg
Carbohydrates	10 g	Potassium	503 mg
Fat	1.4 g	Iron	0.6 mg
Fiber - Dietary	0.8 g	Calcium	38 mg

8% calories from fat

Food Exchanges: 0.5 Veg., 2.5 Meat

RED SNAPPER FLORIDA

Preparation time: 15 minutes   *Chef: Madou Condon*
Cooking time: 10 minutes (broiler)   *Yacht: s/y Tava'e*
Serves: 4

2 shallots, chopped
1/2 cup white wine
1 pink grapefruit, sectioned
4 (4 oz.) snapper fillets
1/4 tsp. ground coriander
1/4 tsp. pepper
1/2 cup plain nonfat yogurt
Garnish: fresh parsley

Preheat oven broiler. Reduce chopped shallots in wine over low heat. Peel grapefruit, section over bowl to catch juice. Broil snapper until it flakes easily with a fork. Mix in coriander with shallots, pepper, and grapefruit sections. Heat slowly in a small saucepan. Remove from heat and stir in yogurt. *Place fish on plate, ladle sauce around and add grapefruit sections and parsley.*

Hint: *To the above, I add wild rice and stewed romaine. Don't use Barbecue sauce, as smoky taste will kill the sauce flavor. If no broiler, cook in aluminum foil or poach the fish.*

Nutrient content per serving:

Calories	231	Cholesterol	44 mg
Protein	26 g	Sodium	97 mg
Carbohydrates	23 g	Potassium	892 mg
Fat	2.2 g	Iron	0.8 mg
Fiber - Dietary	0.1 g	Calcium	120 mg

8% calories from fat

Food Exchanges: 0.1 Milk, 0.4 Veg., 1.1 Fruit, 3.3 Meat

FISH FILLETS IN A JIFFY

Preparation time: 10 minutes   *Chef: Helene Gaillet Neergaard*
Cooking time: 15 minutes (broiler)   *Yacht: Image*
Serves: 2

1 cup sliced red onion
1/2 sweet red pepper, sliced
1/4 tsp. each rosemary, sage and/or thyme
1/4 cup fresh lemon juice
1/2 tsp. fresh ground black pepper
2 (4 oz.) pike fillets (or other white meat fish)
Vegetable cooking spray
Garnish: lemon wedges

Preheat oven on broil. Place onion and red pepper in a shallow baking pan. Sprinkle the herbs, lemon juice, and pepper over and stir well. Broil about 10 minutes stirring often to keep from burning. Wash and dry fish fillets and spray a little cooking spray on them. Place fillets on top of onion mixture. Broil 4-5 minutes; do not over cook! *Garnish. Serve immediately.*

Hint: *Do not worry if onions burn slightly on the edges when the fish is cooking.*

Note: *This recipe is easily expanded or halved.*

Nutrient content per serving:

Calories	134	Cholesterol	45 mg
Protein	23 g	Sodium	46 mg
Carbohydrates	8 g	Potassium	437 mg
Fat	1.3 g	Iron	1.0 mg
Fiber - Dietary	1.2 g	Calcium	82 mg

9% calories from fat

Food Exchanges: 0.7 Veg., 0.1 Fruit, 2.2 Meat

MAI THAI FISH WITH BROWN RICE

Preparation time: 15 minutes   *Chef: Bobbi Fawcett*
Cooking time: 15 minutes (microwave)   *Yacht: Windwalker*
Serves: 4

4 (4 oz.) fillets of sole
1/4 cup fish stock, or other stock, or water
3 cloves garlic, minced
1/2 cup chopped onion
2 tsp. finely chopped fresh ginger
3 Tblsp. less salt soy sauce
3 Tblsp. oyster sauce
4 Tblsp. Tamarind sauce, see note below
2 cups cooked brown rice
Garnish: 1 chopped jalapeño or
**   red chili and fresh cilantro**

Bake, poach or microwave fish. To microwave, place in a single layer in microwave dish (thick sides facing out). Cover and cook on medium heat approximately 5 minutes. Sauté garlic and onion in fish stock. Add ginger, soy, oyster, and Tamarind sauces; bring to a boil then simmer for a few minutes. Heat cooked fish in sauce. *Serve hot over brown rice. Spoon sauce over the rice and fish.*

Garnish with fresh jalapeño, red chilies and fresh cilantro.

Note: *Tamarind sauce may be replaced by 3 Tblsp. plum jam and 1 Tblsp. lemon juice.*

Nutrient content per serving:

Calories	314	Cholesterol	77 mg
Protein	32 g	Sodium	974 mg
Carbohydrates	40 g	Potassium	526 mg
Fat	2.7 g	Iron	1.1 mg
Fiber - Dietary	2.0 g	Calcium	43 mg

8% calories from fat

Food Exchanges: 0.3 Veg., 1.4 Bread, 3.8 Meat

POACHED SALMON
WITH VANILLA DILL SAUCE

Preparation time: 10 minutes　　　　　*Chef: Joan Ruppe*
Cooking time: 15 minutes　　　　　　*Yacht: Windflower*
Serves: 6

Aluminum foil
6 (4 oz.) pink salmon fillets
3 lemons
2 Tblsp. chopped fresh dill weed (or 1 Tblsp. dried dill)

Vanilla Dill Sauce:
1/2 cup nonfat vanilla yogurt
1 Tblsp. chopped fresh dill weed
1-1/2 Tblsp. fresh lemon juice
Garnish: lemon twists and dill weed sprigs

Preheat oven to 350°F. Place fillets on individual sheets of foil. Squeeze juice of 1/2 lemon on each fillet. Sprinkle (lots) of dill on top of fillets, fold pockets air tight and bake on a cookie sheet for 15 minutes, or until cooked. *Garnish.*

Sauce: Mix yogurt, dill and lemon juice. Serve on side.

Hint: This is also great cold for lunch. For dinner, I serve rice pilaf and asparagus with this dish.

Nutrient content per serving:

Calories	167	Cholesterol	60 mg
Protein	25 g	Sodium	100 mg
Carbohydrates	8 g	Potassium	477 mg
Fat	3.9 g	Iron	0.9 mg
Fiber - Dietary	0.1 g	Calcium	69 mg

21% calories from fat

Food Exchanges: 0.4 Milk, 0.1 Fruit, 3.0 Meat

SALMON AND COURGETTE ROULADES WITH MUSHROOM PURÉE

Preparation time: 15 minutes   *Chef: Shirley Gibson*
Cooking time: 10-15 minutes   *Yacht: Flying Scotsman*
Serves: 4

4 (4 oz.) pink salmon fillets
2 cups coarsely grated zucchini (courgette)
1 tsp. finely grated lime peel
1/4 tsp. freshly ground black pepper
2 cups cooked arborio rice

Mushroom Purée:
1 cup finely chopped onion
3/4 lb. fresh mushrooms, washed and roughly chopped
1/3 cup nonfat skim milk
2 Tblsp. lime juice
1/4 tsp. each: freshly grated nutmeg, freshly ground black pepper
1/2 tsp. less salt soy sauce

Flatten each piece of salmon gently between two pieces of cling wrap until escallop sized (use meat mallet or rolling pin). Blanch zucchini in boiling water for one second, cool quickly in cold water, squeeze out water in a clean cloth until nearly dry. Mix with lime and add pepper. Place each escallop on a larger piece of cling wrap, spread with zucchini and roll up tightly, twisting the ends of the cling wrap to seal (like a Christmas cracker). Poach in a covered pan of simmering water until just cooked, 8-10 minutes depending on size. ***Mushroom Purée:*** Sauté onion and mushrooms in nonstick pan, till juices start to run, add milk, simmer till tender, purée, add lime juice and soy sauce to taste, adding a little more milk if necessary to make a thick creamy sauce. *To serve, cut each roll on the diagonal, arrange slices overlapping on individual plates. Serve with mushroom purée, rice and green beans.*

Nutrient content per serving:

Calories	201	Cholesterol	60 mg
Protein	27 g	Sodium	135 mg
Carbohydrates	10 g	Potassium	928 mg
Fat	4.5 g	Iron	2.3 mg
Fiber - Dietary	2.1 g	Calcium	91 mg

13% calories from fat

Food Exchanges: 1.1 Veg., 0.8 Bread, 3.0 Meat

MARINATED DOLPHIN FISH GRILL

Preparation time: 5 minutes   *Chef: Judy Garry*
Marinating time: 20 minutes   *Yacht: Sloopy*
Cooking time: 10 minutes (grill)
Serves: 4

1/4 cup lemon juice
2 Tblsp. less salt soy sauce
1/2 tsp. dill weed
1/2 tsp. ground black pepper
2 Tblsp. dry vermouth
4 (4 oz.) dolphin fish (mahi mahi) fillets

Prepare grill. In a shallow dish, combine lemon juice, soy sauce, dill, pepper and vermouth. Mix well. Add fish steaks in a single layer. Marinate at room temperature for 20 minutes or refrigerate for up to 4 hours, turning at least twice.

Remove from marinade. Grill about 5 minutes on each side. *Drizzle extra marinade over fish before serving.*

Note: *Be careful not to overcook the dolphin or it will be very dry.*

Nutrient content per serving:

Calories	114	Cholesterol	83 mg
Protein	22 g	Sodium	363 mg
Carbohydrates	2 g	Potassium	518 mg
Fat	0.8 g	Iron	1.3 mg
Fiber - Dietary	0.1 g	Calcium	3 mg

7% calories from fat

Food Exchanges: 2.8 Meat

When marinating fish, poultry and vegetables, use a Ziplock bag, or a plastic bag with tie; makes turning easy.

TERIYAKI FISH STEAKS

Preparation time: 10 minutes
Marinating time: 1 hour
Cooking time: 10 minutes (grill)
Serves: 6

Chef: Joyce Pfaff
Yacht: Flash Vert

6 (4 oz.) dolphin steaks (or tuna)

Teriyaki Marinade:
Juice and rind of 1 lime
1/4 cup lite soy sauce
2 Tblsp. low-sodium catsup
1/4 cup water
2 Tblsp. cider vinegar
1 tsp. honey
1/2 tsp. black pepper
2 cloves garlic, crushed

In a shallow non-metallic dish, combine marinade ingredients. Add fish and marinate for approximately 1 hour before grilling. Grill over hot coals about 5 to 8 minutes, or until fish is opaque and flakes easily when tested with a fork at the thickest part.

Serve with brown rice and fresh steamed vegetables for a very low calorie, nutritious meal.

Nutrient content per serving:

Calories	90	Cholesterol	62 mg
Protein	16 g	Sodium	244 mg
Carbohydrates	4 g	Potassium	392 mg
Fat	0.6 g	Iron	1.2 mg
Fiber - Dietary	0.1 g	Calcium	8.7 mg

6% calories from fat

Food Exchanges: 2.1 Meat

Dolphin fish

That's not me

Flipper

GRILLED TUNA
WITH MANGO TARRAGON SAUCE

Preparation time: 5 minutes   *Chef: Penny Knowles*
Cooking time: 5 minutes (broiler)   *Yacht: Golden Skye*
Serves: 6

6 (4 oz.) fresh yellowfin tuna steaks*
1/2 tsp. black pepper

Mango Tarragon Sauce:
1 cup mango, fresh or canned
1-1/2 cups nonfat yogurt
1/4 cup dry sherry
Juice of 1/2 lemon
1-1/2 tsp. dried tarragon
Garnish: Lime slices and fresh parsley

Season tuna with pepper and broil about 2 minutes on each side. While tuna is cooking, pureé remaining ingredients in blender or food processor, then heat for about 1 minute in a small pan.

Place a layer of sauce on each plate. Set a tuna steak on the sauce. *Garnish with lime slices and fresh parsley.*

***Note:** See fish chart. Different types of tuna vary considerably in fat content.*

Nutrient content per serving:

Calories	193	Cholesterol	51 mg
Protein	30 g	Sodium	91 mg
Carbohydrates	12 g	Potassium	735 mg
Fat	1.2 g	Iron	1.1 mg
Fiber - Dietary	0.9 g	Calcium	28 mg

6% calories from fat

Food Exchanges: 0.3 Milk, 0.4 Fruit, 3.7 Meat

Put lot of herbs in marinades for fish, poultry, and vegetables. For an extra dash of flavor, use a rosemary sprig as your basting brush when broiling or grilling.

TUNA IN CITRUS SAUCE

Preparation time: 10 minutes   *Chef: Jan Robinson*
Marinating time: 1 hour or longer   *Yacht: Vanity*
Cooking time: 15 minutes (broiler)
Serves: 4

4 (4 oz.) yellowfin tuna steaks

Citrus Sauce:
1/4 cup frozen orange juice concentrate
2 Tblsp. lemon juice
1 tsp. dried dill weed
1 tsp. paprika
2 Tblsp. minced fresh parsley or 1 Tblsp. dried
1/2 cup water
3 Tblsp. + 3 Tblsp. fruit juice sweetened orange marmalade
1 tsp. arrowroot
Garnish: Fresh orange slices and sprigs of parsley or dill.

Place fish in a Ziplock bag. Combine remaining ingredients (except marmalade and arrowroot) and mix to dissolve orange juice concentrate. Reserve 1/2 cup for sauce and pour remaining mixture over fish. Marinate in refrigerator 1 hour or longer, turning at least once. Preheat broiler. Remove fish from marinade and place on broiler pan. Add 3 Tblsp. of marmalade to sauce and heat. Broil fish four inches from heat 10-15 minutes until fish flakes, basting with marinade several times during cooking. While fish is broiling, heat reserved orange sauce in small saucepan with arrowroot and remaining 3 Tblsp. marmalade until sauce begins to thicken. Transfer fish to serving dish. Pour sauce over fish or serve on the side. *Garnish with fresh orange slices and sprigs of parsley or dill.*

Nutrient content per serving:

Calories	159	Cholesterol	38 mg
Protein	21 g	Sodium	48 mg
Carbohydrates	16 g	Potassium	598 mg
Fat	10 g	Iron	1.2 mg
Fiber - Dietary	0.5 g	Calcium	32 mg

6% calories from fat

Food Exchanges: 0.7 Fruit, 2.8 Meat

CARIBBEAN FISH FILLETS

Preparation time: 10 minutes   *Chef: Jan Robinson*
Cooking time: 5-15 minutes   *Yacht: Vanity*
Serves: 4

4 (4 oz.) grouper fillets, or other mild white fish
1/4 cup orange juice
1 Tblsp. lemon juice
2 tsp. orange marmalade
1/3 cup mashed banana
2 cloves garlic, minced
1 tsp. fresh grated ginger root, or 1/2 tsp. ground
1/2 tsp. black pepper
1/2 cup plain nonfat yogurt
Garnish: Freshly chopped parsley or cilantro

Preheat oven to 350°F. Place fillets in baking pan large enough to hold fish in a single layer. In a medium bowl, combine all other ingredients; pour 1/2 cup mixture evenly over fish. Bake 5-15 minutes, or until fish flakes. Timing will vary depending on thickness of fillets. Remove fish from pan, place on serving dish. Stir yogurt and parsley into the pan then spoon sauce over fish and serve. *Sprinkle with parsley or cilantro.*

Nutrient content per serving:

Calories	148	Cholesterol	41 mg
Protein	24 g	Sodium	87 mg
Carbohydrates	9 g	Potassium	726 mg
Fat	1.3 g	Iron	1.3 mg
Fiber - Dietary	0.5 g	Calcium	391 mg

6% calories from fat

Food Exchanges: 0.1 Milk, 0.1 Veg., 0.3 Fruit, 3.0 Meat

GROUPER STEAKS WITH ORANGE-GINGER SAUCE

Preparation time: 20 minutes   *Chef: Randa Jacobs*
Cooking time: 30 minutes   *Yacht: Blithe Spirit*
Serves: 4

Vegetable nonstick spray
1 lb. Grouper steaks
1/4 cup fat-free chicken broth (page 80)

Orange-Ginger Sauce:
1/4 cup fat-free chicken broth (page 80)
2 green onions, sliced diagonally in 1/2" pieces
1/2 cup orange juice
1 tsp. Worcestershire sauce
1 tsp. grated peeled ginger root (or 1/2 tsp. ground ginger)
1/8 tsp. coarsely ground black pepper
1/8 tsp. hot sauce
1 tsp. arrowroot
Garnish: 2 chopped green onions and thin orange slices

Spray a 12" nonstick skillet. Place over medium heat and cook grouper steaks 2 minutes. Turn fish add 1/4 cup chicken broth and cook 8 minutes more, or until fish flakes easily when tested with a fork. Carefully remove fish to a warm platter. Using same skillet on medium heat, add 1/4 cup chicken broth and onions; cook until tender. Add orange juice, Worcestershire sauce, ginger, pepper and hot sauce to skillet. Cook over high heat, stirring constantly until sauce boils; boil 1 minute. Mix arrowroot with a little water and stir into sauce. Pour some sauce over fish steaks; serve remaining sauce with fish. Garnish with green onions and thin slices of orange.

Nutrient content per serving:

Calories	124	Cholesterol	40 mg
Protein	26 g	Sodium	59 mg
Carbohydrates	4 g	Potassium	491 mg
Fat	2 g	Iron	1.2 mg
Fiber - Dietary	0.4 g	Calcium	26 mg

13% calories from fat

Food Exchanges: 0.2 Fruit, 3.5 Meat

GROUPER WITH TROPICAL SALSA

Preparation time: 10 minutes   *Chef: Jan Robinson*
Marinating time: 2 hours   *Yacht: Vanity*
Cooking time: 10 minutes (grill or broiler)
Serves: 4

4 (4 oz.) grouper steaks
Freshly ground pepper
3 Tblsp. Dijon mustard
4 garlic cloves, crushed
1/4 cup lime juice
1/4 cup soy sauce
1 tsp. dried dill weed or 1 Tblsp. chopped fresh dill

Trim the grouper and season on both sides with pepper to taste. Place in a glass baking dish large enough to hold the steaks in one layer. In a small mixing bowl, combine the mustard, garlic, lime juice, soy sauce, pepper and dill. Mix well and pour over the fish. Cover with plastic wrap and marinate in the refrigerator for at least 2 hours, preferably overnight, turning the steaks occasionally.

Preheat the broiler or light a charcoal fire and let burn to a gray ash. Broil or grill about 6 inches from the heat until firm to the touch and cooked through, about 4 minutes on each side.

Serve with **Tropical Salsa** *(page 114)* **Brown Rice** *(page 205)* **Al Dente Fresh Vegetables** *(page 218) and Whole Wheat Rolls.*

Nutrient content per serving:

Calories	177	Cholesterol	40 mg
Protein	28 g	Sodium	362 mg
Carbohydrates	18 g	Potassium	728 mg
Fat	2 g	Iron	2.4 mg
Fiber - Dietary	2.2 g	Calcium	54 mg

10% calories from fat

Food Exchanges: 0.8 Veg., 0.7 Fruit, 3.0 Meat

LINGUINE WITH CLAM AND BASIL

Preparation time: 20 minutes　　　　　*Chef: Paulette C. Hadley*
Cooking time: 10 minutes　　　　　　　*Yacht: Chardonnay*
Serves: 4

2 (6-1/2 oz.) cans minced clams, drained, reserve liquid
1-1/2 cups chopped onion
2 cloves garlic, minced
2 Tblsp. + 1/3 cup clam juice (or vermouth)
1-1/2 tsp. crushed dried basil
1/2 tsp. white pepper
1 tsp. arrowroot
1/2 cup fresh chopped parsley
12 oz. cooked linguine
1/2 tsp. black pepper
2 Tblsp. plain nonfat yogurt

In a saucepan cook onion and garlic in 2 Tblsp. clam juice. Cook until softened. Add basil, white pepper, clam liquid. Simmer 15 minutes. Dissolve arrowroot in a little water. Add to sauce and stir to thicken. Add clams, heat and stir in parsley. Toss linguine with black pepper and nonfat yogurt. *Put on serving plates and add sauce.*

Note: *Edna Beaman on Yacht Wahsoune uses a very similar recipe - must be good!*

Nutrient content per serving:

Calories	151	Cholesterol	72 mg
Protein	11 g	Sodium	58 mg
Carbohydrates	24 g	Potassium	319 mg
Fat	1.8 g	Iron	5.2 mg
Fiber - Dietary	2 g	Calcium	102 mg

10% calories from fat

Food Exchanges: 0.8 Veg., 1.0 Bread, 0.6 Meat

Pasta can be cooked ahead of time and reheated with hot water.

CORN CRAB CAKES

Preparation time: 30 minutes   *Chef: Beverly Grant*
Chilling time: 1 hour   *Yacht: Safe Conduct II*
Cooking time: 10 minutes
Serves: 4

1 cup fresh cooked corn kernels
1-1/2 cups imitation crabmeat (surimi)
1/2 cup diced onion
1/2 cup diced red pepper
1/2 cup diced celery
1/2 cup nonfat mayonnaise
1/2 tsp. dry mustard
1/4 tsp. cayenne pepper
1/2 tsp. black pepper
2 egg whites, lightly beaten
1-1/4 cups fat-free cracker crumbs
Vegetable cooking spray
Garnish: Lemon wedges

Combine corn, crabmeat, onions, peppers, and celery. Set aside. Mix mayonnaise with mustard, and cayenne pepper. Stir in crab mixture, black pepper, egg whites, and 1/4 cup cracker crumbs. Form into eight patties. Coat with remaining cracker crumbs and chill for one hour.

Spray a large nonstick skillet with vegetable spray; place over medium-high heat until hot. Add crabmeat patties, and cook 3 - 4 minutes on each side, or until lightly browned. *Garnish and serve with a mustard sauce or* **Tofu Curry Dip** *(page 113).*

Nutrient content per serving:

Calories	220	Cholesterol	17 mg
Protein	32 g	Sodium	1137 mg
Carbohydrates	40 g	Potassium	259 mg
Fat	1.8 g	Iron	0.7 mg
Fiber - Dietary	1.6 g	Calcium	27 mg

5% calories from fat

Food Exchanges: 0.4 Veg., 3.3 Bread, 10.1 Meat

LATINA SCALLOPS PROVENCALE

Preparation time: 10 minutes　　　　　　　*Chef: Shirley King*
Cooking time: 10 minutes　　　　　　　　　*Yacht: Latina*
Serves: 6

Vegetable cooking spray
1-1/2 lbs. fresh sea scallops or frozen, thawed
2 Tblsp. fat-free chicken broth (page 80) or water
4 cloves garlic, minced
3 cups peeled and chopped tomatoes
3 Tblsp. chopped fresh basil (or 1 Tblsp. dried)
1/2 tsp. fresh ground black pepper
3 scallions, cut into matchstick thin pieces

Spray a large nonstick skillet with vegetable spray. Place skillet over medium-high heat. Pat scallops dry with paper towels. Cook scallops until opaque, about 5 minutes. Remove scallops to platter; keep warm. Heat chicken broth in skillet, add garlic and cook 1 minute. Add tomatoes, basil and pepper. Cook 3-5 minutes. Return scallops to skillet. Add scallions. Heat through.

Serve with the **Rice, Peas and Parsley** (page 204) along with the **Carrot and Sprout Salad** (page 43) icy pineapple and sparkling water.

Nutrient content per serving:

Calories	113	Cholesterol	45 mg
Protein	20 g	Sodium	235 mg
Carbohydrates	5 g	Potassium	536 mg
Fat	1.8 g	Iron	3.2 mg
Fiber - Dietary	0.7 g	Calcium	120 mg

14% calories from fat

Food Exchanges: 0.3 Veg., 2.7 Meat

Hint: Fastest way to skin a tomato
Spear the tomato with a fork and lower into a pan of simmering water. Hold it there while you slowly count-one-one hundred, etc. until you have counted to ten. The tomato won't be cooked, but the skin will slip off easily when you coax it with a knife.

SAUTÉED SCALLOPS

Preparation time: 15 minutes   *Chef: Edna Beaman*
Cooking time: 5 minutes   *Yacht: Wahsoune*
Serves: 4

Vegetable cooking spray
1 lb sea scallops
1/4 cup fat-free chicken broth (page 80)
2 cloves garlic, minced
1/4 cup chopped fresh parsley
1 tsp. lime juice
1/2 tsp. black pepper

Drain scallops well and pat dry. Heat spray in a non-stick skillet over medium heat. Add scallops and cook 2 minutes. Turn scallops. Add garlic and chicken broth; cook until scallops are opaque (do not over cook), about 2 minutes. Remove skillet from flame and add rest of ingredients; toss together and serve.

Nutrient content per serving:

Calories	108	Cholesterol	45 mg
Protein	20 g	Sodium	242 mg
Carbohydrates	3 g	Potassium	441 mg
Fat	2 g	Iron	2.9 mg
Fiber - Dietary	0.2 g	Calcium	107 mg

17% calories from fat

Food Exchanges: 0.1 Veg., 2.6 Meat

Before cooking frozen scallops, thaw them until they can be separated from one another easily. Dry them carefully if they are to be sautéed.

SHRIMP AND SCALLOP PILAF

Preparation time: 20 minutes
Cooking time: 25 minutes
Serves: 4

Chef: Edna Beaman
Yacht: Wahsoune

1/4 cup + 1 cup fat-free chicken broth (page 80)
1 cup chopped onion
2 cloves garlic, pressed
1/4 tsp. tumeric or saffron
1 cup uncooked long grain white rice
2-1/4 cups water
3 Tblsp. fresh lemon juice
1/2 lb. sea scallops, halved crosswise
1/2 lb. peeled and deveined medium shrimp
1 (10 oz.) pkg. frozen green peas, partially thawed
1/2 tsp. pepper, or to taste

Heat 1/4 cup chicken broth in a large saucepan over medium heat. Stir in onion, garlic, tumeric and rice. Cook about 3 minutes until onion is softened. Stirring, pour in 1 cup broth and water and bring to a boil. Reduce heat, cover and simmer for 10 minutes. Squeeze lemon juice over scallops and shrimp. Add scallop, shrimp, peas and pepper into saucepan. Simmer until scallops are opaque, shrimp pink, rice cooked and peas heated through, about 10 minutes.

Nutrient content per serving:

Calories	341	Cholesterol	106 mg
Protein	27 g	Sodium	422 mg
Carbohydrates	54 g	Potassium	589 mg
Fat	1.6 g	Iron	6.0 mg
Fiber - Dietary	3.9 g	Calcium	110 mg

4% calories from fat

Food Exchanges: 0.6 Veg., 3.1 Bread, 2.4 Meat

To devein shrimp, make a shallow cut lengthwise down the back of each shrimp; remove sand vein with point of knife.

TAHITI SHRIMP

Preparation time: 20 minutes   *Chef: Marion Vanderwood*
Cooking time: 15 minutes   *Yacht: Ocean Voyager*
Serves: 4

3 Tblsp. fresh ginger root, grated
3 cloves garlic, chopped
1/4 tsp. black pepper
1/4 cup white wine
1 (6 oz.) can frozen concentrated orange juice
4 cups + 1 Tblsp. water
1 lb. peeled and deveined shrimp
2 tsp. arrowroot
Garnish: Freshly chopped cilantro

Combine ginger, garlic, pepper, white wine and orange juice in a large saucepan. Simmer 10 minutes. Dissolve arrowroot in 1 Tblsp. water and stir slowly into sauce. In another saucepan bring 4 cups of water to a boil. Add shrimp, bring back to a boil and remove from heat immediately. Drain and add shrimp to sauce.

Place wild rice or fettucine in center of plate. Pour shrimp-sauce over pasta and arrange snow peas. Sprinkle with cilantro.

Nutrient content per serving:

Calories	211	Cholesterol	175 mg
Protein	24 g	Sodium	181 mg
Carbohydrates	20 g	Potassium	539 mg
Fat	2.1 g	Iron	3.0 mg
Fiber - Dietary	0.4 g	Calcium	87 mg

9% calories from fat

Food Exchanges: 0.2 Veg., 1.0 Fruit, 3.2 Meat

GRILLED PRAWN
AND VEGETABLE KABOBS

Preparation time: 15 minutes   *Chef: Randa Jacobs*
Cooking time: 3 - 4 minutes (grill)   *Yacht: Blithe Spirit*
Serves: 4

16 prawns, shelled and deveined (or 16 jumbo-size shrimp)
8 cherry tomatoes
8 mushrooms
8 slices yellow bell pepper
8 slices zucchini
2 Tblsp. balsamic vinegar
1 Tblsp. honey
1/4 tsp. paprika
1/8 tsp. pepper
8 skewers

Preheat grill. Alternately thread each of 8 skewers with 2 prawns and one each cherry tomato, mushroom, slice of yellow pepper and zucchini. Mix vinegar, honey, paprika and pepper. Brush kabobs with mixture and broil on preheated grill 3 to 4 minutes, or until prawns turn pink and vegetables are crisp-tender. Turn once during cooking. *Serve with **Hauté Potato** (page 212).*

Nutrient content per serving:

Calories	175	Cholesterol	175 mg
Protein	24 g	Sodium	180 mg
Carbohydrates	13 g	Potassium	528 mg
Fat	2.3 g	Iron	3.9 mg
Fiber - Dietary	1.4 g	Calcium	71 mg

12% calories from fat

Food Exchanges: 1.0 Veg., 3.2 Meat

Eat a lot of vegetables and fruit in season. Not only are they cheap, but they do the most for you. Beans and grains provide the best protein, and they are inexpensive too.

SEAFOOD KABOB
WITH CURRIED HONEY GLAZE

Preparation time: 15 minutes   *Chef: Sheila Kruse Boyce*
Cooking time: 20 minutes (grill)   *Yacht: Victorious*
Marinating time: 1 hour
Serves: 6

1/3 cup honey
1 Tblsp. curry powder
1/3 cup less salt soy sauce
1/2 lb. sea scallops
1/2 lb. medium shrimp, shelled and deveined
1/2 lb. snapper or grouper, cut in 1-1/2 inch cubes
1-1/2 cups zucchini, cut into 1/4 inch slices
1-1/2 cups yellow squash, cut into 1/4 inch slices
1-1/2 cups red pepper, cut into 1 inch squares
2 cups pineapple, cut into 1 inch squares

Combine honey, curry powder and soy sauce in small saucepan. Heat
to boiling. Simmer 2 minutes. Pour over scallops and marinate 1 hour.
Place shrimp separately on one or two skewers. (It cooks slower than
fish). Place fish, zucchini, yellow squash, red pepper and pineapple in
alternating pattern on skewers. Brush marinade on kabobs, covering
both sides, saving some to pour on scallops in saucepan. Grill until
shrimp and fish are done (about 20 minutes, depending on heat).
Prior to serving place scallops in saucepan, simmer scallops with
marinade (about 4 minutes). Place one fish kabob on plate and divide
shrimp and scallops between plates. *Serve with rice pilaf cooked with
saffron or tumeric (makes rice yellow) and dry white wine.*

Nutrient content per serving:

Calories	203	Cholesterol	85 mg
Protein	24 g	Sodium	515 mg
Carbohydrates	23 g	Potassium	581 mg
Fat	1.9 g	Iron	1.8 mg
Fiber - Dietary	1.7 g	Calcium	61 mg

8% calories from fat

Food Exchanges: 0.4 Veg., 0.4 Fruit, 3.0 Meat

SEAFOOD SYMPHONY

Preparation time: 30 minutes   *Chef: Pam Donnelly*
Cooking time: 40   *Yacht: Shellette*
Serves: 6

1/2 lb. calamari (squid), cut into rings
3/4 lb. snapper (or dolphin) fillets, cut in bite-size pieces
4 oz. can mussels, drained
1 cup dry white wine
1 Tblsp. lemon juice
1 tsp. black pepper
1 tsp. arrowroot, mixed with 1 Tblsp. water
1/2 tsp. ground nutmeg
1/2 cup plain nonfat yogurt
2 Tblsp. chopped parsley
Garnish: parsley and lemon wedges

In a saucepan simmer calamari and fish with wine, lemon juice and pepper for 10 minutes. Stir in arrowroot mixture and nutmeg; simmer 2 minutes. Add mussels and heat through. Stir in yogurt and parsley. DO NOT BOIL. *Garnish with parsley and lemon wedges.*

Serve over brown or white rice.

Nutrient content per serving:

Calories	174	Cholesterol	120 mg
Protein	22 g	Sodium	126 mg
Carbohydrates	11 g	Potassium	513 mg
Fat	1.9 g	Iron	1.5 mg
Fiber - Dietary	0.3 g	Calcium	67 mg

10% calories from fat

Food Exchanges: 0.1 Milk, 0.1 Fruit, 0.3 Bread, 2.8 Meat

For a sweet tender taste, try soaking fish in vinegar and water before cooking it.

CIOPPINO
(ITALIAN SEAFOOD STEW)

Preparation time: 20 minutes   *Chef: Doris Bailey*
Cooking time: 40 minutes   *Yacht: Maverick*
Serves: 8

1/4 cup + 1-3/4 cups fat-free chicken broth (Page 80)
1 cup chopped yellow onion
3 chopped bell peppers (1 ea. red, yellow, and green)
1 Tblsp. dried red pepper
6 garlic cloves, chopped
1 (28 oz.) can puréed low-sodium tomatoes
1 cup white wine
1/2 tsp. dried marjoram
3/4 lb. dolphin fish (mahi mahi) cut in large chunks
3/4 lb. snapper fillet, cut in large chunks
1/2 lb. sea scallops
1/2 lb. shelled and deveined shrimp
Garnish: 2 Tblsp. chopped fresh parsley

In a nonstick skillet sauté onions, bell peppers, dried red pepper, and garlic in a 1/4 cup chicken broth until just tender. Add tomatoes, broth, wine and marjoram. Bring to a boil, then partially cover and simmer 30 minutes. Add the dolphin, snapper, scallops and shrimp. Simmer for approximately 8 minutes, or until seafood is cooked; do not stir. Ladle into wide soup plates. *Sprinkle with parsley.*

*Cioppino is always a big hit on **Maverick**. Serve with bread and a salad.*

Nutrient content per serving:

Calories	175	Cholesterol	53 mg
Protein	26 g	Sodium	203 mg
Carbohydrates	10 g	Potassium	761 mg
Fat	1.5 g	Iron	1.8 mg
Fiber - Dietary	1.8 g	Calcium	96 mg

8% calories from fat

Food Exchanges: 1.6 Veg., 3.2 Meat

Grains and Vegetables

PEPPER PRESSURE COOKER RICE

Preparation time: 10 minutes   *Chef: Jeanne Bach*
Cooking time: 16 minutes   *Yacht: Iemanja*
Serves: 4

1 cup long grain white rice
2 cups vegetable stock (page 81)
1/2 tsp. black pepper

Pour stock into pressure cooker. Add rice; place cooker on high heat, in 1-2 minutes, stir and secure cover on cooker. When valve jiggles or rotates, time for 60 seconds and immediately *remove* from heat. Let it sit for 6 minutes (add 1 minute per extra cup of dry rice; e.g. 2 cups rice cooking time = 7 minutes). Release pressure under running tap water and open cooker once pressure reaches zero. Add pepper, stir and serve.

Caution: *Do not fill the pressure cooker more than half full.*

Nutrient content per serving:

Calories	177	Cholesterol	0 mg
Protein	4 g	Sodium	9 mg
Carbohydrates	39 g	Potassium	113 mg
Fat	0.3 g	Iron	2.2 mg
Fiber - Dietary	1.0 g	Calcium	21 mg

2% calories from fat

Food Exchanges: 0.2 Veg., 2.4 Bread

I'm telling you, I'm under a lot of pressure!

VEGETABLE WILD RICE

Preparation time: 15 minutes　　　　　　*Chef: Diane Delorey*
Cooking time: 45-55 minutes　　　　　　*Yacht: September Morn*
Serves: 6

2 small onions, finely minced
2/3 cup grated carrots
1 cup finely diced celery
1/4 cup + 1-1/2 cups vegetable stock (page 81)
1-1/2 cups uncooked wild rice
4-1/2 cups water

In a medium-size saucepan, sauté vegetables in 1/4 cup vegetable stock. Add rice, 1-1/2 cups stock and water. Bring to a boil and simmer for 40-50 minutes (until rice is cooked.) Remove from heat, let stand 5 minutes, fluff with a fork and serve.

Nutrient content per serving:

Calories	156	Cholesterol	0 mg
Protein	6 g	Sodium	34 mg
Carbohydrates	33 g	Potassium	305 mg
Fat	0.5 g	Iron	1.0 mg
Fiber - Dietary	1.0 g	Calcium	28 mg

3% calories from fat

Food Exchanges: 0.4 Veg., 1.9 Bread,

Every time he eats Wild Rice, he goes banana

CARIBBEAN RICE

Preparation time: 10 minutes   *Chef: Diane Delorey*
Cooking time: 10 minutes   *Yacht: September Morn*
Serves: 8

1/2 cup each sliced red, yellow, and green peppers
1/4 cup onion, diced
1/4 cup water
1 cup spicy salsa
4 cups cooked rice

Sauté peppers and onions in water until softened, but still crisp. Add peppers, onions and salsa to cooked rice.

*Serve with **Caribbean Chicken K-bobs.** (page 165)*

Nutrient content per serving:

Calories	154	Cholesterol	0 mg
Protein	3 g	Sodium	6 mg
Carbohydrates	34 g	Potassium	160 mg
Fat	0.5 g	Iron	1.5 mg
Fiber-Dietary	2.1 g	Calcium	19 mg

3% calories from fat

Food Exchanges: 0.6 Veg., 1.8 Bread

RAISIN RICE

Preparation time: 5 minutes
Cooking time: 20 minutes
Serves: 6

Chef: Helene Gaillet de Neergaard
Yacht: Image

2 cups diced unpared apples
1 cup long grain white rice
2-1/2 cups water
2 Tblsp. fresh lemon juice
1 Tblsp. lemon rind
1/4 cup raisins

Place all ingredients in a saucepan. Bring to a boil, cover and cook over low heat for 20 minutes or until done. Let sit for five minutes, fluff with a fork and serve.

Note: *For extra flavor, use 2-1/2 cups fat-free chicken broth (page 80), or vegetable stock (page 81) in place of the water. Brown rice can also be substituted for white rice, which takes 10 minutes longer to cook.*

Nutrient content per serving:

Calories	160	Cholesterol	0 mg
Protein	4 g	Sodium	198 mg
Carbohydrates	36 g	Potassium	186 mg
Fat	0.4 g	Iron	1.5 mg
Fiber - Dietary	1.5 g	Calcium	15 mg

2% calories from fat

Food Exchanges: 0.6 Fruit, 1.6 Bread

Health Conscious...

BROWN RICE WITH PEAS AND PARSLEY

Preparation time: 10 minutes   *Chef: Shirley King*
Cooking time: 5 minutes   *Yacht: Latina*
Serves: 6

3 cups cooked, long grain brown rice
1/2 cup fresh peas, cooked, or frozen peas, thawed
1/2 cup chopped, fresh parsley

Place cooked rice in saucepan with 1/4 cup water. Stir in peas and parsley. Heat thoroughly, or warm in a microwave oven.

Serve with **Latina Scallops, Provencale,** *(page 191)* **Carrot Sprout Salad,** *(page 43) icy pineapple slices and sparkling water.*

Nutrient content per serving:

Calories	116	Cholesterol	0 mg
Protein	3 g	Sodium	14 mg
Carbohydrates	24 g	Potassium	84 mg
Fat	0.9 g	Iron	0.9 mg
Fiber - Dietary	1.9 g	Calcium	19 mg

7% calories from fat

Food Exchanges: 1.5 Bread

Long grain brown rice when cooked - *firm, separate grains.*
Medium grain brown rice when cooked - *soft, sticks together*
Short grain brown rice (sweet rice) - *very soft and sticky grains*

BROWN RICE

Preparation time: none
Cooking time: 40 minutes, or
Cooking time 20 minutes (microwave)
Yield: 3-1/2 cups

Chef: Jan Robinson
Yacht: Vanity

1 cup raw long grain brown rice
2 cups water

Put rice and water in a pan with a tight-fitting lid. Bring to boil, reduce heat to the *lowest* setting. Cover and cook for 40 minutes. Do *not* check on the rice while it is cooking, and do *not* stir. After 40 minutes the water should be absorbed; if not, cook a few minutes longer. Remove from heat, leave lid on, and let it sit for 15 minutes before serving. *Fluff with a fork and serve.*

Microwave: Put 1 cup rice and 2-1/4 cups water in a microwave dish or bowl with a tight-fitting lid. Place in the microwave and cook on HIGH for 25 minutes. Same instructions as above. Do *not* stir and do *not* peek!

Hint: I usually keep a good amount of brown rice cooked and in the fridge. Great to snack on. Often, I add to 1 cup of cooked rice, a scant Tblsp. of nonfat plain yogurt, and 1 tsp. honey. Mix together, sprinkle a little nutmeg or cinnamon on top, and eat - yummy!

Nutrient content per 1/2 cup serving:

Calories	108	Cholesterol	0 mg
Protein	2.5 g	Sodium	4.9 mg
Carbohydrates	22 g	Potassium	42 mg
Fat	0.9 g	Iron	0.4 mg
Fiber- Dietary	1.7 g	Calcium	10 mg

7% calories from fat

Food Exchanges: 1.4 Bread

MARIA'S SPINACH RICE

Preparation time: 10 minutes
Cooking time: 20 minutes
Serves: 8

Chef: Pam Shea
Yacht: Gwei-Lo

1 cup onion, chopped
1/4 cup + 4 cups vegetable stock (page 81)
1 (10 oz.) pkg. frozen chopped spinach, thawed and drained
2 cups uncooked long grain white rice

Sauté onion in 1/4 cup vegetable stock until soft. Add spinach and 4 cups vegetable stock. Bring to boil and add rice. Cover and simmer over low heat for 20 minutes.

Note: *Jan adds 1-1/2 Tblsp. fresh lemon juice and 1/4 tsp. each of pepper and cumin to the rice before cooking.*

Nutrient content per serving:

Calories 198	Cholesterol .... 0 mg
Protein .... 5 g	Sodium .... 40 mg
Carbohydrates .... 43 g	Potassium .... 260 mg
Fat .... 0.5 g	Iron .... 2.7 mg
Fiber - Dietary .... 1.9 g	Calcium .... 78 mg

2% calories from fat

Food Exchanges: 1.2 Veg., 2.4 Bread

MEDITERRANEAN RICE

Preparation time: 10 minutes   *Chef: Jan Robinson*
Cooking time: 35 minutes (microwave)   *Yacht: Vanity*
Serves: 4

1 cup long grain brown rice
1/2 cup finely diced onion
3 cloves garlic, minced
2-1/2 cups vegetable stock (page 81)
2 Tblsp. chopped fresh parsley, or1 Tblsp. dried
1/4 tsp. black pepper
2 Tblsp. chopped fresh dill, 1 Tblsp. dried
1 (10 oz.) pkg. frozen chopped spinach, thawed
1-1/2 Tblsp. lemon juice
1 Tblsp. honey
Lemon wedges

Rinse rice. Combine with onions and garlic in a 1-1/2 quart microwave dish. Cook uncovered on HIGH until rice dries and becomes aromatic (about 2 minutes.) Add vegetable stock, cover and bring to boil. Add parsley, pepper and dill. Cover and cook for about 30 minutes, or until rice is tender. Squeeze spinach gently to remove excess liquid. Stir into rice and cook for 3 minutes, or until heated through. Stir in lemon juice and honey.

Serve with lemon wedges for additional seasoning at the table.

Nutrient content per serving:

Calories	248	Cholesterol	0 mg
Protein	7 g	Sodium	76 mg
Carbohydrates	54 g	Potassium	473 mg
Fat	1.6 g	Iron	2.5 mg
Fiber - Dietary	5.3 g	Calcium	148 mg

6% calories from fat

Food Exchanges: 1.5 Veg., 2.3 Bread

COUSCOUS SUPREME

Preparation time: 15 minutes *Chef: Judy Garry*
Cooking time: 15-20 minutes *Yacht: Sloopy*
Serves: 4

3/4 cup finely chopped carrot (1 large)
1 cup finely chopped onion (1 medium)
1/2 cup finely chopped celery (2 stalks)
1 Tblsp. less-salt soy sauce
2 Tblsp. + 2-1/2 cups vegetable stock (page 81)
1 cup couscous
***Garnish:* Fresh parsley sprigs**

Sauté finely chopped carrot, onion, and celery in soy sauce and 2 Tblsp. vegetable stock. Add 1/2 cup stock cook until tender. Add remaining 2 cups stock; bring to a boil and stir in couscous. Cover, let sit for 5 minutes until liquid is absorbed. Stir and fluff with fork.

This Moroccan pasta dish is a great substitute for rice or potatoes. It goes great with salmon or lamb, and looks pretty, too, with the color of carrots and parsley garnish.

Nutrient content per serving:

Calories	152	Cholesterol	0 mg
Protein	7 g	Sodium	486 mg
Carbohydrates	31 g	Potassium	340 mg
Fat	0.3 g	Iron	0.7 mg
Fiber - Dietary	5.9 g	Calcium	35 mg

2% calories from fat

Food Exchanges: 1.6 Veg., 1.4 Bread

SWEET AND SOUR PINTO BEANS

Preparation time: 15 minutes   *Chef: Jan Robinson*
Cooking time: 50-60 minutes   *Yacht: Vanity*
Serves: 4

1 cup Pinto Beans
1/4 tsp. Tabasco
1 Bay Leaf
1-1/2 cups water
1 large onion, cut in chunks
1 Tblsp. Brown Rice Syrup (or Barley Malt)
2 Tblsp. red wine vinegar
1 garlic clove, crushed
1/4 tsp. cumin
1 tsp. arrowroot
Garnish: 3 green onions, finely chopped

Clean beans, wash and soak in 3 cups water overnight. Rinse, add Tabasco, bay leaf, and water; bring to a boil. Skim off foam, cover and simmer 1/2 hour. Add onion and continue simmering until beans are almost tender, about 15 minutes. Add syrup, vinegar, garlic, and cumin; stir gently. Dilute arrowroot in little cold water. Add water and arrowroot mixture to beans. Simmer until all beans are soft, about 10-15 minutes. Adjust seasonings and turn off flame. *Sprinkle with green onions.*

This Moroccan pasta dish is wonderful served with rice and carrots garnished with parsley.

Nutrient content per serving:

Calories	207	Cholesterol	0 mg
Protein	11 g	Sodium	5 mg
Carbohydrates	40 g	Potassium	715 mg
Fat	0.8 g	Iron	3.8 mg
Fiber - Dietary	0.5 g	Calcium	81 mg

3% calories from fat

Food Exchanges: 1.1 Veg., 2.2 Bread, 0.5 Meat

LIGHT AND LIVELY MASHED POTATOES

Preparation time: 15 minutes   *Chef: Dawn Barrington*
Cooking time: 20 minutes   *Yacht: Dark Horse*
Serves: 4

4 medium-size potatoes, peeled
1/2 cup fat-free cream cheese, softened
1/2 cup nonfat skim milk
1/2 tsp. black pepper
2 Tblsp. fresh chopped chives, or green onions
2 Tblsp. fresh dill, 1 Tblsp. dried dill weed
***Garnish:* 1/4 cup fresh chopped parsley**

Cut potatoes into large chunks. Put potatoes in saucepan and cover with water. Bring to a boil and cook 20 minutes, or until tender. Drain. Mash potatoes. Add milk and cream cheese. Beat to desired consistency. Stir in chives and dill. *Garnish with parsley.*

Serve with your favorite entrée as a low-fat, low-cholesterol accompaniment.

Nutrient content per serving:

Calories	161	Cholesterol	6 mg
Protein	10 g	Sodium	226 mg
Carbohydrates	31 g	Potassium	577 mg
Fat	0.2 g	Iron	1.1 mg
Fiber - Dietary	1.8 g	Calcium	70 mg

1% calories from fat

Food Exchanges: 0.1 Milk, 1.8 Bread, 0.5 Meat

BAKED POTATOES
WITH HERB COTTAGE CHEESE

Preparation time: 10 minutes   *Chef: Susanne Nilsson*
Cooking time: 1 hour   *Yacht: Falcon*
Serves: 4

4 medium-size Idaho baking potatoes

Topping:
1 cup nonfat cottage cheese
1/3 cup chopped herbs (dill, parsley, chives and chervil)
1/2 Tblsp. lemon juice
1/2 tsp. pepper

Preheat oven to 400°F. Wash and bake potatoes 1 hour. In a bowl, mix cottage cheese, herbs, lemon juice, and pepper. Cut the potatoes open and top with the mixture.

Note: *You can microwave the potatoes, about 12 minutes, turning once.*

Nutrient content per serving:

Calories	265	Cholesterol	5 mg
Protein	12 g	Sodium	205 mg
Carbohydrates	55 g	Potassium	906 mg
Fat	0.3 g	Iron	3.5 mg
Fiber - Dietary	5.1 g	Calcium	44 mg

1% calories from fat

Food Exchanges: 2.9 Bread, 0.4 Meat, 0.2 Fat

HAUTÉ POTATO

Preparation time: 10 minutes   *Chef: Randa Jacobs*
Cooking time: 60 minutes   *Yacht: Blithe Spirit*
Serves: 4

**1/2 cup plain nonfat yogurt
2 green onions, chopped
2 Tblsp. chopped parsley
1/4 tsp. lemon pepper
4 russet potatoes, baked
2 tsp. shredded lemon peel**

Combine yogurt, green onion, parsley and lemon pepper. Mix well. Slit baked potato lengthwise and open by gently squeezing from bottom. Spoon 2 Tblsp. yogurt mixture over potato. Sprinkle with lemon peel.

Serve as accompaniment to **Grilled Prawn and Vegetable Kebabs** *(page 195)*

Nutrient content per serving:

Calories	163	Cholesterol	0.5 mg
Protein	5 g	Sodium	30 mg
Carbohydrates	36 g	Potassium	699 mg
Fat	0.2 g	Iron	0.7 mg
Fiber - Dietary	3.9 g	Calcium	69 mg

1% calories from fat

Food Exchanges: 0.1 Milk, 2.1 Bread

TOFU TATERS

Preparation time: 20 minutes
Cooking time: 60 - 80 minutes
Serves: 4

Chef: Jan Robinson
Yacht: Vanity

4 medium to large baking potatoes
1-1/2 cups finely chopped onion
1-1/2 cups finely chopped mushrooms
1/2 tsp. sage
1 tsp. freshly ground black pepper
5 oz. low fat tofu, drained and mashed
3 Tblsp. finely chopped parsley
1 Tblsp. prepared mustard, spicy or dijon
1 Tblsp. honey
1/8 tsp. paprika

Bake potatoes in preheated 425°F. oven for 40-60 minutes (until soft). Combine onion, mushrooms and sage in skillet. Cover and simmer for 5 minutes over medium heat, until mushrooms become tender and release their juices. Season with pepper. Cut baked potatoes in half, lengthwise and scoop out insides, leaving a shell that is about 1/4 inch thick. Combine scooped out potato with tofu, parsley, mustard and honey. Mash together, making the mixture as smooth as possible. Stir in mushroom-onion mixture. Fill potato skins with tofu-potato mixture, mounding the filling above the shell. Sprinkle potatoes generously with paprika. Place on baking sheet and bake for 20 minutes.

Note: *I often cook the potatoes in the microwave for about 15 minutes or until cooked. These can be done ahead.*

Nutrient content per serving:

Calories	225	Cholesterol	0 mg
Protein	7 g	Sodium	23 mg
Carbohydrates	47 g	Potassium	830 mg
Fat	1.9 g	Iron	1.4 mg
Fiber - Dietary	6.0 g	Calcium	29 mg

7% calories from fat

Food Exchanges: 1.0 Veg., 2.1 Bread, 0.2 Fat

FRENCH ROAST POTATOES

Preparation time: 10 minutes　　　　　　　*Chef: Regina Jordan*
Cooking time: 40 minutes　　　　　　　　　　*Yacht: Prelude*
Serves: 6

12 small, new red potatoes
Vegetable cooking spray
2 Tblsp. Dijon mustard
2 Tblsp. grainy prepared mustard
2 Tblsp. crushed fresh rosemary, 1 Tblsp. dried
1/4 tsp. black pepper

Preheat oven to 375-400°F. Cut potatoes in 4 pieces. Place in pot and cover with water. Cook approximately 15 minutes. (Test with fork: should penetrate potato with slight resistance) Drain and place skin side up in baking dish coated with vegetable spray. Spray skins with vegetable spray. Mix the Dijon and grainy mustard and brush skins with mixture. Sprinkle rosemary on each. Bake for 20 minutes or until skins are crisp. Pepper to taste.

These also make a tasty snack!

Nutrient content per serving:

Calories	126	Cholesterol	0 mg
Protein	2.9 g	Sodium	86 mg
Carbohydrates	28 g	Potassium	525 mg
Fat	0.8 g	Iron	0.6 mg
Fiber - Dietary	2.1 g	Calcium	14 mg

5% calories from fat

Food Exchanges: 1.7 Bread

CARROT / GRAPE FESTIVAL

Preparation time: 5 minutes
Cooking time: 10 minutes
Serves: 6

Chef: Gretchen Fater
Yacht: Maranatha

Vegetable cooking spray
1/2 lb. carrots, julienned
1/2 lb. seedless green grapes (about 1-1/4 cups), halved

Coat saucepan with vegetable spray and sauté carrots. Cover carrots with water and simmer for 8 minutes. Drain. Add grapes and heat. *Serve immediately.*

Nutrient content per serving:

Calories	42	Cholesterol	0.0 mg
Protein	0.6 g	Sodium	24 mg
Carbohydrates	10 g	Potassium	151 mg
Fat	0.5 g	Iron	0.3 mg
Fiber - Dietary	0.6 g	Calcium	16 mg

9% calories from fat

Food Exchanges: 0.7 Veg., 0.4 Fruit

I heard you guys make a great festival!

AMARETTO CARROTS

Preparation time: 15 minutes　　　　　　　　*Chef: Betty Goss*
Cooking time: 15 minutes　　　　　　*Yacht: Champagne Lady*
Serves: 4

1 lb. (3 cups) medium-size carrots
1 Tblsp. brown rice syrup
1/4 cup Amaretto
***Garnish:* Mint leaves or watercress**

Clean carrots. Cut in desired shape (harmonize with other food shapes on the menu). In a medium saucepan, heat 1/4 cup water and add carrots; sauté until crisp tender. Add brown sugar and Amaretto. Cover with a lid and cook on very low heat until the carrots are glazed and tender.

Garnish with mint leaves or watercress. I serve as an accompaniment to
Tombstone Chicken *(page 166)*

Hint: *Susan Nilsson on Yacht Falcon uses honey to glaze baby carrots for a similar side dish.*

Nutrient content per serving:

Calories	104	Cholesterol	0 mg
Protein	0.4 g	Sodium	13 mg
Carbohydrates	23 g	Potassium	136 mg
Fat	0.5 g	Iron	0.2 mg
Fiber -Dietary	0.9 g	Calcium	8.7 mg

5% calories from fat

Food Exchanges: 0.5 Veg.

CURRIED CARROTS

Preparation time: 15 minutes   *Chef: Jan Robinson*
Cooking time: 12 minutes   *Yacht: Vanity*
Serves: 4

1 lb. (3 cups) carrots, sliced diagonally into 1/4-inch pieces
1/3 cup raisins
1/4 cup water
2 Tblsp. honey
1 tsp. prepared mustard, spicy or dijon
1 tsp. curry powder
1 Tblsp. lemon juice

Combine carrots, raisins and 2 Tblsp. water in heavy skillet. Bring to boil. Cover and cook 8-10 minutes, until barely tender. Add more water if necessary to keep from burning. Add remaining ingredients. Cook, stirring constantly, about 2 minutes or until carrots are glazed.

Nutrient content per serving:

Calories	138	Cholesterol	0 mg
Protein	2 g	Sodium	46 mg
Carbohydrates	35 g	Potassium	521 mg
Fat	0.4 g	Iron	1.1 mg
Fiber - Dietary	4.8 g	Calcium	43 mg

2% calories from fat

Food Exchanges: 2.3 Veg., 0.9 Fruit

Use lemon juice, herbs and spices, garlic, and flavored vinegars instead of rich sauces to accent the flavor of vegetables.

AL DENTE FRESH VEGETABLES

Preparation time: 10 minutes   Chef: Jan Robinson
Cooking time: 10 minutes   Yacht: Vanity
Serves: 10

2 cups broccoli florets
2 cups chopped carrots
2 cups shredded red cabbage
Dash of Tabasco sauce
1 cup sliced onions
1 cup julienned green bell pepper
1/4 cup vegetable stock (page 81)
Freshly ground pepper

Put a dash of Tabasco in the water to steam the vegetables. Bring water to boil and add carrots. A couple of minutes later add broccoli; 3 minutes later add cabbage and steam until tender. Set aside. Simmer onions and pepper in a little vegetable stock until softened; add pepper to taste. Drain carrots, broccoli and cabbage, and add onions and green pepper. Sprinkle with pepper to taste.

I like to squeeze fresh lemon juice over all the vegetables, or sprinkle a little Balsamic vinegar. Or I add 2 Tblsp. of nonfat yogurt and toss.

Nutrient content per serving:

Calories	89	Cholesterol	0 mg
Protein	5 g	Sodium	107 mg
Carbohydrates	19 g	Potassium	586 mg
Fat	0.6 g	Iron	1.6 mg
Fiber - Dietary	6.6 g	Calcium	90 mg

6% calories from fat

Food Exchanges: 3.2 Veg

DILLY DIJON VEGETABLES

Preparation time: 10 minutes   *Chef: Jan Robinson*
Cooking time: 10 minutes   *Yacht: Vanity*
Serves: 4

**2 cups each of carrot rounds, cauliflower and
       broccoli florets**
3 Tblsp. Dijon mustard
3 Tblsp. honey
1 tsp. dried dill weed
***Garnish:* 2 Tblsp. freshly chopped parsley**

Steam vegetables 8-10 minutes, until barely tender. Combine mustard with honey and dill to make a smooth sauce. Dribble sauce over hot cooked vegetables, so sauce is evenly distributed. *Sprinkle with parsley.*

Nutrient content per serving:

Calories	123	Cholesterol	0 mg
Protein	4.5 g	Sodium	106 mg
Carbohydrates	28 g	Potassium	632 mg
Fat	0.6 g	Iron	1.7 mg
Fiber - Dietary	6.4 g	Calcium	84 mg

4% calories from fat

Food Exchanges: 2.7 Veg

Run! he's hungry again!

SESAME CHARD

Preparation time: 10 minutes   *Chef: Julie Simspon*
Cooking time: 15 minutes   *Yacht: Adela*
Serves: 6

1 lb. Swiss chard (or small head Chinese cabbage, i.e. bok choy)
2 Tblsp. less-salt soy sauce
1 Tblsp. Oriental Blend Spice

Cut and discard white stems. Place green tops and small amount of
water in a large fry pan. Cook for 15 minutes, or until tender. Sprinkle
with soy sauce and Oriental Blend Spice.

Sometimes I add carrots and use a tiny bit of honey.

Nutrient content per serving:

Calories	35	Cholesterol	0.0 mg
Protein	3 g	Sodium	481 mg
Carbohydrates	6 g	Potassium	629 mg
Fat	0.7 g	Iron	2.7 mg
Fiber - Dietary	2 g	Calcium	77 mg

12% calories from fat

Food Exchanges: 0.6 Veg., 0.1 Fat

*Chop extra onion, green onion, green and red peppers;
and snip extra parsley, dill, basil, and chives. Put
them in airtight containers or ziplock bags, label and
freeze them. These are then good to use in stews,
soups, and gumbos, etc.*

EGGPLANT STUFFED WITH SWEET ONIONS

Preparation time: 30 minutes　　　　　　　　　*Chef: Josie Gould*
Cooking time: 45 minutes　　　　　　*Yacht: Amalthea of Sark*
Serves: 4

4 small eggplants (called Japanese or Chinese eggplants)
1/4 cup + 1/4 cup vegetable stock (page 81)
2 cups onions, chopped
4 cups tomatoes, chopped and drained
1/2 cup chopped Italian parsley
8 garlic cloves, finely minced
1 tsp. dried oregano leaves
1 tsp. dried basil leaves
1 tsp. ground cinnamon
1 tsp. ground nutmeg

Cut eggplants in half. Soak in water for 15 minutes, rinse well and drain then dry thoroughly. Sauté eggplants, cut side down in 1/4 cup vegetable stock until just soft. Remove from pan and lay flat, cut side up, in large, lidded skillet. Sauté the onion in remaining 1/4 cup vegetable stock until soft, but not brown. Remove from heat and add drained tomatoes, chopped parsley, garlic, herbs and spices. Spread mixture on top of eggplants, cover bottom of skillet with water. Cover skillet and simmer gently for 45 minutes, or until eggplants are soft.

Serve lukewarm or cold with fresh bread. Makes an excellent light lunch dish or buffet.

Nutrient content per serving:

Calories	119	Cholesterol	0 mg
Protein	4 g	Sodium	25 mg
Carbohydrates	27 g	Potassium	796 mg
Fat	1.2 g	Iron	2.5 mg
Fiber - Dietary	3.0 g	Calcium	82 mg

8 % calories from fat

Food Exchanges: 3.4 Veg., 0.2 Bread

SEASONED VEGETABLES

Preparation time: 10 minutes   Chef: Jan Robinson
Cooking time: 10 minutes   Yacht: Vanity
Serves: 4

2 turnips, cut in large pieces (approx. 2 cups)
1 cup Brussels sprouts
2 carrots, cut in large pieces (approx. 1 cup)
1 cup broccoli florets
1 cup cauliflower pieces

Steam all vegetables for only a few minutes until crisp and tender. Strain and put aside in a bowl. Marinate with the recipe below. This also makes a healthy appetizer.

Tamari Marinade:
2 Tblsp. Tamari
4 Tblsp. water
2 tsp. lemon juice
2 Tblsp. sherry

Mix all ingredients together.

This recipe was given to me by my friend Becca.

Nutrient content per serving:

Calories	81	Cholesterol	0 mg
Protein	4.6 g	Sodium	595 mg
Carbohydrates	16 g	Potassium	558 mg
Fat	0.5 g	Iron	1.6 mg
Fiber - Dietary	6.4 g	Calcium	77 mg

5% calories from fat

Food Exchanges: 2.7 Veg

MEXI–CORN

Preparation time: 10 minutes   *Chef: Jan Robinson*
Cooking time: 10 minutes   *Yacht: Vanity*
Serves: 4

2 green onions, finely sliced
1/2 cup chopped green pepper
1/2 cup chopped red pepper
1 cup chopped fresh tomato
1 Tblsp. balsamic vinegar
2 Tblsp. water
1 tsp. chili powder
1/8 tsp. cayenne pepper
1 (10 oz.) pkg. frozen corn, thawed
1 tsp. honey
***Garnish:* 2 Tblsp. chopped fresh cilantro**
       Juice from 1 lime

In large skillet over medium heat, cook green onions, peppers and tomato in vinegar and water for 5 minutes. Add chili powder and cayenne, and cook briefly. Add corn and honey, stirring occasionally for 5 minutes. *Squeeze fresh lime juice over all and sprinkle with cilantro.*

Goes well with **Vegetable Tacos,** *(page 133)* **Black Bean Burritos** *(page 131) or other south of the border recipes.*

Nutrient content per serving:

Calories	84	Cholesterol	0 mg
Protein	3 g	Sodium	15 mg
Carbohydrates	21 g	Potassium	239 mg
Fat	0.3 g	Iron	0.9 mg
Fiber - Dietary	2.6 g	Calcium	11 mg

3% calories from fat

Food Exchanges: 0.4 Veg., 0.9 Bread

MARINATED ASPARAGUS SPEARS

Preparation time: 15 minutes   *Chef: Sheila Kruse Boyce*
Cooking time: 4 minutes   *Yacht: Victorious*
Chilling time: 2-4 hours
Serves: 4

1 lb. (16-20 stalks) thin asparagus spears
1 cup vegetable stock (page 81)
1/4 cup water
1 tsp. paprika
2 Tblsp. Grand Marnier
2 Tblsp. red wine vinegar
1 tsp. black pepper
1/2 tsp. thyme leaves
2 cloves garlic, sliced
2 tsp. chopped parsley
2 bay leaves
2 Tblsp. slivered onion

Place asparagus in skillet and just cover with mixture of stock and water. Simmer 3-5 minutes; asparagus should be tender, but still crisp. Rinse with cold water to arrest further cooking. Drain well and place in gallon Ziplock bag. Combine rest of the ingredients, mix well and pour over asparagus in bag. Seal bag and turn over and over to coat asparagus with marinade. Chill for 2-4 hours, turning bag now and then. (Do not marinate overnight, as asparagus will lose color.)

The marinated asparagus is good served as a chilled vegetable with grilled fish.

Nutrient content per serving:

Calories	98	Cholesterol	0 mg
Protein	3 g	Sodium	10 mg
Carbohydrates	20 g	Potassium	429 mg
Fat	0.5 g	Iron	1.6 mg
Fiber - Dietary	1.9 g	Calcium	48 mg

4% calories from fat

Food Exchanges: 1.4 Veg

EPINARD IMPERIAL
(Spinach, Onions and Potatoes)

Preparation time: 5 minutes   *Chef: Helene de Neergaard*
Cooking time: 5 minutes   *Yacht: Image*
Serves: 6

1/4 cup + 1/4 cup vegetable stock (page 81)
2 cloves garlic, minced
2 medium onions, chopped
2 (10 oz.) pkgs. frozen chopped spinach, thawed and drained
2 (10 oz.) cans small white potatoes, rinsed and quartered
1/2 tsp. freshly ground black pepper
3 Tblsp. lemon juice

In a skillet heat 1/4 cup vegetable stock and sauté onions and garlic until transparent. Add spinach, potatoes and remaining vegetable stock. Stir over medium heat until ingredients are well heated and blended. Season to taste with pepper and lemon juice. *Serve.*

Nutrient content per serving:

Calories	109	Cholesterol	0 mg
Protein	5 g	Sodium	330 mg
Carbohydrates	24 g	Potassium	607 mg
Fat	0.5 g	Iron	2.8 mg
Fiber - Dietary	5.4 g	Calcium	158 mg

4% calories from fat

Food Exchanges: 1.8 Veg., 0.5 Bread

GREEK BEANS

Preparation time: 5 minutes   *Chef: Jan Robinson*
Cooking time: 8 minutes   *Yacht: Vanity*
Serves: 2

1 cup coarsely chopped onions
2 cloves garlic, crushed
1/4 cup water
4 oz. green beans, sliced
2 medium tomatoes
1/4 tsp. pepper

Garnish:
2 Tblsp. freshly chopped parsley and
2 Tblsp. fresh lemon juice.

Place onion, garlic and water in a 1-1/2 quart microwave dish. Cook uncovered on HIGH power, 1 minute. Add beans, cook covered, HIGH power 3-5 minutes, or until tender. Add tomatoes and pepper. Cook covered, HIGH power 1-1/2 minutes, until heated through.

Nutrient content per serving:

Calories	66	Cholesterol	0 mg
Protein	2.8 g	Sodium	15 mg
Carbohydrates	15 g	Potassium	521 mg
Fat	0.7 g	Iron	1.5 mg
Fiber - Dietary	3.3 g	Calcium	47 mg

8% calories from fat

Food Exchanges: 2.4 Veg.

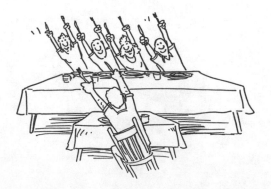

Desserts

AIR SOUP AND WIND PIE

Preparation time: 5 minutes   *Chef: Gillian Pfister*
Cooking time: 30 minutes   *Yacht: Effects*
Serves: 6

Fresh Air
Pie Crust
Caribbean Wind
Crewed Charter Yacht

Take one pot of fresh air, ladle small servings into soup bowls. Take pie crust up to the bow of the boat, fill with fresh Caribbean wind. Place pastry cover over ingredients. Bake till golden brown.

Serve cool "Air Soup", followed by "Wind Pie" in the shade of the cockpit in a beautiful Virgin Island Anchorage. This makes a great Crash Diet.

"Air Soup and Wind Pie" is also a fun answer for the curious guest who wants to know, "What's for dinner?"

Nutrient content per serving:

Calories	0	Cholesterol	0 mg
Protein	0 g	Sodium	0 mg
Carbohydrates	0 g	Potassium	0 mg
Fat	0 g	Iron	0 mg
Fiber - Dietary	0 g	Calcium	0 mg

0% calories from fat

Air Soup!

NONFAT YOGURT CHEESE

Preparation time: 5 minutes
Chilling time: 4-24 hours depending on
       consistency desired
Yield : about 2 cups

Chef: Jan Robinson
Yacht: Vanity

1 (32 oz.) carton plain nonfat yogurt

Before the advent of "Free" dressings and cheeses, this was our only choice in making creamy dressings and desserts. While we encourage you to experiment with new products, this is a good natural standby.

Any one of several different methods may be used to drain the yogurt:
1. Line a large strainer with cheesecloth, paper towels or coffee filters. Spoon yogurt into the strainer, refrigerate and let drain into a large bowl or jar.
2. You can use the same method with a drip coffee maker lined with double paper coffee filters.
3. A special yogurt cheese funnel designed for this specific purpose is available in some health food and gourmet stores.

Drain for the desired time:
    4-6 hours for sour cream consistency;
    12 hours or longer for whipped cream cheese consistency
        and for dessert toppings;
    24 hours or longer for cream cheese consistency
        (appropriate for cheesecake recipes).

Hint: *For every cup of yogurt cheese desired, use two cups of yogurt. Discard the liquid that drains off. Yogurt cheese will keep in the refrigerator for up to five days. This "drained yogurt" is used frequently for dip, dessert and dressing recipes, so you might want to keep some in the refrigerator.*

Nutrient content per 1 cup serving:

Calories	254	Cholesterol	8 mg
Protein	26 g	Sodium	348 mg
Carbohydrates	35 g	Potassium	1156 mg
Fat	0.8 g	Iron	0.4 mg
Fiber - Dietary	0 g	Calcium	903 mg

3% calories from fat

Food Exchanges: 2.7 Milk

ARRANGED TROPICAL FRUIT

Preparation time: 40 minutes   *Chef: Vanessa Owen*
Serves: 4   *Yacht: Dream On*

2 passionfruit
1 large ripe mango, peeled and sliced
3 Tblsp. orange juice
Tropical fruit: starfruit (carambola), pineapple
      persimmon, grapefruit, kiwi

Prepare each fruit to its best advantage, i.e. cut starfruit crosswise to
show star, etc. Purée mango, mix with orange juice and passion fruit,
adjust consistency so it is of "flooding" consistency (if it is too thick add
more orange juice). Chill. Pour onto (or flood) pudding plates. Arrange
prepared fruits, keep each type together, its better to the eye. Don't be
too fussy-the simplest arrangements get most praise!

*Hint: All the preparation for this can be done in advance. Just assemble
at the last minute. This is stunning enough (if carefully done) to serve
the most discerning of gourmet diners.*

Nutrient content per serving:

Calories	133	Cholesterol	0 mg
Protein	2 g	Sodium	26 mg
Carbohydrates	34 g	Potassium	428 mg
Fat	0.8 g	Iron	0.9 mg
Fiber - Dietary	4.2 g	Calcium	26 mg

5% calories from fat

Food Exchanges: 2 Fruit

CARIBBEAN FRUIT MÉLANGE
WITH GINGER SAUCE

Preparation time: 20 minutes   *Chef: Jan Robinson*
Cooking time: 2 hours   *Yacht: Vanity*
Serves: 4

1 (12 oz.) fresh pineapple peeled, cored and cubed
2 large mangoes or papayas, peeled and cubed
2 oranges, peeled, sectioned and pith removed
1 pint blueberries, washed and sorted
1 banana, sliced

Ginger Sauce:
2 cups plain nonfat yogurt
3 Tblsp. freshly grated ginger
1 Tblsp. honey

Combine first four ingredients in a large bowl. Combine yogurt, ginger and honey in a small bowl. Chill both for several hours. Slice banana into fruit mixture and dollop sauce on top before serving.

Nutrient content per serving:

Calories	298	Cholesterol	2 mg
Protein	9 g	Sodium	95 mg
Carbohydrates	68 g	Potassium	900 mg
Fat	1.4 g	Iron	0.9 mg
Fiber - Dietary	7.3 g	Calcium	285 mg

4% calories from fat

Food Exchanges: 0.7 Milk, 0.1 Veg., 3.6 Fruit

Use herbs and spices to enhance the taste of fat-free or nonfat dairy products. Use nonfat yogurt or light soy milk.

EVE'S TEMPTATION

Preparation time: 10 minutes
Chilling time: 1 hour
Serves: 4

Chef: Evelyn Rogers
Yacht: Anne Marie 2

1 cup nonfat cream cheese
1/2 cup nonfat plain yogurt
1/2 tsp. vanilla
1 Tblsp. grated lime rind
2 tsp. fructose

Blend the cream cheese and yogurt in blender or food processor until very smooth. Blend in all the rest of the ingredients. Chill for 1 hour before serving. *Place a bowl of the topping on a platter and surrond with a colorful array of fresh fruit.*

Nutrient content per serving:

Calories	50	Cholesterol	5 mg
Protein	7 g	Sodium	213 mg
Carbohydrates	6 g	Potassium	34 mg
Fat	0.007 g	Iron	0.02 mg
Fiber - Dietary	0.02 g	Calcium	1 mg

0% calories from fat

Food Exchanges: 0.1 Bread, 0.5 Meat

GUILTLESS PEACH PERFECTION

Preparation time: 5 minutes   *Chef: Margot Drybrough*
Serves: 6   *Yacht: Dingbat*

1 commercial nonfat golden loaf cake
       (Sara Lee or Entennman's)
2 ripe peaches or nectarines
1 (8 oz.) container nonfat peach yogurt
1/2 tsp. cinnamon

Cut 6 generous portions from loaf onto dessert plates. Slice up fruit and place 3 to 4 wedges across each piece of cake. Spoon even amounts of yogurt over each serving and then sprinkle cinnamon on the top.

This is so simple, but tastes elegant. Now you can have your cake and eat it, too! Experiment with different fruits, yummy with strawberries.

Nutrient content per serving:

Calories	175	Cholesterol	0.8 mg
Protein	6 g	Sodium	175 mg
Carbohydrates	39 g	Potassium	141 mg
Fat	0.03 g	Iron	0.1 mg
Fiber - Dietary	0.5 g	Calcium	70 mg

0% calories from fat

Food Exchanges: 0.4 Milk, 0.1 Fruit, 1.7 Bread

TROPICAL ANGEL

Preparation time: 10 minutes   *Chef: Joan Ruppe*
Serves: 8   *Yacht: Windflower*

1 cup plain nonfat yogurt
1 tsp. fructose
1 tsp. vanilla extract
1 commercially available nonfat anglefood cake
1 (12 oz.) can unsweetened pineapple chunks
2 pints strawberries

Stir fructose and vanilla into yogurt, set aside. Layer cake and fruit (in glass loaf pan or large wine glasses) starting with cake, ending with fruit (cake, fruit, cake and fruit). Just before serving put a dollop of yogurt on top of each. *Garnish with unsweetened pineapple, kiwi or strawberry.*

This is a fantastic low-fat dessert. Very light and refreshing. Fresh fruit is always best, but if not available, canned or frozen fruit also works great!

Hint: *Another variation is to pour 1/4 cup coconut rum over all before serving to soak through. (Be sure to add the extra calories to your nutrition.)*

Note: *For an alternative topping, try* **Eve's Temptation** *on page 232.*

Nutrient content per serving:

Calories	154	Cholesterol	5 mg
Protein	5 g	Sodium	104 mg
Carbohydrates	35 g	Potassium	355 mg
Fat	0.6 g	Iron	0.8 mg
Fiber - Dietary	4.6 g	Calcium	81 mg

4% calories from fat

Food Exchanges: 0.1 Milk, 1 Fruit, 0.9 Bread

Substitute 2 oz. soft tofu for 4 oz. butter in baked goods and desserts.

MARINATED PINEAPPLE WEDGES

Preparation time: 10 minutes *Chef: Gretchen Fater*
Cooking time: 3 minutes (microwave) *Yacht: Maranatha*
Marinating time: 12 hours
Serves: 4

1/4 cup water
1/4 cup unsweetened frozen apple juice concentrate,
thawed and undiluted
1 Tblsp. freshly squeezed lime juice
1/2 tsp. grated lime rind
1/2 tsp. ground allspice
2 Tblsp. Grand Marnier
1 (12 oz.) fresh pineapple

Combine first five ingredients in a 2-cup glass measure. Microwave uncovered on HIGH for 2-1/2 to 3 minutes, or until boiling. Let mixture cool, stir in liqueur and set aside. Cut pineapple lengthwise into four 3 oz. wedges. Peel and trim eyes from pineapple, reserve leaves. Place wedges in a shallow container and pour marinade over pineapple. Cover and refrigerate overnight. Drain wedges, discard marinade and serve.

Garnish with pineapple leaves.

Nutrient content per serving:

Calories	93	Cholesterol	0 mg
Protein	1 g	Sodium	6 mg
Carbohydrates	20 g	Potassium	173 mg
Fat	0.4 g	Iron	0.5 mg
Fiber - Dietary	0.9 g	Calcium	11 mg

4% calories from fat

Food Exchanges: 1 Fruit

PINEAPPLE RUM FOOL

Preparation time: 20 minutes   *Chef: Betty Goss*
Cooking time: 8 minutes   *Yacht: Champagne Lady*
Chilling time: 1-2 hours
Serves: 6

3 cups fresh pineapple, peeled and chopped
2 Tblsp. + 1 tsp. fructose
3 Tblsp. dark rum
2 cups evaporated skim milk
1 tsp. nutmeg

In medium saucepan mix pineapple and 2 Tblsp. fructose. Add rum and bring to a boil, stirring occasionally, for 8 minutes. Remove from heat, place in a covered container and place in refrigerator, 1 to 2 hours. At the same time, chill the evaporated milk in a bowl in the freezer until ice crystals just begin to form, about 20 minutes. Then, just before serving, whip using chilled beaters gradually adding the 1 tsp. fructose. Mix drained pineapple with whipped milk and mound into 1/2 the scooped out pineapple shell, or serve in a stemmed glass with dollop of whipped milk and a sprinkle of nutmeg on top.

I use this dessert with any meal where the acid content has been low and when the menu calls for a light dessert. Canned pineapple doesn't work well in this recipe.

Nutrient content per serving:

Calories	136	Cholesterol	3 mg
Protein	6 g	Sodium	99 mg
Carbohydrates	23 g	Potassium	371 mg
Fat	0.6 g	Iron	0.6 mg
Fiber - Dietary	0.9 g	Calcium	253 mg

4% calories from fat

Food Exchanges: 0.7 Milk, 0.6 Fruit

Substitute whipping cream with evaporated skim milk (chilled and whipped) or egg whites beaten until stiff.

HONEYED BANANA SAUTÉ

Preparation time: 5 minutes　　　　　　　*Chef: Gretchen Fater*
Cooking time: 5 minutes　　　　　　　　*Yacht: Maranatha*
Serves: 6

3 Tblsp. Rum
1/2 tsp. grated lemon rind
1 Tblsp. lemon juice
2 Tblsp. honey
1/8 tsp. nutmeg
3 bananas, split lengthwise, and halved

Add all ingredients, except bananas, to medium-size sauté pan. When heated through, add bananas and cook 2 to 3 minutes; then spoon the honey sauce over the bananas. Serve immediately.

Can be served as is, or over any of the commercially available nonfat cake, like Angel Food Cake. Also good on breakfast pancakes.

Nutrient content per serving:

Calories	91	Cholesterol	0 mg
Protein	1 g	Sodium	1 mg
Carbohydrates	19 g	Potassium	233 mg
Fat	0.3 g	Iron	0.2 mg
Fiber - Dietary	0.9 g	Calcium	4 mg

3% calories from fat

Food Exchanges: 0.9 Fruit

CITRUS POACHED PEARS

Preparation time: 15 minutes   *Chef: Jan Robinson*
Cooking time: 30-45 minutes   *Yacht: Vanity*
Serves: 4

4 firm, ripe pears
1/2 cup honey
2 Tblsp. lime juice
1/4 tsp. ground ginger
1-1/2 cup unsweetened apple juice

Topping:
1 tsp. + 1 tsp. grated lime peel
1 Tblsp. honey
1 cup nonfat plain yogurt*

Core whole, unpeeled pears. In a broad saucepan with tight-fitting lid, combine honey, lime juice, ginger and apple juice. Bring to boil over medium heat. Place pears upright in boiling liquid. Cover, lower heat and simmer for 30-45 minutes, until pears are tender. Remove pears carefully and transfer to serving dish. Spoon 1-2 Tblsp. cooking syrup over each pear.

Topping: Mix lime peel and honey into drained yogurt.

Serve pears hot or cold, with a dollop of topping and a sprinkle of lime peel over all at serving time.

* *The night before, put yogurt in a sieve lined with a paper towel or coffee filter over the bowl in the refrigerator to drain.*

Nutrient content per serving:

Calories	339	Cholesterol	1 mg
Protein	4 g	Sodium	50 mg
Carbohydrates	84 g	Potassium	547 mg
Fat	0.8 g	Iron	1.3 mg
Fiber - Dietary	4.5 g	Calcium	136 mg

2% calories from fat

Food Exchanges: 0.3 Milk, 2.6 Fruit

BAKED PEARS

Preparation time: 10 minutes
Cooking time: 25 minutes
Serves: 4

Chef: Bobbi Fawcett
Yacht: Windwalker

2 or 3 fresh Bartlett pears (or other ripe, but firm pear)
3/4 cup orange juice
1-1/2 Tblsp. raisins or currants
1/2 tsp. lemon rind
1 tsp. arrowroot
1/8 tsp. allspice
1/4 tsp. cinnamon

Preheat oven to 350° F. Peel, halve and core pears. Pierce inside with a fork. Cook rest of ingredients on stove top about 4 to 5 minutes. Distribute sauce evenly over cut side of pears and bake 20 minutes. Basting optional. *Garnish with fresh mint leaves.*

Nutrient content per serving:

Calories	83	Cholesterol	0 mg
Protein	1 g	Sodium	1 mg
Carbohydrates	21 g	Potassium	224 mg
Fat	0.5 g	Iron	0.4 mg
Fiber - Dietary	2.7 g	Calcium	18 mg

4% calories from fat

Food Exchanges: 1.3 Fruit

CURRIED PEARS

Preparation time: 10 minutes   *Chef: Gretchen Fater*
Cooking time: 10 minutes   *Yacht: Maranatha*
Serves: 6

4 pears, peeled, cored and cut into wedges
1/2 cup unsweetened apple juice
1 Tblsp. honey
1 Tblsp. lemon juice
1 Tblsp. curry

Combine all ingredients in a saucepan and bring mixture to a boil. Cover, reduce heat and simmer 8 to 10 minutes, or until pears are tender. Serve hot.

Hint: *This is a good luncheon dessert served with a salad, it can also substitute apples for pears.*

Nutrient content per serving:

Calories	93	Cholesterol	0 mg
Protein	1 g	Sodium	2 mg
Carbohydrates	24 g	Potassium	194 mg
Fat	0.6 g	Iron	0.7 mg
Fiber - Dietary	3.2 g	Calcium	18 mg

5% calories from fat

Food Exchanges: 1.3 Fruit

When you burn yourself in the galley or kitchen, vanilla will help ease the pain (apply, don't drink it.)

APPLE PEACH RASPBERRY CRISP

Preparation time: 30 minutes   *Chef: Marion Vanderwood*
Cooking time: 1 hour   *Yacht: Ocean Voyager*
Serves: 6

4 cups peeled, sliced apples
2 cups peeled, sliced peaches
1 cup + 1 cup unsweetened frozen raspberries, thawed
2 Tblsp. + 1 Tblsp. Fructose
2 Tblsp. flour
1 tsp. allspice

Topping:
1 cup rolled oats
1/4 cup brown sugar
1 tsp. cinnamon
Vegetable cooking spray

Preheat oven to 350°F. In two pie plates or an 8x12-inch baking pan combine sliced apples, peaches, and raspberries. In a small bowl, combine fructose, flour, allspice; add to fruit. Toss to mix.

Topping: Combine oats, sugar and cinnamon. Sprinkle over fruit. Spray topping with vegetable cooking spray. Bake 3/4 to 1 hour, or until bubbly.

Purée: Blend 1 cup raspberries with 1 Tblsp. fructose and press through cheesecloth to strain out the seeds.

Tip: Serve with raspberry purée either poured over the slices or pooled on the plates under the crisp. You can substitute available fruits, but raspberries give an excellent flavor.

Nutrient content per serving:

Calories 263	Cholesterol .... 0 mg
Protein .... 6 g	Sodium .... 4 mg
Carbohydrates .... 58 g	Potassium .... 410 mg
Fat .... 2.5 g	Iron .... 2.2 mg
Fiber - Dietary .... 7.9 g	Calcium .... 44 mg

8% calories from fat

Food Exchanges: 1.3 Fruit, 1.2 Bread

THE BEST RICE PUDDING

Preparation time: 10 minutes   *Chef: Jan Robinson*
Cooking time: 1 hour   *Yacht: Vanity*
Serves: 8

2-1/4 cups nonfat skim milk
1/2 cup honey
5 egg whites
1 Tblsp. vanilla
3/4 tsp. cinnamon
3 cups cooked brown rice
1/2 cup raisins
1 tsp. freshly ground nutmeg

Preheat oven to 325°F. With a rotary mixer or hand beater, mix milk, honey, egg whites, vanilla and cinnamon together in a bowl. Stir in rice and raisins. Spoon mixture into an 8" x 8" baking dish, sprinkle with nutmeg, and place in a larger pan 3/4 filled with water. Bake for 1 hour, or until set in the center. Remove baking dish from pan of water to cool. Serve warm or chilled.

Note: *Cool the pudding to room temperature before putting in the refrigerator.*

Nutrient content per serving:

Calories	215	Cholesterol	1 mg
Protein	7 g	Sodium	76 mg
Carbohydrates	45 g	Potassium	257 mg
Fat	0.9 g	Iron	0.7 mg
Fiber - Dietary	1.8 g	Calcium	102 mg

4% calories from fat

Food Exchanges: 0.2 Milk, 0.4 Fruit, 1.0 Bread, 0.3 Meat

SUMMER PUDDING

Preparation time: 20 minutes   *Chef: Vanessa Owen*
Chilling time: overnight   *Yacht: Dream On*
Serves: 8

**2 lbs. (4-5 cups) fresh mixed berries: raspberries,
        strawberries, blackberries**
1 cup water
2 tsp. fructose
8 slices sourdough bread
1/4 cup nonfat plain yogurt

Cover berries with water and cook until berries are soft but still bright.
Drain and reserve juice. Dip slices of bread into juice and line 8
ramekins with bread. Divide fruit into ramekins. Reduce remaining
juice to syrup and cool. Cover ramekins with waxpaper disc, weight.
Chill overnight. Turn out; pour syrup over and feather with yogurt.

*Tip: Tinned fruits are equally good in this recipe; combine all the
syrups, dip bread and reduce. The fruits should not be heated as they
will mush up and lose color. I often do a **Tropical Summer Pudding**
using mango, banana, pineapple, etc., but use at least one berry to
set the color.*

Nutrient content per serving:

Calories	131	Cholesterol	0 mg
Protein	3 g	Sodium	123 mg
Carbohydrates	28 g	Potassium	190 mg
Fat	1.3 g	Iron	1.5 mg
Fiber - Dietary	5.3 g	Calcium	56 mg

9% calories from fat

Food Exchanges: 0.9 Fruit, 0.7 Bread

*Fructose is often considered the principal fruit sugar;
and since it is twice as sweet as sugar, use half the
quantity.*

SOURSOP SOUFFLÉ

Preparation time: 35 minutes   *Chef: Vanessa Owen*
Chilling time: 2 hours   *Yacht: Dream On*
Serves: 4

1 medium, very ripe soursop
1 lemon, juice and zest
3/4 cup egg substitute
3 egg whites
2 Tblsp. fructose
1 Tblsp. unflavored gelatin

Prepare 4 ramekins with a waxpaper "collar" that extends 1-1/2 inches above rim (not essential but creates stunning "soufflé" effect). I use a folded strip of waxpaper and a rubberband to hold it. Put the soursop through a sieve. Whisk egg substitute and fructose until fluffy and pale. Sponge gelatin in lemon juice and zest, heat until gelatin is dissolved. Fold soursop into egg mixture and add gelatin. Allow mixture to reach setting point (when you can draw a spoon through the mixture and it parts so you can see the bottom of the bowl). Whisk egg whites until stiff but not dry, and fold carefully into soursop mixture. Pour into prepared ramekins and chill for 2 hours. Remove waxpaper collar and serve.

This is wonderful and light and a very good introduction to the soursop fruit, without the hassle of pips!

Nutrient content per serving:

Calories	102	Cholesterol	0 mg
Protein	10 g	Sodium	113 mg
Carbohydrates	18 g	Potassium	299 mg
Fat	0.3 g	Iron	0.7 mg
Fiber - Dietary	0.3 g	Calcium	26 mg

2% calories from fat

Food Exchanges: 0.8 Fruit, 0.8 Meat

STRAWBERRY SOUFFLÉS

Preparation time: 5 minutes   *Chef: Penny Knowles*
Cooking time: 15 minutes   *Yacht: Golden Skye*
Serves: 6

1 (10 oz.) pkg. unsweetened frozen strawberries, thawed
1/2 tsp. fructose
3 large egg whites
Vegetable cooking spray
1 Tblsp. powdered sugar

Preheat oven to 425° F. Purée strawberries in blender adding the fructose. Beat egg whites in large bowl until stiff, but not dry. Gently fold egg whites into half of purée. Spray 6 ramekins with vegetable spray and lightly powder with sugar. Pour in soufflé mix. Bake for 15 minutes.

Serve immediately, garnished with powdered sugar and remaining purée as sauce.

Nutrient content per serving:

Calories	78	Cholesterol	0 mg
Protein	2 g	Sodium	30 mg
Carbohydrates	18 g	Potassium	140 mg
Fat	0.2 g	Iron	0.6 mg
Fiber - Dietary	4.9 g	Calcium	14 mg

3% calories from fat

Food Exchanges: 1 Fruit, 0.2 Meat

COLD RUM SOUFFLÉ

Preparation time: 30 minutes   *Chef: Jill Christiansen*
Cooking time: 20 minutes   *Yacht: Emerald Zephyr*
Chilling time: 3 hours
Serves: 10

**1 Tblsp. cornstarch
2 Tblsp. + 1/4 cup cold water
1 cup nonfat evaporated milk
1 cup fat-free egg substitute
1/4 cup fructose
1 tsp. unflavored gelatin
1/2 tsp. vanilla
1/2 cup rum
1/8 tsp. fresh nutmeg, grated
Garnish: Mint sprig**

In a saucepan mix cornstarch with water and stir into evaporated milk. Cook, stirring constantly over low heat, until thickened, approximately 10-15 minutes. Set aside. Beat egg substitute with the fructose until well combined. Sprinkle the gelatin on 1/4 cup cold water to soften. Add the gelatin and the egg mixture to the milk mixture and cook, stirring over very low heat for 5 minutes. Remove from heat, add the vanilla, rum and nutmeg, stirring to blend well. Beat the egg whites until they stand in peaks. Fold into the other mixture. Pour into individual serving dishes. Sprinkle with more grated nutmeg. Chill until set (3 hours in my galley refrigerator in the coldest spot.)
Garnish with mint sprig.

Nutrient content per serving:

Calories	82	Cholesterol	1 mg
Protein	6 g	Sodium	111 mg
Carbohydrates	8 g	Potassium	113 mg
Fat	0.1 g	Iron	0.1 mg
Fiber - Dietary	0.01 g	Calcium	75 mg

1% calories from fat

Food Exchanges: 0.2 Milk, 0.4 Meat

FROZEN FRUIT DESSERT

Preparation time: 5 minutes   *Chef: Jan Robinson*
Serves: 2   *Yacht: Vanity*

1 cup frozen peeled banana, chunks
1 cup frozen unsweetened strawberries, raspberries or peaches
1/2 to 1 cup apple juice, unsweetened

Blend all ingredients in blender until well blended. Enjoy!

I keep a couple of bananas (overripe bananas) and bags of different frozen fruit in the freezer for emergencies.

Nutrient content per serving:

Calories	158	Cholesterol	0 mg
Protein	2 g	Sodium	4 mg
Carbohydrates	40 g	Potassium	632 mg
Fat	0.6 g	Iron	1.2 mg
Fiber - Dietary	3.8 g	Calcium	19 mg

3% calories from fat

Food Exchanges: 2.6 Fruit

MANGO YOGURT ICE CREAM WITH RASPBERRY SAUCE

Preparation time: 10 minutes   *Chef: Susanne Nilsson*
Chilling time: 6 hours   *Yacht: Falcon*
Serves: 6

2 large, very ripe mangos
2 cups nonfat plain yogurt
1 Tblsp. fructose

Raspberry Sauce:
1 (12 oz.) pkg. unsweetened frozen raspberries
1 Tblsp. fructose
Garnish: Fresh mint leaf

Peel the mangos and remove the flesh from stone. Cut in small pieces and blend it to a purée. Add yogurt and blend it for a minute. If you have an ice cream maker, put the purée in the bowl and turn it on. If you do not have an ice cream maker, put the purée in a large bowl, cover and freeze for about 6 hours, or until almost firm (it will freeze quicker in ice cube trays). Then, just before serving put in food processor and blend for 2-3 minutes for a real ice-creamy texture.

Raspberry Sauce: Defrost raspberries and blend them in a blender with the fructose. To remove seeds from purée, press through cheesecloth. Make a mirror with sauce on the plates and put one scoop of ice cream in the middle. *Garnish with a fresh mint leaf.*

Nutrient content per serving:

Calories	114	Cholesterol	1 mg
Protein	5 g	Sodium	59 mg
Carbohydrates	24 g	Potassium	347 mg
Fat	0.5 g	Iron	0.3 mg
Fiber - Dietary	3.0 g	Calcium	164 mg

4% calories from fat

Food Exchanges: 0.4 Milk, 0.9 Fruit

FRUIT DESSERT DRESSING

Preparation time: 5 minutes *Chef: Diane Delorey*
Serves: 4 *Yacht: September Morn*

1-1/2 cup nonfat plain yogurt
2 Tblsp. honey
1 Tblsp. fresh lime juice

Mix together and pour over sliced fruit.

Hint: *This dressing is especially tasty on melons, but can also be use for fruit salads.*

Hint: *Blend fresh or frozen berries into this dressing and serve with fresh whole strawberries over commercially available fat-free golden loaf cake.*

Nutrient content per serving:

Calories	81	Cholesterol	2 mg
Protein	5 g	Sodium	66 mg
Carbohydrates	15 g	Potassium	227 mg
Fat	0.2 g	Iron	0.1 mg
Fiber - Dietary	0.03 g	Calcium	170 mg

2% calories from fat

Food Exchanges: 0.5 Milk

STRESS MENU

Preparation time: all day　　　　　　　　　　Chef: *Ms. Binge*
Chilling out time: all day　　　　　　　　　　Yacht: *Fudge It*
Serves: 1

Breakfast:
Power Breakfast
Herbal Tea

Morning Snack:
Oat Bran and Blueberry Muffin

Lunch:
Vegetable Lasagna
Fat Free Sourdough Bread
Fresh Fruit Salad
1 Oreo Cookie

Mid-Afternoon Snack:
All of the Oreo Cookies

Hors d'oeuvres:
2 Piña Coladas
Chips and Dips

Dinner:
Caesar Salad
Stuffed Pork Tenderloin
Baked Potato with Sour Cream
Asparagus with Hollandaise Sauce
Bottle of Wine
Baked Alaska (triple portion)

DIET TIPS

1. If no one sees you eat, it contains no fat.
2. If you break the food in pieces, the calories fall out.
3. When eating with someone else, the sodium is halved.
4. Food used for medicinal purposes (hot chocolate, brandy,
   Sarah Lee cheesecake) never counts.
5. If you fatten up everyone else around you, then you look thinner.
6. If it's frozen, the fat is suspended in space.

Potpourri

FOURTEEN–DAY SUGGESTED MENU

ONE

Power Breakfast #1

Chicken Curry Salad
with Pineapple

Vegetarian Roti
Steamed Brown Rice
Carrot/Grape Festival
Arranged Tropical Fruit

TWO

Three Melon Breakfast
Oat Bran and Blueberry
Muffins

Chilled Tomato Soup
Tuna Pita Pockets

Upside-Down
Vegetarian Chili Pie
Eve's Temptation

THREE

Mango French Toast

Caribbean Black Beans
with Rice
Bread Rolls

Dozy Girl Delight
Marinated Asparagus Spears
Mango Yogurt Ice Cream with
Strawberry Sauce

FOUR

Power Breakfast #2
Herbal Tea

Tuna Pita Pockets
Dilly Dijon Vegetables

Grilled Prawn and
Vegetable Kabobs
Haute Potatoes
Summer Pudding

FIVE

Chicken Fritatta

Cream of Broccoli Soup
Wheat Bread

Sundried Tomatoes
with Basil Pasta
Mexi-Corn
The Best Rice Pudding

SIX

Oatmeal and Raisin Pancakes

Ratatouille Strudel
Green Beans and Baby
Corn Salad

Orient Express Salad
Epinard Imperial
Tropical Angel

SEVEN

Layered Healthy Fruit
Salad Parfait
Raisin Bran Muffin

Greek Turkey Burger in
Pita Bread

Sweet and Sour Vegetabkes
with Ginger and Tofu
Caribbean Rice
Guiltless Peaches

FOURTEEN–DAY SUGGESTED MENU

EIGHT

Off-The-Hips Omelette

Cioppino (Italian Fish Stew)

Carrot Soup with
Spicy Yogurt
Pasta Primavera
Frozen Fruit Dessert

NINE

Tropical Fruit Compote
with Raspberry Sauce
Hearty Breakfast Muffins

Wild Rice-Apple-Mint Salad

Chicken Freight Train
Amaretto Carrots
French Roast Potatoes
Honey Banana Sauté

TEN

Potato Omelette

Vegetable Tacos with Salsa
Mexi-Corn

Teriyaki Fish Sticks
Baked Potatoes with
Herbed Cottage Cheese
Steamed Vegetables
Marinated Pineapple Wedges

ELEVEN

Caribbean Low Fat Fritatta

Artichoke Mushroom
Marinara Sauce on Pasta
Mexican Mango Salad

Szechuan Fish
Brown Rice with Peas and
Parsley
Cold Rum Soufflé

TWELVE

Fruit and Oatmeal Muffins
Autumn Muffins

Vegetarian Chili
Carrots with Yogurt

Lantina Scallops
Brown Rice, Peas and Parsley
Carrot Sprout Salad
Apple Peach Raspberry Crisp

THIRTEEN

Upside-Down Apple Pancake

Tropical Chicken Salad
Vegetable Basil Bean Soup
Fruit Dressing Dessert

Rigeletto Sauce Dark Horse
Cucumber Orange Salad
Fruit Dressing Dessert

FOURTEEN

Egg-A-Muffin

Black Bean Burritos
Tangy Tomato Slaw

Caribbean Chicken Kabobs
Brown Rice
Piña Colada Pudding

STOCKING A HEALTHY KITCHEN

This is a guide. Look for new products that come on the market daily and be sure to read the labels. Manufacturers are denoted by *italics*.

Beverages
Fruit Juice, no added sugar
Herbal Teas
Vegetable Juice, low sodium
Waters: fruit flavored, mineral,
   sparkling, spring

Breakfast Cereals
Amaranth Flakes: *Health Valley*
GrapeNuts: *Post*
Hi Fiber
Oatmeal
Raisin Bran
Wheatgerm

Breads and Crackers
Corn Tortillas
Cracker Meal, no salt or fat: *Nabisco*
Graham Crackers
Hi Fiber Muffins
Hi Fiber Whole Wheat Bran
   and Honey
Melba Toast
Natural Bran
Natural Herbs Crackers, fat-free:
   Health Valley
Pita Bread, whole wheat
Premium Cracker Crumbs, fat-
   free:*Nabisco*
Premium Crackers, fat-free:*Nabisco*
Pumpernickel
Rice Cakes
Sour Dough Bread

Canned Beans
Black, very low sodium
Garbanzo, very low sodium
Kidney, very low sodium
Navy, very low sodium
Pinto Beans, very low sodium
   by *Eden*
Vegetarian *Health Valley*
Fat-free Chili with Black Beans
   by *Healthy Valley*

Condiments
Calypso Queen Products:
   Caribbean Kicker BBQ Sauce
   Down Island Seafood Sauce
   Hotsa Salsa
   Jamaican Jerk Marinade
   Jamaican Curry Dill Sun Sauce
Chutney
Horseradish
Mustards, low sodium
Ketchup, low sodium
Sunny Caribbean Products:
   Caribbee Hot Sauce
   Kuchela
   Herb Mustard
   Caribbean Curry Powder
   Herb Pepper Blend

Dairy Products
Buttermilk, low fat
Cheese, fat-free or low fat:
   cheddar, mozzarella, ricotta,
   romano by *Healthy Choice, Kraft,
   Smart Beat, Borden, Heart Beat*
Cottage Cheese
Cream Cheese, fat-free
Evaporated Milk, skim, low fat
Skim Milk
Sour Cream, nonfat
Yogurt, plain, nonfat

Eggs Substitutes, fat free
Egg Beaters *Fleishmanns*
Second Nature *Real Egg Products*

Fish, canned in spring water

Flour
All-purpose, whole wheat
Bread Flour *Pillsbury*
Buckwheat
Pastry
Rye *Arrowhead Mills*
Hi Lysine Cornmeal *Arrowhead*

Fruit
Canned, in water or natural juice
Citrus
Dried
Fresh
Frozen

Grains
Amaranth
Barley
Bulgur
Cornmeal
Kasha
Oat Bran
Quinoa
Rolled Oats
Wheat berries
Herbs and Spices - see page 254
Legumes
Adzuki beans
Black beans
Great Northern beans
Kidney beans
Lima beans
Navy beans
Pinto beans
Black-eyed peas
Chick-peas (Garbanzo)
Lentils - brown, red, green
Split Peas - yellow, green
Miscellaneous
Baking Powder, no sodium
Baking Soda
Barley Malt
Broth or Stock, canned: low fat,
  low sodium
Brown Rice Syrup
Cooking Sherry
Cooking Wine
Fructose
Guiltless Chips
Honey
Ketchup, low sodium
Maple Syrup, Lite
Mayonnaise, fat-free
Mustards, low sodium
Salsa, *Calypso Queen*
Soy Sauce, low sodium
Tahini
Tamari, low sodium
Tabasco Sauce
Tofu, low fat

Vegetable Cooking Spray
Worcestershire Sauce
Black Pepper
White Pepper
Pastas and Noodles:
Couscous
Farfalle
Fettuccine
Lasagne
Macaroni
Penne
Rotini
Spaghetti
Tortellini
Vegetable Base
Vermicelli
Whole Wheat Base
Rice
Arborio
Basmati
Brown: long and short grain
White, whole grain, unbleached
Wild
Vinegars
Balsamic
Cider
Raspberry
Red wine
Rice
Vegetables
Artichoke Hearts, in water
Fresh Vegetables
Frozen Vegetables
Tomatoes, sun-dried
Tomato Paste, low sodium
Water Chestnuts

* Sunny Caribbee and
Calypso Queen products
*Call **toll free 1-800-338-6072***

HERBS AND THEIR USES

Breads - Aniseed, basil, caraway, chives, dill, fennel, poppy seed, rosemary, sunflower seed, thyme.

Casseroles - Bay, chicory, chives, coriander seed, dill seed, fennel, garlic, marjoram, mint, oregano, parsley, sage, savory, thyme.

Desserts - *General:* aniseed, cinnamon, sage, rosemary, saffron, and green seeds; *Custards:* lemon thyme, mint; *Fruit salads:* aniseed, mints, rosemary; *Fruit compotes:* mint with pears; aniseed, caraway, dill with apples; savory with quinces.

Egg Substitutes - Basil, chervil, chives, dill, parsley, tarragon, marjoram, oregano.

Fish - *General:* basil, bay, caraway, chervil, chives, dill, fennel, lemon thyme, marjoram, mint, parsley; *Baked or grilled:* all the above, savory, tarragon, thyme; *Oily fish:* fennel, dill; *Salmon:* dill seed, rosemary; *Seafood:* basil, bay, chervil, chives, dill, fennel seed, marjoram, rosemary, tarragon, thyme; *Soups:* bay, sage (though this should be used sparingly,) savory, tarragon, thyme.

Marinades - Basil, bay, coriander seed and leaves, cumin, dill, fennel, garlic, mint, onion greens and bulbs, parsley stems, rosemary, tarragon.

Poultry - *Chicken:* chervil, chives, fennel, marjoram, mint, parsley, savory, tarragon, thyme; *Turkey:* parsley, sage, sweet marjoram, tarragon, thyme.

Salads - *General:* basil, caraway, chervil, chicory, chives, coriander leaves, dill, fennel, marjoram, mint, mustard seedlings, parsley, savory, sorrel, tarragon, thyme, watercress.

Soups - *General:* chervil, garlic, marjorams, mint, green onions, parsley, rosemary, savories, sorrel, tarragon, thyme; *Minestrone:* basil, rosemary, thyme; *Pea:* basil, dill, marjoram, mint, parsley, rosemary, savory, thyme; *Potato:* bay, caraway, parsley; *Tomato:* basil, dill, marjoram, oregano, tarragon, thyme.

Vegetables - *Artichokes:* bay, savory, tarragon; *Asparagus:* chervil, chives, dill, tarragon; *Avocado:* dill, marjoram, tarragon; *Brussels sprouts:* dill, sage, savory; *Cabbage:* caraway, dill seed, marjoram, mint, oregano, parsley, sage savory, thyme; *Carrots:* chervil, parsley; *Cauliflower:* chives, dill weed and seed, fennel, rosemary; *Green beans:* dill, marjoram, mint, oregano, rosemary, sage, savory, tarragon, thyme; *Lentils:* garlic, mint, parsley, savory, sorrel; *Mushrooms:* basil, dill, marjoram, parsley, rosemary, savory, thyme, tarragon; *Onions:* basil, marjoram in soup, oregano, sage, tarragon, thyme; *Peas:* basil, chervil, marjoram, mint, parsley, rosemary, sage, savory; *Potatoes:* basil, bay, chives, dill, marjoram, mint, oregano, parsley, rosemary, savory, thyme; *Sauerkraut:* dill, fennel seed, savory, tarragon, thyme; *Spinach:* chervil, marjoram, mint, rosemary for soup, sage, sorrel, tarragon; *Summer squash:* basil, dill, marjoram, rosemary, tarragon; *Tomatoes:* basil, bay, chervil, chives, dill seed, garlic, marjoram, mint, oregano, parsley, sage, savory, tarragon; *Turnips:* dill seed, marjoram, savory.

Vinegars - Basil, bay, chervil, dill leaves, fennel, garlic, marjoram, mint, rosemary, savory, tarragon, thyme.

KNOW YOUR HERBS AND SPICES
Characteristics and Uses

Allspice - Grown in the West Indies. A sharp-flavored berry, tastes similar to cinnamon and cloves. Uses: consommé, boiled fish, relishes, tomatoes, eggplant, baked beans, pickles, fruit preserves, puddings.

Anisé - Highly aromatic with a peppery-sweet scent and licorice-like flavor. Whole or ground anisé goes well with fruit. Popular for use in bread, spice cakes, cookies and desserts.

Basil - Member of the mint family with a mild sweet tasting leaf. Essential to Italian cooking, blends well with tomatoes and garlic. Complements any type of poultry, shellfish, many vegetables, and salads.

Bay Leaf - Dried leaf of the laurel family, strong, aromatic flavor. Uses: shrimp, shish kebab, chicken, stews, pickles, beets, carrots, potatoes, stewed tomatoes, eggplant, soups.

Caraway seeds - Small aromatic seeds of a parsley-type plant Uses: flavor breads, cheese, cabbage dishes, turnips, sauerkraut, rice, potato salads and pancakes, cole slaw, beets, baked pears and apples, clam chowder, or over cooked noodles.

Cardamom - Belongs to the ginger family. Seeds enclosed in small pod. Uses: pickling, coffee cake, curries, soups, peas, jellies.

Cayenne Pepper - Also called red pepper or chili pepper, powder has a hot, biting taste. Uses: fish and cheese dishes, spicy sauces, Lima beans, Mexican dishes.

Celery Seed - A mild celery flavor is contributed by the seeds of this familiar salad vegetable; they can be used in pickling, salads, fish, salad dressings, cream cheese spread, croquettes, cabbage, cauliflower, onions, cole slaw.

Chervil - Is one of the classic *fines herbes* much used in French cuisine. It has a delicate flavor and is suitable wherever parsley is used. Chop the fresh leaf into omelettes, salads, dressings, tomatoes, beets, eggplant, peas, potatoes, spinach, garnish or seasoning for poultry.

Chili Powder - Blend of chili peppers, oregano, cumin and garlic, sometimes with cloves, allspice and salt. Uses: sauces, stews, enhances Mexican dishes.

Chives - Hollow green tips of an onion family plant. Uses: garnish, salads, baked potatoes, sauces, cheese dishes, vegetables.

Cinnamon - Has an aromatic, sweet, pungent taste, available in stick or ground forms. Uses: fruit pies, compotes, Middle Eastern dishes, fruits and vegetables.

Cloves - Aromatic, spicy, pungent tasting dried buds, available whole or ground. Uses: desserts, mulled wines and teas, beets, cabbage, carrots, yellow squash, fruits, soups.

Coriander - Flavor like lemon peel and sage. Comes in leaf and seed forms. The seeds are indispensable in tomato chutney and curries. Excellent flavoring for vegetables, soups, sauces. The leaves have an earthy pungency, delicious in salads, vegetables, poultry dishes.

Cumin - A nutty, peppery flavored seed related to the parsley family, often an ingredient in chili and curry powders. Uses: soups, cabbage dishes, egg dishes, fish, and meat.

Curry Powder - A blend of many ground spices. Uses: Indian-style dishes, soups, sauces, stews, chicken, seafood, and vegetables dishes.

Dill - Has a totally unique, spicy green taste and distinctive aroma. Available as dill weed or dill seed. Add whole seeds to potato salad, pickles, bean soups, salmon dishes, and apple pies. The leaves go well with fish, cream cheese, and cucumber.

Fennel - Has a pronounced aniseed flavor, and is said to be an excellent digestive aid. Chop the stems when tender into salads. Finely chop the leaves and sprinkle on salads and cooked vegetables. Add the seeds to sauces, breads, biscuits, and the water for poaching fish.

Garlic - A bulb plant with a strong, distinctive aroma and flavor for many dishes, hot and cold. Available in many forms. Rub a clove around a salad bowl to subtly flavor salads; add one or two cloves to dressings and marinades, or make garlic vinegar. It can also be baked as a vegetable.

Ginger - This root of a tropical tree has a sweet and spicy flavor, available in many forms. The fresh finger-like root has beige flesh covered with a thin tan skin; you peel the skin before grating or slicing the root. Wrap fresh ginger well and store in the freezer, where it will keep for months; there is no need to thaw it before using. Try ginger in Oriental dishes, in marinades for chicken or fish, stir-fries, and fruit-salad dressings.

Horseradish - White-fleshed pungent root. A relative of the radish. The root is commonly grated and eaten raw as a condiment. Choose firm roots with no soft spots; they will keep in the refrigerator for up to a week when stored in a plastic bag. Before grating the roots, scrub them and scrape away the outer skin.

Mace- From the fruit membrane of the nutmeg tree, a little more pungent than nutmeg - warm and spicy. Mace can be used in the same ways as nutmeg. The classic spice for poundcake.

Marjoram - Has a distinctive savory flavor, is closely akin to oregano and has a related but more delicate flavor. Available in leaf or ground forms. Suitable for thick vegetable soups, pasta, fish, and chicken; tomatoes, zucchini, potatoes, and peppers. Also use in omelettes.

Mint - A widely grown herb with a delightfully cool, pungent flavor. Fresh mint adds zest to sweet dishes, fruit salads and soups; melon, berries, and cold fruit beverages; appetizing garnish. Add to new potatoes, carrots or peas; in fresh pea soup or chilled yogurt soup, and in cold grain salads to enhance flavor.

Mustard - Hot, sharp flavor, available in seed, ground or paste forms. Mustard is often used in sauces Uses: cheese, steaks, chops, ham, baked and green beans, macaroni, cole slaw, mixed greens, salad dressings, cabbage, celery, peas, potato soup.

Nutmeg - A seed with a sweet, spicy flavor. May be freshly ground with a small grater, although most people use it already ground. Used in baking, puddings, sauces, vegetables, fruits.

Oregano - Leaf has a strong but pleasantly bitter taste. Add it to tomato sauces, salad dressings, tomato-based soups or marinades. Used in Italian, Greek and Mexican dishes.

Paprika - A variety of red pepper, slightly sweet and tangy. Uses: decorative, Hungarian dishes, roasts, poultry, eggs, soups, corn, cauliflower, onions, potatoes.

Parsley - The mild flavor and bright green leaves make it the most useful and popular kitchen herb. Comes in flat-leaf and curly-leaf forms. Has a slightly bitter, sweet taste. When cooked it enhances the flavor of other foods and herbs. Use in salads, sandwiches and soups.

Pepper - Pungent, hot tasting, dried berry. Black pepper is from the whole, ground peppercorn and has a more intense taste. White pepper is ground after the outer covering is removed from the seed and is preferred for pale colored foods. Use whole peppercorns and grind them yourself as needed. Once ground, pepper rapidly loses its flavor.

Poppy Seeds - Tiny seeds of poppy plant, about 900,000 seeds to the pound. Imported from Holland, Rumania, Turkey, Poland. Sprinkle on bread, cake, biscuits, mashed potatoes and in salad dressings.

Rosemary - A branch of fresh rosemary looks like a small sprig of evergreen, and is just as fragrant. Available dried or fresh, both need to be crushed or crumbled before using as their needle-like leaves are quite hard. Use in breads, marinades, soups; with salmon fish and vegetables.

Saffron - The most expensive of spices, saffron comes from the dried golden stigmas of a variety of crocus. The spice is sold as "threads" use sparingly, only a pinch is needed to add a brilliant yellow color and an exotic, slightly bitter flavor to seafood, poultry, Spanish, French, Italian or Indian-style rice dishes. Before using, crush the required number of threads and infuse in a small amount of warm water before adding it to the dish.

Sage - Leaves have a pungent slightly bitter taste. Sold as whole leaves or crumbled. Most familiar as a seasoning for poultry stuffing; other uses are in soups, chicken, minestrone, pea, potato, tomato, vegetable; and with halibut, sole, salmon, carrots, eggplant, Lima beans, or onions.

Savory - Summer savory is more subtle than winter savory which is similar to Thyme. Cook with fresh or dried beans and lentils. Sprinkle finely chopped leaves on soups and sauces. Use savory to flavor vinegar. Use savory with vegetables, salads, and in dressings. This herb also enhances the flavor of fish and poultry.

Sorrel - A sharp-flavored leaf with the tangy zest of lemon, sorrel adds piquancy to bland dishes and sauces. Shredded and added to lettuce, makes lemon juice or vinegar unnecessary. Sorrel is often cooked and served like spinach.

Tarragon - An aristocratic herb with a mild flavor and hidden tang. Essential to French cooking, tarragon has a slight flavor of licorice or anise. It can be overpowering and may overshadow other herbs, so use it with discretion. Tarragon is excellent with poached, baked, or broiled fish or poultry, and with shellfish; use in vinaigrettes and other salad dressings, and with cooked potatoes, peas, or asparagus.

Thyme - Common thyme is used in a bouquet garni with parsley and bay. Thyme, though quite strong in flavor, is compatible with many foods and is essential in Creole recipes. Add a little thyme to fish and poultry dishes, tomato sauce, chowders, stuffings, vegetables such as summer squash and green beans.

Turmeric - Member of the ginger family, important in curry powder. Uses: curries, fish dishes, sauces, cauliflower, peas and tomatoes.

TOOLS OF THE TRADE

Blender - For pureeing soups and creating breakfast beverages, make creamy low-fat sauces from ingredients such as non-fat cottage cheese, fruits and vegetables. Use one that has several speeds.

Colander/Sieve - For draining excess liquid from foods.

Essential Gadgets - wooden spoons, wire whisks, vegetable peeler, stainless steel grater, pastry brush, zester, spice grinder, mortar and pestle, melon scoop, measuring spoons and cups.

Food processor - Does everything from julienning to mixing bread dough to pureeing cottage cheese in a minimum of time.

Kitchen scale - Check portion size to keep a watch on calories and fat.

Knives - At least three, high quality, stainless steel knives are essential for removing fats from meat and slicing lots of vegetables and fruits quickly (don't forget a knife sharpener!).

Microwave oven - These have become indispensable for quick, healthy cooking since they retain nutrients, have shorter cooking times (resulting in less nutrient loss), and require no added fat. Cooking times will have to be adjusted to your microwave's power and wattage output. Follow manufacture's suggestions for cookware.

Nonstick Pans - Allow you to sauté and bake with no added fat. Purchase the best you can since the surface of inexpensive brands tend to flake and chip, use plastic and wooden utensils to preserve the finish.

Wok - Allows you to quickly and easily cook all types of meat and vegetables, requires a minimum of liquid for sauteing and allows vegetables to retain their bright colors and stay crisp.

Yogurt Cheese Funnel - Allows you to make nonfat yogurt cheese; a cheesecloth-lined sieve or strainer will accomplish the same result.

GLOSSARY OF FOOD AND COOKING TERMS

Arrowroot: Starch made by grinding the root of a plant of the same name; used mainly for thickening.

Bake: Cook in an oven or oven-like appliance. Always bake a dish uncovered unless recipe specifies otherwise.

Beat: Use a brisk up-and-over motion to add air to a mixture and make it smooth; or use an electric mixer or rotary beater.

Blanch: To briefly boil or steam a food to prevent spoilage during freezing, loosen skins for peeling, remove strong, bitter flavors, to set the color of food.

Blend: Process a food in an electric blender to mix, chop, or purée. Or, combine by hand with a stirring motion to make a uniform mixture.

Boil: Cook in liquid that is heated until bubbles rise to the surface and break. In a full rolling boil, bubbles form rapidly throughout.

Chill: Refrigerate to reduce temperature of a food.

Cool: Let stand at room departure to reduce the temperature of a food. When a recipe says, "cool quickly," the food should be refrigerated or set in a bowl of ice water to quickly reduce its temperature.

Cream: Beat with spoon or electric mixer to make mixture light, fluffy.

Dice: To cut into small cubes.

Dissolve: Stir a dry ingredient into a liquid until the dry ingredient is no longer visible.

Garnish: Decorate a food, usually with another food.

Grate: Rub across a grater to break a food into fine particles.

Julienne: To cut into thin strips.

Legumes: Vegetables that have seed pods such as peas and beans.

Marinate: Allow a food to stand in a liquid that adds flavor to the food.

Mix: Combine ingredients by stirring.

Partially set: A term used to describe gelatin mixtures at the point in setting when the consistency resembles raw egg whites.

Patty: Small flat, round or oval cake of food.

Pit: Remove the seed from a piece of fruit.

Poach: Cook in hot liquid, being careful that the food holds its shape.

Purée: Use a blender, food processor, or food mill to convert a food into a liquid or heavy paste.

Reduce: Boil rapidly to evaporate liquid so mixture becomes thicker.

Sauté: Sweating vegetables or other food in water or stock.

Score: Cut shallow grooves or slits through the outer layer of a food.

Simmer: Cook in liquid that is just below the boiling point. Bubbles burst before reaching surface.

Steam: Cooking food in the steam rising from boiling water.

Steep: Extract the flavor or color from a substance by letting it stand in hot liquid.

Stir: Combining ingredients with a spoon in a circular or figure-8 motion.

Tofu: A white custard-like substance made from coagulated soy milk (soybean curd). For more information see page 78.

Toss: Mix ingredients lightly by lifting and dropping with a spoon, or a spoon and fork.

Whip: Beat lightly and rapidly, incorporating air into a mixture to make it light and to increase its volume.

Zest: Colored oily outer skin of citrus fruit; grated or peeled, it is used to flavor foods and liquids.

TABLE OF EQUIVALENTS
United States and Metric

U. S.	Equivalents	Metric *volume-milliliters*
Dash	Less than 1/8 tsp.	
1 teaspoon	60 drops	0.5 ml.
1 Tablespoon	3 teaspoons	15 ml.
2 Tablespoons	1 fluid ounce	30 ml.
4 Tablespoons	1/4 cup	60 ml.
5-1/3 Tablespoons	1/3 cup	80 ml.
6 Tablespoons	3/8 cup	90 ml.
8 Tablespoons	1/2 cup	120 ml.
10-2/3 Tablespoons	2/3 cup	160 ml.
12 Tablespoons	3/4 cup	180 ml.
16 Tablespoons	1 cup or 8 oz.	240 ml.
1 cup	1/2 pint or 8 oz.	240 ml.
2 cups	1 pint	480 ml.
1 pint	16 oz.	480 ml.
1 quart	2 pints	960 ml.
2.1 pints	1.05 quarts	1 liter
2 quarts	1/2 gallon	1.9 liter
4 quarts	1 gallon	3.8 liters
		weight - grams
1 ounce	16 drams	28 grams
1 pound	16 ounces	454 grams
1 pound	2 cups liquid	
1 kilogram	2.20 pounds	

Participating Yachts

Adela - *Captain Tom Drewes, Chef Julie Simpson* - Adela is a sleek 50' sailing yacht, comfortably equipped for the cruising vacation you'll never forget. Enjoy owner/chef Julie Simpson's culinary delights, while Captain Tom Drews sails you to the many beautiful beaches and coves. Snorkeling, sunbathing, beachcombing, windsurfing, rendezvous scuba diving and fishing. Adela has it all!

Ambience - *Captain and Chef Joyce Bearse* - Share the Sunny Caribbean in our spacious 51' Morgan and take home a video of yourselves waterskiing, windsurfing, snorkeling and fishing. We have two guest staterooms plus crew's quarters, air conditioning, VCR, TV and plenty of tapes. Joyce will tempt your palette with her endless gourmet cuisine.

Anne Marie 2 - *Captain Russell Rogers, Chef Evelyn Rogers* - Anne Marie II is a 47' Sparkman and Stevens custom built sloop. Enjoy the richness of teak and leather below decks and Russ and Eve's warm hospitality. Anne Marie II sails the blue waters of the Caribbean while her guests relax and enjoy the beauty of nature, islands, sea, and sky.

Amalthea of Sark - *Captain Richard McGowan, Chef Josie Gould* - "Amalthea of Sark" is a 78' Jonget ketch. Luxurious appointed for six guests comfort and enjoying.

Ariel - *Captain and Chef Judy Knape* - Ariel is a comfortable, yet fast 60' Morgan schooner, accommodating 6 guest in 3 guest cabins with private heads. Captain Judy Knape doubles as chef, while first mate/chief engineer Mike Folster keeps things humming. Join them for a delightful cruise through paradise!

Blithe Spirit - *Captain Jim King, Chef Randa Jacobs* - Blithe Spirit's guests have choices Columbus never had. Join us aboard our spacious and comfortable 2 cabin sailing yacht, for a fun vacation-island hopping through the Virgin Islands. Enjoy your favorite water sorts. Eat , drink, and be merry. Go home with the finest memories of your life!

Capricious - *Captain and Chef Shirley Keahey* - Spend a romantic holiday aboard the magnificent yacht Capricious and let your senses come alive. Enjoy stunning scenery, feel ocean breezes, smell exotic island flowers and savor gourmet delicacies prepared by your personal chef. Thrill to the excitement of Capricious as you fly across the waves aboard your beautifully appointed sailing ship.

Champagne Lady - *Chef Darrel and Betty Goss* - Champagne Lady, a 44' cutter/sloop in pristine condition cruises the Virgin and Windward Islands. The Lady is beautifully appointed for two guests in the oversized aft stateroom with private ensuite shower. Owners Darrel and Betty take great pride in caring for you. Gourmet foods and wines.

Chardonnay - *Captain William Hadley, Chef Paulette C. Hadley* - Bill and Paulette own and operate a superbly maintained and luxurious cutter/ketch that is well known for its warmth and relaxed environment.

Chardonnay accommodates up to two couples in total comfort. They tailor their menus and activities so you leave as friends who just had their vacation fantasies realized.

Coral Sea - *Capt. Jim Steel, Chef Mary Ruppert* - 60' Morgan

Cruise Forever - *Captain Peter Pajarinen, Chef Elayne Pajarinen* - We welcome you to a sailing experience of adventure with Peter's knowledge of the Caribbean Islands. Enjoy superb cuisine from Elayne's Galley. They have pleased many guests from Nicholson's Yacht Charters with their warm hospitality. Find out for yourself why you too will want to '*Cruise Forever*'.

Dark Horse - *Captain Bob White, Chef Dawn Barrington* - Dark Horse is a 44' Sparkman Stephens design sloop called the Freya 44. She was built in 1969 and remains a sleek black hulled racer/cruising boat. Although Dark Horse is not chartering at this time, you are bound to see her slicing her way through the magical Caribbean water.

Dingbat - Chef Margot Drybrough

Domus - *Captain David Clark, Chef Donna Clark* - Domus, a Morgan 41 ketch, specializes in chartering with one couple. David and Donna enjoy pampering their guests by offering them exciting menus, private accommodations and a charter customized to the wants of the couple.

Dozy Girl - *Captain Tony Messon, Chef Jenny Meston* - Dozy Girl is a 37' French crafted, aluminium cutter with lifting keel, becoming luxury and a pleasure afloat. Cruising the nearby Caribbean Islands and enjoying our 2'6" shallow draft for perfect anchorages. It's PARADISE here.

Dream On - *Chef Vanessa Owen*

Eclipse - *Captain David Ackermann, Chef Dara Drew*

Effects - *Captain Graham Pfister, Chef Gillian Pfister*

Emerald Zephyr - *Captain Larry Christiansen, Chef Jill Christiansen* - Sail on our new 51' Hans Christina Cutter to the sunny Caribbean isle of your choice, secluded beaches, and hidden coves with spectacular coral reefs. Aboard the Emerald Zephyr you will experience romantic evenings, fun-filled days, vibrant sunsets, fine cuisine, and a crew to pamper you.

Encore - *Captain Marvin Glenn, Chef Ann Glenn* - Encore's 53' length x 27 beam provide great space and privacy for 6-8 guest in 4 double cabins, as well as great stability under sail and at anchor. Ann and Marvin Glenn's 14 years chartering Encore in the Virgin Islands ensures you'll join the ranks of guest who rave about their best vacation ever.

Falcon - *Captain Magnus Falk, Chef Susanne Nilsson* - Falcon is a 80' Formosa ketch with five double cabins, beautifully appointed with customized teak interior, she takes six to ten guests with maximum comfort. She is owned and operated by Magnus Falk and Susanne Nilsson, a Swedish couple with four years of charter experience. Enjoy fine cuisine and beautiful sailing.

Flash Vert - *Captains and Chefs Doug and Joyce Pfaff* - Flash Vert is a 46' performance Beneteau that can accommodate up to 4 passengers. Doug and Joyce Pfaff, your hosts, have been a sailing team for the past 21 years. Together they will share with you their joy for sailing, allowing you to raise the sails, assume the helm or simply relax with them in charge.

Flying Scotsman - *Captain Peter Bradshaw, Chef Shirley Gisson* - Privately owned. Winner of Antigua Race Weeks 1989 and 1991. Also renowned for excellent food.

Freight Train II - *Captain George Banker, Chef Candice Carson*
A boat who sails as fast as her name.
Operated by owners in the charter game.
Escape the cold, the frazzles, and the mundane.
Let your body grow healthy, your mind grow sane.
If you have gotten this far, you know poets we're not.
But good cooks and fun people reside on this yacht.

Golden Skye - *Captain Winton Evans, Chef Penny Knowles* - Golden Skye, a new name on the charter scene but a familiar boat. It is a 63' aluminium ketch designed especially for chartering in the Caribbean. Come and discuss the day's delights, on her superb after deck, over sunset cocktails before enjoying sumptuous cuisine in her spacious saloon.

Gwei-Lo - *Captain Gene Coste and Pam Shea* - An impeccably maintained Choey-Lee Offshore 47' ketch. Relax with a cocktail in her spacious teak cockpit and soak up the sun or the many compliments on Gwei-Lo's classic beauty, while captain/owner Gene and chef Pam pamper you with delights for all your senses. Let dive master Gene lead you on an underwater adventure and you'll soon realize that "America's best kept vacation secret" will lure you back again and again.

Iemanja - *Captain Rob Clark, Chef Jeanne Bach* - Presently on board the lovely Irwin 68' Iemanja who comfortably carries up to six guests, served by four crew. Jeanne's Economic Degree from California has been utilized for over eight years now as a charter yacht chef. Jeanne and Capt. Rob Clark welcome guest to cruise and enjoy the various toys to enhance your holiday.

Illusion II - *Captain Roger Perkins, Chef Ronnie Hochmand* - Illusion II is a flush deck, 55' sailing ketch. Three double staterooms, carry up to 6 guest. Our speciality is windsurfing and diving. Lots of flat deck space for rigging up gear or just plain sunbathing.

Image - *Captain William de Neergaard, Chef Helen Gaillet de Neergaard* William and Helen sail on their 26' San Juan as often as possible and have taken it up the Hudson River, all over Long Island sound. Helen is the author of "The Boat Book" to be published Spring of 1993.

Jersey Girl - *Chef Dan McLaughlin* - The Jersey Girl charter-adventure 38' Island Package; Miami to Key West, Bahamas or Cuba. Seven days or more. Includes Captain guide, all food, soft drinks, etc. Snorkel equipment. Just bring yourselves, shorts and T-shirts. Everything else is supplied. For a brochure, call 305-745-2260. Captain Dan McLaughlin.

Lady Privilege - *Chef Cathleen Couatski*

Latina - *Captain Boris King, Chef Shirley King* - Latina is a classic designed 110' ketch reminiscent of the sailing ship of days gone by. Two feature set Latina apart from the fleet; her immense deck and spacious stateroom! She accommodates 6-16 people and has rightly earned the reputations of being "the fun ship!"

Majestic Lady - *Captain Bob Edwards, Chef Dena Edwards* - Our 70' sailing yacht offers exquisite cuisine, three fully air-conditioned staterooms with private baths, windsurfing, fishing, snorkeling, jet skiing, scuba diving, or just laying in the lap of luxury on one of "Majestic Lady's" ample decks. Leave your worries behind and enjoy!!

Maranatha - *Captain Rob Fortune, Chef Gretchen Fater* - Maranatha is a 62' ketch, offering charters in New England and the Caribbean. Designed by the captain for openess and space. Spacious main salon feels like a living room at sea. Chef Gretchen also prepares meals for intimate dining and private, catered parties aboard her Boston Harbor "B/B Afloat" 40' Chris Craft.

Maverick - *Captain and Chef Doris Bailey* - Sail aboard 100' Maverick-the legendary windjammer of the Caribbean. Maverick's traditional design, cozy clean interior and friendly crew (not to mention cuisine) create a wonderful atmosphere to experience your sailing vacation come true! She accommodates 6-10 fun loving people.

Moorea - *Captain Jay Crothers, Chef Elaine Gregory* - Moorea is 42' of Fun in the Sun for up to four persons. Captain Jay, a retired Coast Guard Commander, PADI Scuba Diving Instructor and chef Elaine, a Dive master, together with Moorea's on board compressor will offer unlimited diving and sailing in the gin-clear waters of the Caribbean.

Ocean Voyager - *Captain Martin Vanderwood, Chef Marion Vanderwood* - Martin and Marion Vanderwood, your knowledgeable Canadian crew since 1984, promise you an unforgettable vacation aboard Ocean Voyager, a luxurious Ocean 60, accommodating 4 to 6 guests.

Perfection - *Captain Skip Lookabaugh, Chef Beth Avore* - A 60' sloop and Gulfstar's show boat in 1986. With her roomy salon, deluxe master stateroom, and spacious cockpit, she's perfect for a leisurely cruise through the Virgins or a down island charter, while providing the comforts of home. Beth's dessert won "Best of Show" at the 1991 Grand Marnier Cooking competition.

Prelude -*Captain Ed Bacon, Chef Regina Jordan* - Prelude is a roomy 45' ketch with two staterooms, two head with showers, crew quarters, a large main cabin and a spacious deck. You can sail according to your service package. Available on New York Harbor for summer charters. Members VICL (212) 873-7558.

Promenade - *Chef Fiona Dugdale* - You'll be voyaging on the sleekest trimaran there is and dining on the best cuisine around. Built especially for your chartering comforts, Promenade offers a rare spaciousness not often found. Up to five couples can enjoy her delightfully stable sailing, while others can only watch in envy from the shore.

Redhead - *Captain Richard Peery, Chef/Mate Sharon Peery* - Your fantasy dream vacation comes true aboard "Redhead" which is a 60 ft. luxury sailboat designed for charter accommodating up to 8 guests in 4 private staterooms. A seasoned captain with a passion for fine wine, combined with an award-winning chef to show you the most beautiful beaches, snorkeling and anchorages in the Virgins!

Relax - *Captain Henry Metz, Chef Iris Mosing* - Relax is an excellent sailing yacht with a large spinnaker. She has a roomy cockpit, lots of deck space, hatches, fans and natural ventilation. Specially designed for charter business. Relax offers comfortable accommodation for four guests in two identical cabins. The large head and shower is shared by both cabins.

Renegade - *Captain James Ringland, Chef Lisa Ringland* - Renegade offers a spacious interior as well as an aft steering cockpit and a large center cockpit for entertaining. Both have full bimini tops for a shady respite. Below decks, Renegade has 3 guest cabins, 2 heads with showers, flexible crew's quarters, and a roomy main salon for your comfort.

Safe Conduct II - *Captain Kevin McLean, Chef Beverly Grant*

September Morn - *Captain and Chef Diane Delorey* - September Morn is a owner-operated nautical 60' ketch.

Shellette - *Captain Mike Donnelly, Chef Pam Donnelly* - A 55' Catamaran. Mike and Pam offer you space, style, and luxury aboard their distinguished floating home. Fun-filled days, daring sunset cocktails and a taste of Pam's 'aquacuisine'. *We capture the difference.*

Sloopy- Captain Ed Doll, Chef Judy Garry - Sloopy, the owner, operated Morgan 46' is customized for comfortable Caribbean cruising year round for 2-4 guest. The roomy "Honeymoon" aft cabin is great for that private getaway. Most of our guests prefer the scenic beauty of dining in the spacious cockpit. Air-conditioned and outfitted with all the extra toys. Sloopy is an outstanding charter choice.

s/y Tava'e -*Captain Gerald A. Condon, Chef Madou Condon* - Gerald and Madou left one paradise: the South Pacific, for another paradise: the Virgin Islands. Their souvenirs are Hiva Oa, Raiatea, Bora

Bora, Easter Island, Sepik River, Pitcairn, etc... Thanks to Tava, their 50' cold molded ketch.

Tri World - *Captain James Eldridge, Chef Kate Chivas* - Tri World, a 58' trimaran, welcomes you to a Virgin Islands vacation filled with diving, sailing, swimming, snorkeling, wind surfing, water skiing, beachcombing or just relaxing. Our yacht has three spacious guest cabins with private head and shower. Kate has been chef on Tri World for four years.

Valkyrie - *Captain Bob Campbell, Chef Judith Pear* - We enjoy sharing the Caribbean sailing experience with one couple. There's lots of time for a personalized charter and we make so many new friends. Valkyrie is perfect for honeymoons, anniversaries and getaways. The large aft cabin and head offer complete privacy. Come join us!

Vanity - *Captains Bob and Jan Robinson, Chef Jan Robinson* - Vanity, a luxurious 60' motorsailer cruised the azure waters of the Caribbean with wonderful charter guests for more than twelve years. Jan has retired from chartering; she now travels, is a speaker and writes the ***Ship to Shore*** cookbook collection.

Victorious - *Captain Tom Boyce, Chef Sheila Kruse Boyce* - A delightful blend of modern (Hood Stowaway Masts, microwave, air conditioning, all the watersports toys) and traditional (beautiful teak interior, schooner rig). This 62' blue water sailor caters to total luxury. Your crew will see that all your sailing fantasies come true, with their rich knowledge of the entire Caribbean: its wonderful sights and gourmet cuisine.

Wahsoune - *Chef Edna Beaman*

Whisper - *Captain and Chef Gwen Hamlin* - A 44' sky cutter, Whisper combines two vacations - sailing and scuba diving in one. Captain-owner, Gwen designs Whisper's menu to offer simple, and nutritious meals that complement the boats active nature, while keeping sight of that touch of indulgence one expects.

Windflower - *Captain Ken Tomczuk, Chef Joan Ruppe* - Luxurious customized 52' yacht, 3 private staterooms with adjoining heads and showers. Equipped specifically for charter, exceptional deck space, windsurfing, snorkeling, scuba, VCR and island hopping. Relax top side for breakfast, lunch and tropical sunsets treats enjoy. Enjoy gourmet cuisine by candle light at dinner in our spacious salon.

Windwalker - *Captain John Norris, Chef Bobbi Fawcett* - Have a real adventure...charter Windwalker. Join Australians John and Bobbi proud owners of their spacious CT 54. A comfortable traditional clipper style built in 1982 with all modern amenities-air compressor for diving. Known as a fun boat with its relaxed atmosphere and occasional sing alongs.

BIBLIOGRAPHY

Computer Program - Nutritionist III™ Ver 6.2

1. *Agricultural Handbook #8*, vol. 1-21. USDA, 1977-1990.
2. *USDA Nutrient Data Bank* (on-line database). USDA 1990.
3. *Agricultural Handbook 456: Nutritive Value of American Foods in Common Units.* USDA, 1975.
4. *Provisional Table on the Nutrient Content of Bakery Foods and Related Items.* USDA, 1981.
5. *Nutrient Content of Beverages.* USDA, 1982.
6. *Provisional Table on the Nutrient Content of Frozen and Canned Vegetables.* USDA, 1979.
7. *Table of Amino Acids in Fruits and Vegetables.* USDA, 1983.
8. *Vitamin E Content of Foods.* USDA, 1979.
9. *Folacin in Selected Foods.* USDA, 1979.
10. *Recommended Dietary Allowances.* Tenth Edition. National Research Council, 1989.
11. *Nutrition Recommendations: The Report of the Scientific Review Committee.* Health and Welfare Canada, 1990.
12. *Apple Human Interface Guidelines: The Apple Desktop Interface.* Apple Human Interface Group and Technical Publications Group. Addison-Wesley, 1987.

Where a source of data for a food item was not listed in the program, the data was provided from the manufacturing company.

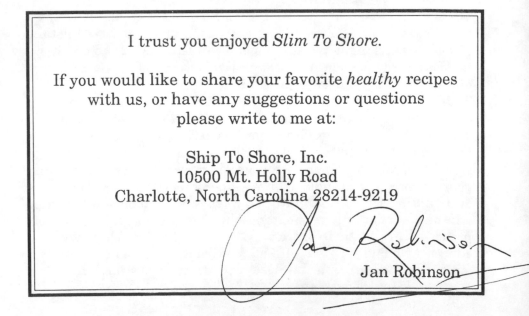

I trust you enjoyed *Slim To Shore*.

If you would like to share your favorite *healthy* recipes with us, or have any suggestions or questions please write to me at:

Ship To Shore, Inc.
10500 Mt. Holly Road
Charlotte, North Carolina 28214-9219

Jan Robinson

RE-ORDER ADDITIONAL COPIES

Quantity	Description	Price	Total
	Ship To Shore I	$14.95	
	Ship To Shore II	$14.95	
	Sip To Shore	$10.95	
	Sea To Shore	$14.95	
	Sweet To Shore	$14.95	
	Slim To Shore	$14.95	
	6% Tax (N.C. Only)		
	Gift Wrap $2.00 Each		
	Freight $2.50/Book		
	TOTAL		

AUTOGRAPH TO: _____

_____

SHIP TO: _____

_____

_____

AUTOGRAPH TO: _____

_____

SHIP TO: _____

_____

_____

Call to order **TOLL FREE**
1-800-338-6072

Make **Checks** and **Money Orders** payable to:
SHIP TO SHORE, INC.

Please charge my: ☐ VISA
☐ MasterCard   ☐ AmEx

Card Number:

_____

Signature:

_____

Expiration Date: _____

AUTOGRAPH TO: _____

_____

SHIP TO: _____

_____

_____

_____

SHIP TO SHORE
10500 Mount Holly Road
Charlotte, NC 28214-9347
(704) 392-4740

RE-ORDER ADDITIONAL COPIES

Quantity	Description	Price	Total
	Ship To Shore I	$14.95	
	Ship To Shore II	$14.95	
	Sip To Shore	$10.95	
	Sea To Shore	$14.95	
	Sweet To Shore	$14.95	
	Slim To Shore	$14.95	
	6% Tax (N.C. Only)		
	Gift Wrap $2.00 Each		
	Freight $2.50/Book		
	TOTAL		

AUTOGRAPH TO: _____

_____

SHIP TO: _____

_____

_____

AUTOGRAPH TO: _____

_____

SHIP TO: _____

_____

_____

Call to order **TOLL FREE**
1-800-338-6072

Make **Checks** and **Money Orders** payable to:
SHIP TO SHORE, INC.

Please charge my: ☐ VISA
☐ MasterCard   ☐ AmEx

Card Number:

_____

Signature:

_____

Expiration Date: _____

AUTOGRAPH TO: _____

_____

SHIP TO: _____

_____

_____

_____

SHIP TO SHORE
10500 Mount Holly Road
Charlotte, NC 28214-9347
(704) 392-4740

Share a taste of
the Caribbean with your friends!
FREE !

We will send your friends a beautiful color brochure of our Caribbean products including spices, sauces, and an exotic collection of home accents. Simply fill out and mail the form below or call us at 1-800-338-6072.

Name:_____   Name: _____

Address:_____   Address:_____

_____   _____

City: _____   City: _____

State, Zip: _____   State, Zip: _____

The perfect gifts for any occasion.

_____

Share a taste of
the Caribbean with your friends!
FREE !

We will send your friends a beautiful color brochure of our Caribbean products including spices, sauces, and an exotic collection of home accents. Simply fill out and mail the form below or call us at 1-800-338-6072.

Name:_____   Name: _____

Address:_____   Address:_____

_____   _____

City: _____   City: _____

State, Zip: _____   State, Zip: _____

The perfect gifts for any occasion.